T0244113

Archive Activism

ARCHIVE
ACTIVISM

Archive Activism

A Memoir of a
"Uniquely Nasty" Journey

Charles Francis

University of North Texas Press
Denton, Texas

©2023 Charles Francis

All rights reserved.
Printed in Canada
10 9 8 7 6 5 4 3 2 1

Permissions:
University of North Texas Press
1155 Union Circle #311336
Denton, TX 76203-5017

The paper used in this book meets the minimum requirements of the
American National Standard for Permanence of Paper for Printed Library
Materials, z39.48.1984. Binding materials have been chosen for durability.

Library of Congress Cataloging-in-Publication Data

Francis, Charles C., 1951- author.
  Archive activism : a memoir of a "uniquely nasty" journey / Charles Francis.
  Includes bibliographical references and index.
  ISBN-13 978-1-57441-908-5 (cloth)
  ISBN-13 978-1-57441-920-7 (ebook)
1. LCSH: Francis, Charles C., 1951—Political activity. 2. Mattachine Society
of Washington, D.C.—History. 3. Archivists—United States—Biography.
4. Political activists—United States—Biography. 5. Sexual minorities—
Archives—Political aspects—United States. 6. Homophobia—United States.
7. BISAC: SOCIAL SCIENCE / LGBTQ Studies / Gay Studies 8. LANGUAGE
ARTS & DISCIPLINES / Library & Information Science / Archives & Special
Libraries 9. LCGFT: Autobiographies.

  CD997.F73 A3 2023
  020.92/3092 [B]–dc23
                        2023023558

The electronic edition of this book was made possible by the support of
the Vick Family Foundation.

Typeset by vPrompt eServices.

To those who save everything and donate
it all to great libraries. Without them,
"Hey, it didn't happen."

"What it boils down to is that most men look upon homo-sexuality as something 'uniquely nasty,' not just a form of immorality."

US Civil Service Commission attorney John Steele, 1964

"Injustice is routinely documented by those who perpetrate it."

Mark A. Greene, author and American archivist
"A Critique of Social Justice as an Archival Imperative"

"Dear Rev. Phelps, I just want to alert you to the fact that some dizzy son of a bitch is sending out mailings and emails from the Westboro Baptist Church and using your name! . . . I know you are a god fearing, Christian person filled to the brim with forbearance, tolerance and love . . . and this other goofy homophobe nut must be something opposite."

Senator Alan Simpson, on being called a "senile old fag lover" by Rev. Fred Phelps

Contents

Acknowledgments

I took on the humbling challenge of writing a memoir because of a discovery: Archive Activism, a cause much bigger than me. Recovering erased, sealed, and often deleted LGBTQ history is of vital importance and is a cause worth sharing with everyone armed only with a library card. Thanks to scores of colleagues, student volunteers, friends, pro bono attorneys, donors, supervisory and reference archivists, and librarians, we arrived at this place of LGBTQ citizen archivery where research = activism (R = A).

This never would have happened without Pate Felts, my decades-long friend, cofounder and treasurer of the repurposed Mattachine Society of Washington, DC. With the combined brilliance of a master's degree CPA and the humor of a Southern Gothic novelist, Pate kept Mattachine on course as a nonprofit corporation in the District of Columbia while conducting labyrinths of searches in reading rooms across the country. Thank you, Pate.

I also wish to thank the international law firm McDermott Will & Emery partners Lisa Linsky and Paul Thompson for their belief in Archive Activism backed by their legal talents. Our ten-year partnership with the McDermott team, which grew to some twenty associates and partners, recovered reams of erased history. Lisa and Paul taught us everything we know about evidentiary history and its power to strengthen democracy with FOIA (Freedom of Information Act) requests, exacting and organized research, briefs, white papers and litigation. I am deeply appreciative to them and the incredible McDermott Archive Activist team.

In the beginning was Rande K. Joiner. She served as pro bono legal counsel to the original Kameny Papers Project back in 2005, helping my dear friend Bob Witeck and me save Frank Kameny's papers and memorabilia for donation to the Library of Congress and the Smithsonian National Museum of American History. It was Rande who connected the new Mattachine Society of Washington, DC, with her friend Lilli Vincenz, making possible the donation of Lilli's papers and iconic films to the Library of Congress. I am so grateful for Rande's friendship and wise counsel that helped us donate the Vincenz archive.

The doors of the Library of Congress opened wide for LGBTQ collections in the Manuscript Division thanks to the former chief of the division, Jim Hutson; Janice Ruth, now chief of the division; and the library's historian at the time, John Haynes. All three recognized the importance of LGBTQ collections (and the gap in their LGBTQ collecting). When we contacted them regarding the Kameny Papers, they immediately understood the importance of the primary materials generated by our movement. John Haynes explained to me how abstraction was often an enemy of historical understanding. Thanks to them for leading the Manuscript Division into a new era.

Storage vaults deep inside the Smithsonian National Museum of American History contain the greatest collections imaginable. In one vault are Division of Medicine and Science collection items, including a classic straitjacket with all the buckles, and lobotomy tools we associate with the horrors at St. Elizabeths Hospital. In another vault is the most complete collection of political and campaign artifacts in the country, including suffragist Alice Paul's "Jail for Freedom" pin shared with Frank Kameny. We thank historian/curators Katherine Ott and Harry Rubenstein for allowing us into these inner sanctums.

Then comes the real work of identifying the RGs (Record Groups). Our gratitude goes to all of the supervisory archivists, research archivists, and librarians across the country who listened, understood, and developed successful strategies to recover the LGBTQ erased past. This stuff is buried, often quite purposefully, and they understood that. Our thanks to Supervisory Archivist Rick Peuser and to Tab Lewis in the research room at the National Archives in College Park, Maryland, for helping us break the code of the Office of the General Counsel at the US Civil Service Commission. (It was "suitability" all along.)

Thank you to Supervisory Archivist (retired) Claudia Anderson at the LBJ Presidential Library. Archivist Anderson alerted us to the opening of Mildred Stegall's Walter Jenkins / Bob Waldron files. She and Research Archivist Brian McNerney went forward, after the library's many years of honoring John Macy's donor agreement, to process and open his personal papers. At the JFK Presidential Library, we thank Reference Archivist Stacey Chandler, who discovered Frank Kameny's unanswered plea to include everybody in the "New Frontier" of American space exploration. So there's your answer, Frank. No New Frontier for LGBTQ Americans. I greatly appreciated the assistance of Carla Carlson, assistant curator, Historical Manuscripts at the University of Southern Mississippi in Hattiesburg, for help exploring the papers of the segregationist Mississippi governor Paul Johnson Jr. Finally, thank you to Lisa Vecoli, curator emeritus of the Tretter Collection at the University of Minnesota, for allowing us to review the papers of St. Elizabeths Hospital Chief Psychotherapist Dr. Benjamin Karpman, including his yellowed, wince-to-read essay on "The Normal Pervert."

My thanks to Omar Encarnación, professor of political studies at Bard College and author of *The Case for Gay Reparations*, who taught us how to think about Archive Activism on an international scale. From Queen Elizabeth's royal pardon for codebreaker Alan Turing and the subsequent passage of the Turing Law, pardoning thousands, to Germany's financial reparations and the Comunidad Homosexual Argentina search for the gay disappeared, we learned Archive Activists are a global community.

For her encouragement and help in the donation of my personal papers to the Special Collections of the UNT Libraries, I sincerely thank Morgan Gieringer at the University of North Texas.

Most of all, love and early morning songs to husband Stephen and son Thomas for time traveling with me through all of this. Without them there would be no memoir—and no life—from Frank Kameny Way in Dupont Circle to Kachemak Bay in Alaska. Thank you for letting "Pops" raise high those old pickets.

Introduction

Uniquely Nasty?

T hat's me grinning at FBI director J. Edgar Hoover's grave on the
cover photo. I am relishing this moment. Like the millions of
tourists who annually visit Washington for selfies and pics in front of
their favorite attractions, I chose a grave for a feel-good image of my
own. I, a citizen "sex deviate"—the pejorative and crime invented by
Director Hoover decades ago—returned for a reckoning of my own.
It took a lifetime for me to be able to stand here with a smile, no trace
of anger, on my face. I could have chosen other places and moments
to tell my story—from White House ceremonies and holiday parties to
Supreme Court hearings and events at the Library of Congress and
the Smithsonian Institution exhibiting our work. Or maybe standing
before a bower of plastic flowers with my husband at our marriage at
the DC Superior Court. But this place is it—J. Edgar's neatly fenced
grave, a packaged plot for the tourists and dog walkers at Congressional Cemetery in Washington, DC. Here I can mark the distance
LGBTQ Americans have traveled since his creation of the FBI Sex
Deviates program in 1951, the year of my birth in Dallas.

I hold my bound copy of the Mattachine Society of Washington, DC's amicus brief submitted to the Supreme Court in the case of *Obergefell v. Hodges*, the same-sex marriage victory that opened the door for a million LGBTQ Americans to marry those whom they love.[1] That victory is now protected by federal law. This "friend of the court" brief presents our case for same-sex marriage. Dubbed the "animus amicus" by the *Washington Post*,[2] it steadies and delights me because it tells stories of endurance and courage we uncovered because they were erased or forgotten. "Animus, therefore, was a culture," our brief declares. "And with that culture came a language. For decades, government officials referred to homosexuality in official, often highly confidential or privileged communications, as 'unnatural,' 'abnormal,' 'immoral,' 'deviant,' 'pervert(ed).' An 'abomination.' 'Uniquely nasty.'"[3]

From where I stand, going back in time to J. Edgar's Sex Deviates program, one can measure the distance between our era and his. I was once so enmeshed and implicated in the long history of hiding that the liberation side of life's equation would only come decades later, like a late blooming. For me it started atop a rickety pull-down ladder into a dusty attic—and with a new way to converse with history we call Archive Activism.

We all know the well-worn observation "Those who cannot remember the past are doomed to repeat it."[4] But what if you cannot find the past? What happens when all evidence, every shred, has been erased, deleted, sealed, or purposefully forgotten? What if the past is torched or stuffed into garbage bags and dumpsters? For LGBTQ Americans this has been the way of our world. "This Didn't Happen" is the sign over the iron gate. *Homosexual* is an adjective, not a noun. You don't exist. You are a behavior. Your uncle's old love letters embarrass the family. No politics for you. History is for a people, not for queers. Breaking through this was the challenge of the first generation of pioneering LGBTQ community historians and activists who succeeded beautifully at confronting the invisibility and the lies. But it is never over. The historic animus has seeped down into the dark and

violent corners of American life. Today, a This Didn't Happen movement called Don't Say Gay flourishes.

Archive Activism is a rescue mission for primary archival materials located in archives and libraries, large and small, worldwide.
It is preservation-minded movement to recover and protect historical queer memory. Archive Activism is a populist mission to recover
the erased past and to document the government animus that continues to course through LGBTQ political and policy history. It is a
popular brand of citizen archivery representing those living or passed
who were wrongly investigated or silenced, their lives and careers
thwarted or destroyed. Internationally, Archive Activists uncover the
names of those killed or "disappeared." This is not an approach for
scholars or professional historians. It is freeing not to hoard research
or wait for book deals or seek tenure. Rather, Archive Activists use
their discoveries and the power of history to fight for social justice,
equality, and even our own safety. We believe it is possible to be
armed with library cards. Archive Activists wield documents and let
them speak for themselves. The Latin phrase "vox populi," the voice
of the people or public opinion, may be less important than the power
of the documentary evidence itself, the "vox docs."

***

"What it boils down to is that most men look upon homosexuality as
something 'uniquely nasty,' not just a form of immorality," wrote US
Civil Service Commission lawyer John Steele in his influential 1964
policy memorandum addressing gay and lesbian "suitability" for federal
employment. His rationale banned us from earning a living—and a life.
From postal clerks and air traffic controllers to soldiers, we were done;
"once a homo, always a homo," he wrote.[5]

Uniquely nasty.

Worse than plain nasty. Really?

How did that happen?

In my youth I did some mean things and had some "nasty" thoughts,
but *uniquely* so?

In Dallas in 1964, I am working on my Eagle Scout, preparing to run for student council president, and starting to crush on a guy in my class. My seventh-grade friends and I are all into British director Richard Lester's black-and-white film *A Hard Day's Night*, especially the Beatlemania shot of the band sprinting through a London tube station. I imagine myself running with them, definitely not on the Elvis side of the continental divide. The Beatles, sucking up to Texas, wore cowboy hats when they arrived at Dallas Love Field. This was probably their gay manager Brian Epstein's idea. He loved to dress them up. This set my adolescent energy in motion. I join an all-night line with a bedroll at the Preston State Bank in University Park to buy my Beatles tickets. The kid next to me is wearing his Beatles wig, and I like that better than the cowboy hats.

We are in a new world, teen sixties Dallas. Running fast in a mania of our own, past questions without answers, it has been one year since Dallas's darkest day, the day on which John F. Kennedy was assassinated. Are we truly a City of Hate?[6] Confronted by historic hatreds, it is our teenage time of innocence lost. Taking a lot of our cues and all of our soul off Dallas white radio (white radio? even radio is segregated) from breakthrough Black DJ Cuzzin' Linnie,[7] we keep running. Cuzzin' Linnie is not about Liverpool; he's playing Memphis. We know it is time, our time for change. Still, so many are dead set against LBJ and his "communist" ideas like civil rights. Our congressman Bruce Alger voted against the Civil Rights Acts of 1957 and 1960—and he will do so again.

How could we know in such a time that an epithet like "uniquely nasty" struck at one's core, deeper than just "immorality"? Immorality we could do something about. We realized that, according to the papers we unsealed and the boxes we discovered many decades later in people's attics, the National Archives, and elsewhere, this insult was an organized, bipartisan federal assault. I and millions more like me, spanning generations, Black and white, invisible and unknown to one another, were assigned to this subaltern place before we even knew the words used to denigrate us.

Archive Activism, finding words and documents that are rattlesnake ugly.

In the years to come, we would uncover those words to examine them not as lies, but as living things. Still used to shock and stun, a lot of them are rattlesnake ugly, discovered under flipped rocks. We find them inside classified, sealed, hidden files that are part of the vast American archive. We breathe deeply the dust and blood rising off the old carbons with traces of that mimeograph smell that make you dizzy. Words like *deviate, pervert, revulsion, suitability, insanity, disordered, dishonorable, disloyal,* and *groomer* anger us—and then inspire our work to ensure none of this is erased or can ever happen again.

Our activism was born in these forgotten papers—and lies—generated decades ago, retooled and weaponized for our time. Whether slimed as perverts in the fifties, compared to "man on dog"[8] years later in Texas, or defiled as pedos and groomers today, it is the same personal and political calumny.

Running still, I hit the intersection of history and memory. It was in Dallas where I first engaged with the idea of history itself.

Chapter 1

Big D and Me

It's the early fifties, and I am slowly coming to consciousness inside a steam-filled oxygen tent at Baylor Hospital. I've had a gasping night of asthma—before inhalers. Not a "nasty" bone in my body. My greatest defender, my mom, Liz, is blowing kisses with her best friend, Aunt Lenora. They are pressing a set of Hopalong Cassidy six-shooters against the womb-like tent. This is "Big D," as Dallas became known in the fifties. They think they are cheering little Charles up, waving those toy guns. What normal Texas boy would not jump at that, even in an oxygen tent? Not me. I am trying to stay calm and not tear at the zipper, just glad to see my young, cute mother waving at me while managing Hopalong's holster. She is not into guns. She just loves me, and that is my rescue from asthma town; it's what helps me survive.

Beyond surviving early childhood, the greatest thing I remember about my upbringing in Dallas—that anyone would care about— is my connection to its history in a town where history often dies. I had vibrant connections to the nineteenth century through my two grandmothers.

Dallas Cowboy, 1953.

Born two years apart, they were both vivid originals, one secular, the other old-school religious. Nothing "Hopalong Cassidy" for these two. About the time I was in that oxygen tent, my cousin Clay recalls that Grandmother Francis (b. 1887) hosted a small recital for a celebrated young pianist from Kilgore, Texas—a gay prodigy who later won the Tchaikovsky Piano Competition in 1958 in Moscow. In her 1920s Spanish revival mansion in Highland Park, Harvey Van Cliburn—born Harvey Lavan Cliburn Jr.—played Grandmother's nearly seven-foot tall parlor grand piano for a select group brought together by pianist and Music Director of the Dallas Symphony Orchestra Walter Hendl. Van Cliburn had a long relationship with the Dallas Symphony conductor.[1] Grandmother, Frances Lysaght Francis—yes, Frances Francis—born and raised in Weatherford, Texas, was a strong financial supporter of the Dallas Symphony and created for herself a world of classical music and Methodism in Highland Park.

Yet in summers for nearly thirty years, she would decamp to the Chautauqua Institution, a 750-acre, gated compound that began as a Methodist retreat on Lake Chautauqua, New York. There she would enjoy the lectures, sermons, symphony concerts, and company of ladies under the influence of Thomas Edison's wife Mina, the staunch Methodist "Maid of Chautauqua" who frowned on dancing.[2] Grandmother Francis was a lovely, serious Christian lady who sponsored her own Francis Memorial Sermons featuring ministers and theologians she would meet in Chautauqua and bring to the Highland Park Methodist Church. The traveling cultural tent shows named the Chautauqua Movement that came to small towns across Texas in the nineteenth and early twentieth centuries certainly influenced her. The Chautauqua tent show first visited Weatherford in 1890 where today there is a Chautauqua Park. I cannot imagine Grandmother Francis at a golf enclave like Hobe Sound, Florida, with East Coast–establishment types like the Mellons, Dukes, Bushes, and Doubledays. She was an authentic slice of nineteenth-century Texas.

From Weatherford, Texas, to Highland Park, Frances L. Francis
at the front gate in the fifties. Charles Francis collection.

No dancing. No drinking. No smoking. And no pretension. Nor could
those folks handle Chautauqua. I escorted her there once.

Van Cliburn liked the acoustics in her huge living room on
Armstrong Parkway across from the century-old grand pecan tree that
divides the parkway. He wanted to buy the place. The answer was no.
She likely asked Van to join her in Chautauqua.

My other grandmother, born Florence Carter in 1889, was more fun. She would never say good-bye to me. Only, "Charles, I'll see you in the funny papers," with a cackle-laugh and a kiss. I thought it was hilarious she called comic strips "the funny papers." It was that long ago. She was one of six girls and four boys raised in a Romanesque mansion that looked like a courthouse built by her father, Charles Carter, on the corner of Ross Avenue and Crockett Street. She married my grandfather in 1911 in the entrance hall.

Today, the Carter house is no more, transformed into the Trammell Crow Tower, a postmodern skyscraper that looms above the Dallas Arts District. Charles Carter (1848–1912), for whom I am named (Charles Carter Francis), was "one of the best known and most esteemed cotton brokers"[3] in Dallas who served two terms as a city councilman. Born in Talladega, Alabama, Carter prospered along with the Dallas regional expansion into the biggest cotton producer in the United States and one of the world's largest cotton spot markets.[4] Carter arrived in Dallas in 1878 (population 10,000) from Vicksburg, Mississippi, where he was a cotton grader. According to his obituary in the Talladega, Alabama paper, Carter's father, Charles (b. 1803), served three terms in the Alabama legislature that concluded with Alabama's secession. Charles Sr. was an Andrew Jackson supporter: "I cast my first vote for Andrew Jackson in 1824 . . . and he whipped the Indians. I voted for him three times. I think Jackson was one of the best presidents we ever had."[5] Never mind the bloody Trail of Tears where the Cherokee and Creek Indians were force marched—many in fetters and chains—out of the South, clearing the way for King Cotton and slavery.

If this reads like a Faulkner novel, that's because it is.

The Carters are soaked in Southern history going back to Albemarle County, Virginia (home to Jefferson's mountain kingdom, Monticello, and the University of Virginia) and a tobacco plantation society of Enlightenment ideas—and the horrors of chattel slavery. I engaged a genealogist referred by the Library of Virginia to write a report on our branch of the FFV (First Families of Virginia) Carters. Known for writing reports for those seeking to social climb into hoity-toity lineage societies like the Jamestown Society (for acceptance one's family had to own land there pre-1700), the genealogist helped me decode our past. He explained that the Carters include "King" Carter, a Virginia colonial governor of immense wealth and vast plantation holdings with hundreds of enslaved people, and Robert Carter, who was moved by his Christianity to emancipate them. Then come other Carters, who include a plantation overseer without land or tax records. Since we could not verify exactly which Carters are mine, I accept all of them as part of me. The researcher explained, "Anyone with colonial Southern roots likely has all of this in their pedigree."[6] The only way to cope is to not flinch and to own up. Historical truth telling is the first requirement of racial justice. The archive took me there to reckon. (It would be a lot easier to claim the Carters from Poor Valley, Virginia, discovered in the 1920s playing traditional Appalachian music at what is now called the Carter Family Fold, the family of singer-songwriter June Carter—who married Johnny Cash.) FFV or Poor Valley, what will it be, mate?

Charles Carter arrived in Dallas ten years after the surrender of General Lee at Appomattox Courthouse, a surrender that shook the Alabama Carters to their roots—enough to propel young Charles and his wife, Susan Tanner, to Texas. It is estimated that some thirty-five thousand Alabamians died in the war, with many thousands disabled and orphaned, leaving the state physically and spiritually mangled.[7] Unwilling to formally accept defeat, Alabama had to be occupied in 1867 by the US military. Was it all for a romantic "Lost Cause"? The Civil War, according to the Lost Cause explanation, was about secession, not slavery. I was taught that. "GTT," Gone to Texas, was Charles Carter's answer, a total history wash. His father, Charles Carter Sr., said, "'All of our bad people left us and came to Texas,' saying which he laughed."[8] Dallas was a perfect place to erase and start over—with a rail terminal back East to the cotton markets of the world and the future. I picture Charles Carter walking through hundreds of cotton bales, dodging horses and wagons on Elm Street, Dallas's curb cotton market.

The Carters at home with their catch. Charles Francis collection.

By the time I was with grandmother Florence Carter Leachman, she was a modern-era lady of the 1950s. She loved to fish with a cane pole at Ferndale, an old-time East Texas bass fishing club in Pittsburg, Texas—with screen porches high up in the pines and lunches with the best ever deep-fried corn bread they call "hush puppies," an East Texas delicacy. Florence helped manage the very

With couple #4 at a 1950s Dallas dinner dance. *Left to right*:
James Francis, Florence Carter Leachman, Elizabeth Leachman Francis,
and Thomas Leachman. Charles Francis collection.

successful family-owned laundry business founded in 1885 (before
people had washing machines). At their magical Tudor mansion in
Greenway Parks, Florence and Tom Leachman, who served as president of the Dallas Country Club in 1930, raised their family. They had
a special Dallas elegance. There is a photograph of them with my
mom and dad at a black-tie dinner dance in 1950, Grandmother

(dance tag #4) wearing a stylish corsage so large it looked like it might take flight.

Florence and Tom had four wonderful children and, later, a menagerie of parakeets. She would teach her special chosen ones—the parakeets—how to speak parakeet-English (no more mimicry of the ever-squawking blue jays). Family reunions in her garden were special affairs decorated with a collection of classic, hand-painted Japanese chochins, paper and silk lanterns with electric lights inside them. For her good manners were everything. She would have talent shows featuring my gay cousin Bobby who could beautifully play her baby grand. We would perform in a well-mannered way, conducted and enforced by her bird perch. I remember she bopped me on the head with that perch. I probably got it for being a smart aleck. Like her birds, we were being schooled for our time of post–World War II affluence and optimism that made possible the oxygen tent that saved my life.

I did not know it then—raised in the rarified 1950s Dallas oxygen of privilege—but my ticket had already been stamped "homosexual": mentally ill, according to psychiatry; soon criminal, according to the coming 1973 Texas Homosexual Conduct law; and damned, according to most of their churches. A surprise was coming this kid's way. It would take more than fifty years after my birth for that burden to be lifted by society, the Supreme Court . . . and me. When my mother died, she well knew I was gay and had met my partners in Dallas and New York. But still, her last words to me, with a squeeze of her hand, were, "Figure it out, Honey."

Over a lifetime I did figure it out to gain a wider perspective both on being an LGBTQ American and on my rare upbringing and privilege. I would have to learn about a new kind of activism, an activism rooted in research and history itself—LGBTQ American history, which is often sealed or erased. Without knowing how to rescue, learn, and use this history, especially in a time of peril for our democracy, we are surely lost. Given all of the advantages I had, without suffering from war or racial discrimination or dramatic personal affliction—or celebrity—why would anyone care to read my story about Archive Activism? I think because it has been such a "uniquely nasty" journey not just for me but also for millions of Americans.

***

Mother and Grandmother Francis knew I was different. "All offspring are startling to their parents,"[9] but what to do with this asthmatic boy who didn't like Texas's state sport (football) and glazed over when the men discussed those Longhorns. I was like Wheezer, the funny and mean nickname given the kid who wheezed after running around the set in the old Our Gang comedy series in reruns on television. In one episode the kids (was it Spanky? Alfalfa? Farina?) mistakenly rub a stinky Limburger cheese on Wheezer's chest to help him breathe, when his parents had been using goose grease. I have not forgotten how the kids ran away from poor Wheezer.

Grandmother had an idea. Perhaps classical music appreciation might be a key for me to find my way. Hey, it worked for Van Cliburn, right? She knew a lady who taught piano and music appreciation for cousin Clay. I took all of this as a sign of love, and it was. So off I went to Elizabeth McClarty's house near Southern Methodist University (SMU). There I learned all about a German composer named Johann Sebastian Bach; a Hungarian tenor, Lauritz Melchior (I thought it was Lawrence Melchior and was corrected); violinist Yeheudi Menuhin; and, thankfully after Yehudi, Marian Anderson. Of course I loved Marian Anderson and her interpretation of "He's Got the Whole World in His Hands." For the right answers, I would be rewarded with sugar cookies. Still, like guns, classical music appreciation did not resolve my malady, as she would see it, of difference. I would have to find my own way.

Sunday lunches at Grandmother Francis's were the cement that held our family together in those years. Fried chicken, tomato aspic, homemade cinnamon rolls. Surrounded by lots of love and meals cooked with perfect East Texas style and verve by Grandmother's staff, her maids Ruby and Elizabeth and served by Romeo and

Roy—those Sundays gathered the Francises together over decades. I recall being seated toward Grandmother's end of the long table, where I might ask for seconds or salt from a silver salt cellar, too much salt being a no-no. If she approved, as if by magic Elizabeth or Roy would appear to serve us. How does that happen?, I marveled. She showed me. There was this slight rise in the rug beside her chair. It was a hidden, silent kitchen buzzer. She would press it with her lace-up Victorian shoe and out would come her help—our friends—to serve their fabulous Texas-style Sunday lunch. ·

"Let me. Let me?" I would ask to press the buzzer myself.

"Absolutely not, it is for my use only. Now, Charles, get off the floor. Eat your lunch." That buzzer, it was for Grandmother only: the silent, invisible symbol of her culture, her world—and her control.

The Francises purchased that house in 1930. My grandfather, W. H. Francis, was born and raised in nineteenth-century Denton, where he attended Denton High School and became city attorney after attending the University of Texas Law School. Long dead by my time, for nearly thirty years he served as vice president and general counsel of Dallas's Magnolia Petroleum Company.[10] Magnolia's symbol was the bright red, mythic flying horse—Pegasus—which became a symbol of Dallas itself.[11] The Dallas economy had evolved from cotton oil to the real thing, "Texas tea" as went the silly "Ballad of Jed Clampett." Dallas, indeed all of Texas, became drenched. It was the gusher age after our blackland prairie got cottoned out. My friend Dwight Hunter, born in 1911 into a pioneer family from San Angelo, recalled wearing his dress-up white shirt and driving to the ranch with his dad to witness a new well. That white shirt got splattered with the black goop.

Grandmother Francis enjoyed watching me flash-memorize Bible verses, for which she would pay me a dollar. "The Lord is my shepherd, I shall not want," and we did not. I would run through verse after verse. "Seek and ye shall find." Faster. "Knock and the door shall be opened unto you, Matthew 7." She would talk to my brothers and me about President Kennedy—not his awful politics, but how voraciously and rapidly he could read. And the Rockefellers. Oh, how they sought, found, and *tithed*. "Now, Charles, willful waste makes woeful want," she would quote the old Scottish proverb, then tell us she was just "tired of all these 'isms'"—communism and socialism, not capitalism.

My two grandmothers vibrated history. Just by exploring their old houses with winding staircases into the dark, my imagination would run free. Grandmother Leachman read to me the 1885 poem "Little Orphant Annie" by James Whitcomb Riley. When Orphan Annie was bad, she "mocked and shocked" their visitors, and one day the goblins swept her and her brother "away upstairs."

"Charles Carter, the GOBBLE-UNS'll git YOU if you don't watch out."

Ohh nooooo! I wanted more.

At my grandmothers' houses I could connect with one simple idea—usually erased in the fifties—that there was such a thing as the past in Dallas. It was away upstairs, beyond imagining, but it was a past we could not escape. And who knew? Dallas had one. For the first time in my child's imagination, I could connect with that past. Knowing these two ladies, I could feel the mystery.

***

Mother put me in my place. "Honey, I don't know whether you are a genius or a moron," she would laugh and threaten to hand me over to the Baptist Buckner's Orphanage in East Dallas.

"Oh, *please* don't send me to Buckner's," I would play along. Genius or moron, she told me Einstein himself needed reminding to put on a coat. "Me? Einstein?," I would howl laughing.

Elizabeth Leachman, my mother, was a combination of Texas governor Ann Richards and Auntie Mame. One can know something about people in the sixties by their favorite vinyl album. Hers was *Ella in Berlin*, West Berliners cheering for Ella Fitzgerald, jazz, and America in the Cold War. I thought they must be cheering for all of us in Dallas, too.

After my parents' divorce, she married Dr. Manning Shannon, "Doc" to us. Over the years, our mother became less Ella and more Liz Taylor in the alcoholic epic *Who's Afraid of Virginia Woolf?* However, after going through her Alcoholics Anonymous program, Elizabeth (Liz) Shannon rose again to become a mentor to many. Throughout her life my mother set her Dallas world on fire with humor and plain good sense. She knew how to make things fun while leading us ever onward in our lives.

I was given the green light by my two brothers, sister-in-law, half-brother, and half-sister to speak at her funeral, delivering a eulogy in a pulpit overlooking her coffin at the Highland Park Methodist Church. Eulogies are beyond difficult, especially praising Mother and her ability to lead our family, working together with my patriarchal big brother and younger brother, too.

Dad left as a result of their divorce, when divorce was rare. His leaving style could best be described as emotional detachment. He was there for the bimonthly weekends, but never for the highs or lows. Thanks to Mother, we stayed on course. But this came with a price. For me the price was a partial wipeout of my "Francis-ness," a loss of frame. There was my Uncle Bill Francis (Grandmother always called him "Billy") who worked for General Eisenhower at the Supreme Allied Headquarters in London and later served as his assistant secretary of defense; and my Uncle Charlie Francis (b. 1893), whom I did not know, from Denton, an old-school Texas Democrat and part of LBJ's inner circle in his senate days.[12] I became hardened to the distancing from our family history. It did not sting so much as deaden—or maybe protect me from the loss.

So in my eulogy I dispensed with family history and instead told a funny story about Mother and her best friend Ruth Sharp Altshuler, who was in the sanctuary that day. In 1945, after the war, Mother and "Aunt Ruth" were living it up in New York City at New York's most famous women's hotel, the Barbizon on East Sixty-Third. The Barbizon was "packed full with aspiring actresses, models, singers, artists, and writers,"[13] and men were not even supposed to be part of the picture. "Men are definitely not allowed upstairs," I read from one of mother's old letters to her father who demanded by telegram that she and Ruth have an educational experience in New York. The mourning shifted to laughter. People loved hearing about Liz and Ruth, who became one of Dallas's most influential women and leaders at the Barbizon. After the funeral I received a note from Aunt Ruth. She wrote, "Our educational experience consisted of going to the Village to Café Society every night to hear a black piano player named Phil Moore."[14] Café Society on Sheridan Square in Greenwich Village was the first racially integrated night club in the United States, showcasing, among many others, American jazz pianist Phil Moore. Café Society was where Billie Holiday first sang "Strange Fruit."[15]

"There will Never, NEVER be anyone with her warmth and wit," Ruth's note concluded about her friend, my mom.[16]

That'll Be a "D"

Even though there were no words besides pejoratives like *queer* or *homo*, I knew I was gay beginning with my first crushes on cowboys—the real ones like Ed and Rodney, who wrangled horses at our favorite dude ranch. Or, when I became a magician on the kids' birthday party circuit, I was thrilled by pictures of Harry Houdini bound, like the classical Greek sculpture Laocoon, attacked by chains of serpents. I could make things vanish or materialize at will, spending my allowance for illusions. At my favorite store in the world, Magicland downtown on Ervay Street, I learned about the Magician's Oath: "As a magician I promise never to reveal the secret of any illusion to a non-magician, unless that one swears to uphold the Magician's Oath in turn."[17] Translated: Swear to me you won't tell.

So there I am on the gay side in Big D coming out of the chute in the early sixties. All gay youth develop survival strategies to cope with this profound sense of otherness. Some withdraw. They don't want to be noticed, just left alone. Some hide. Some truly flame

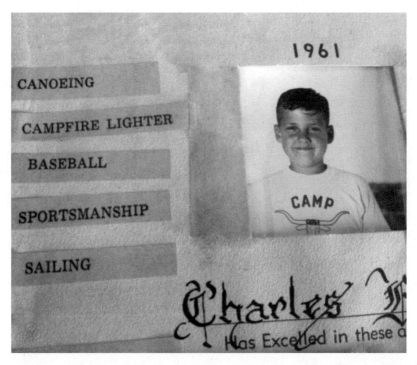

CANOEING

CAMPFIRE LIGHTER

BASEBALL

SPORTSMANSHIP

SAILING

1961

CAMP

Charles

Has Excelled in these

"Hail to That Campfire Lighter," Camp Longhorn, Burnett, Texas, 1961.

with amazing flamboyance and courage. Far too many, tragically, don't make it. Suicide, the idea and reality of it, is very real for these kids. I went the other way, the way of the magic act toward popularity. I had inherited a small piece of my mother's spark, and I used it. If I was feeling like an alien or got pulverized against the gym wall in a brutal game of bombardment, I could smile a bit brighter, be a bit funnier, practice to become a better magician, or be more outgoing to "win friends and influence people," like the eponymous bestseller of the day by Dale Carnegie. The most important word in the world to people? According to Carnegie, it's their name. Learn their names.

What's it like to be a gay kid in Texas? I learned my lessons well at one of the wellsprings of white Texas culture in the fifties and sixties: Camp Longhorn in Burnett (pronounced Bern-it).

Camp Longhorn was founded in the late 1930s by the dazzling (if you are gay) and charismatic twice–All American collegiate swimmer at the University of Michigan, and for thirteen years the University of Texas swim coach, Julian William "Tex" Robertson from Sweetwater, Texas.[18] In Texas it is the rare few who can get away with being a Tex. Robertson invented himself as a Tex if ever there was one. Camp Longhorn was his swimming camp situated on beautiful Hill Country Inks Lake in the burning central Texas heat. There the prime goal for campers was to be awarded for their good deeds with merits by the counselors, which could be used at a merit store to buy things like a hatchet, knife, or water skis. These merits were pins you would hang on your shorts. Think of summer camp as one big Skinner box, devised by behavioral scientist B. F. Skinner, dispensing pellets to reinforce desired behavior in mice. One could also get Ds, demerits, for bad behavior, or even a sandy bunk. Get five Ds in one day? You could be sent to Tex himself—a total disaster for a good Camp Longhorn boy. "That'll be a D," they would say. Who knew if you might even get a paddling from Tex?

Ranked among the low in a high-competition camp, my strategy was merit-driven to just "Love it," as one of the counselors would scream as his trademark until his voice was pure gravel. "Love it," he would preach. Years later, one lifelong friend accused me of having been a "merit hound" at Camp Longhorn, a funny and damning criticism. The hail-fellow greeting at Longhorn was "Attaway-to-go," and I became an attaway-to-go kind of kid. I studied this kind of Texas cool watching my favorite senior camper, a track star named Bobby "Rabbit" Whittington from Dallas. Rabbit was the ultimate Longhorn camper—a funny, athletic swimmer, elected Longhorn Carnival King, a popularity contest even at summer camp; it never stops. I learned my Camp Longhorn chops from Rabbit.

Each evening at Longhorn there was a camp-wide campfire lighting ceremony, where one camper would be named Campfire Lighter because of some outstanding contribution or accomplishment on that one day. A Cabin 2 Cherokee my moment came at age ten when

I was invited to perform a song from Rodgers and Hammerstein's *Oklahoma!* My mom had taken me to see the show at the Dallas Summer Musicals at the State Fair of Texas, and I sang it everywhere. I had no clue how gay I was. So I sang to the whole camp "Pore Jud is daid, pore Jud Fry is daid," a singing eulogy delivered at Jud's funeral. I recited how Jud loved "everything and everybody . . . so nobody ever know'd it." Jud was just so "big-hearted," I declaimed.[19] I am surprised I was not booed out of the campfire ring, but the kids and my counselor Jack loved it—or felt sorry for me. They even nicknamed me Big-Hearted Charlie Francis. They loved my Jud Fry enough to name me camper of the day, Campfire Lighter. Even now husband Stephen, son Thomas, and I even sing "Hail to that Campfire Lighter" for moments worthy of special recognition.[20] Even though my Jud Fry performance is one of those mortifying memories of a blooming gay kid, I still think *campfire lighter* could be a great calling.

But I did not tell my parents or brothers about being Big Hearted. I was already editing myself.

Many years later, I was walking down Fifty-Seventh Street in New York, in front of Carnegie Hall, and there strode Bobby Whittington himself. I yelled, "Hey, Rabbit." He cracked up laughing and told me about his life in New York as a fashion photographer with his studio above Carnegie Hall. He gave me the tour with his trademark easy twang glamour. He was the first member of his high school class of '65 who was openly gay. It was heartbreaking to learn Rabbit fell to the AIDS epidemic in 1988—before there were any meds. Somehow, I was spared—but for what, I wondered.

That Speech on Popularity

Reviewing my school days papers saved over the years, one letter sent me reeling back to the world of junior high school popularity, my old survival strategy. It is a handwritten letter addressed to me in 1965 as student council president. "Dear Charles," it begins, "Thank you for the wonderful speech you gave on popularity."

The fifties Highland Park look in the sixties. Student council
president at the podium (*corner right*).

Oh my God.

"We didn't give you a long time to make a speech, but we think
you did it well. We are proud to have leaders like you in our school.
Thanks again for giving us some of your valuable time!" signed
by three kids from room 228. I probably said something about our
winning school spirit (the jocks and cheerleaders) and how best to
be "true to your school," as the Beach Boys' Brian Wilson wrote.
One day I was called upon to do just that when the fifties sex-symbol
Jayne Mansfield ("The Girl Can't Help It," 1956) visited our junior
high (she had attended Highland Park). The principal summoned
me, as student council president, into his office to greet Mansfield
and her shady looking husband. We walked into the hallway for the
standard walk-by of trophies and awards, and suddenly the hallway
bells began clanging. The hall jammed with kids, who could not
believe their adolescent eyes when they saw Mansfield, a former
Playboy bunny, wearing an insane pink sweater that dared you to
look away. Some bad boy jumped over the crowd and touched her;

she screamed, and we ran for cover in the principal's office. I am still processing this.

I knew there were two of me: the true-to-my-school student council president who would greet Jayne Mansfield and introduce the prom queen, and the me who crushed on guys. I even managed to have a first-love/special relationship for years with a classmate, beginning one summer night in a sauna and swim that we kept secret—a memory we enjoy to this day. Still, back then I prayed this would all magically one day go away—maybe when I went to college later, at the University of Virginia, then all male.

Right.

***

It was 1969 when I walked into my first gay bar. Atlantis was downtown on Field Street, just blocks from the shuttered Carousel Club, the infamous burlesque bar owned by Jack Ruby, the killer of Lee Harvey Oswald. The reason why I highlight my first gay bar is that this was a weird rite of passage for gays and lesbians in the day when we were still criminalized aliens in Texas. There were zero organizations or civic ways to meet. LGBTQ youth were pushed down into a netherworld without family, friends, or support. It was sink or swim. You might think a bar named Atlantis would have some sea-related décor. Not this place, with its white plaster statue at the front door of Michelangelo's *David*, the patron saint of old-time queer bars. How did I ever get here?

There was this cool young guy—I'll call him Jules—in my high school trigonometry class. Perhaps Canadian or French, Jules mesmerized me with his European-style demeanor and fishnet T-shirt. I reasoned if he was named Jules and dressed like that—so un–Highland Park—then perhaps he was like me, since I had no words for *gay*. Obviously I was not paying sufficient attention to trig sine and cosine rules. I fell behind in my studies and appealed to our teacher Catherine Walters, a no-nonsense, military-tough lady. Walters blasted me, and deservedly so. "Who do you think you are?"

she crisply upbraided me in her military style before the class. "The Oracle at Delphi?"

Somehow I convinced Jules to let me go home with him to study trig, and he liked that idea. Unfortunately, when we got to Jules's place, we realized his mother was home—a buzzkill that ended that. But Jules was cool about it all and quietly handed me a book of matches, saying nothing but knowingly pointing to the matchbook's cover. It said Atlantis.

So the Oracle at Delphi went to Atlantis. The police pressure was always in the background, and I imagined (but ignored) how they might identify and expose this underground and underage student council president. It is hilarious to look back at that Atlantis underworld. How can I forget the SMU student athletes, guys who would call each other "Miss Thing"; women who would call one another "dykes" (although you better not), shooting pool with smokes tucked into their tees; country boys from Tyler and queens from Abilene; Tammy Wynette and Judy Garland on the same juke? It was a Texas gay and lesbian sixties, with a cast of characters as varied as the Star Wars cantina. Amid all of this difference, there was tons of love and self-respect in the room. Although, ominously, this was only a borderline safe place. At any moment the lights could come on and it would be ID time, or the police would note our license plate numbers. This was the real, after-dark world in downtown Dallas, a million miles from Grandmother's.

There was another gay bar down the block named Tara, as in *Gone with the Wind*. In the coming years, a new gay dance bar opened in Dallas near Lee Park (yep, named for Robert E. Lee). The bar was The Old Plantation. What was with these Texas gays and lesbians, I often wondered, with their attraction to Old South tacky? Gay and lesbian liberation was slowly making its way to Dallas.

I got over the Old South stuff (and my own fears) soon enough to lay aside the quest to be liked—in order to love.

Namath. Namath.

We could all sense big changes coming our way as the culture colli-sions of the sixties rolled across the small farm and ranch commu-nities in North Texas. My best friend David Sands and I knew this storm coming our way was a "big 'un" when we joined his grandmother's side of the family for Sunday lunch near Corsicana. Granny Sands's family invited us to join them at her homeplace on a farm road, a Depression-era farmhouse with a screened back porch and ceiling fans for family gatherings. David was a hand-some, former junior high school football player who decided to move out of the Brylcreem era to let his hair grow out a bit, with some low-key sideburns. He looked fantastic.

We walked through Granny's front parlor, decorated with those souvenir plates country folks once collected on their road trips, into the smell of jalapeno and bacon-wrapped dove and the buzz of family on the back porch. We stepped out to the back screened porch to greet everyone, and walked into some serious family friction. When they saw David, there was a sudden quiet, then a low gasp. We froze. David's West Texas aunt cracked the moment wide open.

"Namath. Namath," she declared.

"He looks like Namath. Joe Namath." And she wasn't laughing. She was serious, almost in shock. David was caught off guard, and I scrambled for a comeback. I knew almost nothing about college or professional "ball," as they called football, only a little more about the New York Jets quarterback Joe Namath. I liked his looks.

"David, your hair," his aunt pressed. "It looks like shit," she judged in her country candor. "I just think 'Joe Namath,' I cain't help it," she explained, all hunkered down now. Oh, Lord, I thought what if she knew my personal story? We had spun off the farm road and were now trapped at this table, thrown into a rabid discussion of "ball" and Namath. To change the subject, I asked, "Please pass some of that chow chow."[21] The scene was right out of a story by Texas's *Best Little Whorehouse* humorist Larry King.[22]

Somehow, David and I got the folks laughing because we knew this was not about ball. It was about the New York Jets' Joe Namath daring to grow some hot curly locks with sideburns, defying the old standards of masculinity. His aunt had a problem with that. Of course, this was even before Namath went full gender queer in 1974, appearing in a silk pantyhose commercial.

"Namath looks pretty good these days, don't you think so, Dave?" I said.

That broke the fever. And that's what got us through the, ahem, misunderstanding. It was a table fight with plenty of love all around.

David's father's family, Granny's side, was farm and cattle. David's dad told me about the Depression-era days when he would trade eggs for school pencils. Loyd Bowmer Sands was a dashing carrier-based fighter pilot in World War II who made it back alive. Distinctions of wealth or class were dissolved in the heroism of that generation. Loyd Sands was one of those heroes. But David's mom's side "had money" as people would say. "Had money" meant "rich as Texas sin." David's mom, Caroline Hunt, a daughter of the infamous oil billionaire H. L. Hunt, had money, all right. Decades later she would found Rosewood Hotels and Resorts, owning and operating properties like Dallas's famous Mansion on Turtle Creek and the Carlyle Hotel in New York City. She blossomed into one of Dallas's leading citizens—grandmother, philanthropist, and business leader. I loved her so.

The thing about the crack-up at Granny's, why I will never forget it, was that this was not just about masculinity. It was layered with the collision of Texas country and city affluence at one family table. Poor Joe Namath and David's burns were the lightening rod. How dare Namath, who played ball for the University of Alabama, transform himself into a new-style celebrity quarterback who had money in (*eyeroll*) New York? These were FDR Depression-era, farm and cattle people who once swapped eggs for school supplies folded in with the Hunts from El Dorado, Arkansas. That Sunday at Granny's, courtesy of Joe Namath, I got a preview of the culture wars to come.

"Big D, Little A, Double L, A, S"

Is Dallas a town where history dies? Big D definitely was, maybe because it is so young compared to cities like New Orleans or Philadelphia. "Oh, we're from Big D, my oh yes" became our Dallas theme song written in 1956 by Broadway tune composer Frank Loesser. Popularized by Bing Crosby, it was "Big D, little A, double L, A, S." All that fifties white "nice" came crashing down on November 22, 1963, the darkest day in Dallas history. The trauma of the assassination on Dallas and our lives as school kids was agonizing, so we moved on—as Texans will—focusing on the future rather than a past easily erased. This is part of Dallas's dynamism and its damnation. Paul Crume, the *Dallas Morning News* page-one columnist for decades, wrote a final pronouncement: "Two ghosts will hover in the plaza in Dallas, the ghost of a President and the ghost of old hopes and dead dreams."[23]

So many years beyond the sixties, Dallas was still a "jug of white milk," according to former mayor of Dallas Mike Rawlings when he moved there in 1976.[24] Rawlings served as mayor of Dallas from 2011 to 2019. In 2013, for the fiftieth anniversary of the Kennedy assassination, he asked Ruth Altshuler to chair the President John F. Kennedy Commemorative Foundation, which was organizing a city-wide observance and commemoration ceremony at Dealey Plaza. "On my hands and knees, I begged Ruth to take this on," he told me. Thanks to Rawlings and Ruth, it was time for Dallas to do some serious remembering.

Who could be better than Ruth Altshuler to bring the various Dallas communities together to support such a remembrance? Her civic commitment to Dallas was truly all-inclusive. On a special wall in her Dallas home, amid the many mainstream charity plaques like the prestigious Linz Award, one honor greatly moved me. It was given by one of Dallas's original AIDS charities, active when people with AIDS were total pariahs. She told me it was one of her favorites. "Ruth Sharp Altshuler, *Quietly* you have single-handedly provided support for the critical basic needs of people with AIDS in the North Texas area over the last ten years. . . . You have taken care of the basic necessities, leaving people to concentrate on health, wellness, quality of life and enabling them to continue to be contributing members of society. The board, staff, volunteers and clients of the AIDS Resource Center extend our heartfelt appreciation (June, 1996)." The center's parent organization was the Dallas Gay Political Caucus, later to become the Dallas Gay and Lesbian Alliance. According to William Waybourn, president of the Dallas Gay Alliance in those years, "When there was a shortfall . . . Ruth helped keep its AIDS programs afloat when no government agency would touch us."[25] She was there for them.

Mike Rawlings continued with his explanation of why he chose Ruth to chair the commemorative foundation: "I explained to Ruth how this was an opportunity to put a new stake in the ground for Dallas, a chance to redefine the brand." Rawlings, a Democrat, believed it equally important to focus on the legacy of JFK, after decades of official nonrecognition of the date in deference to the wishes of the Kennedy family. Characterized as "one of the most consequential, community-minded figures in Dallas history,"[26] Ruth agreed to do this on the condition that she would not have to raise the money. As things turned out, she raised nearly all of it. She was too emotionally invested in the success of the project and speaking about her personal and our collective trauma as Dallasites and the journey forward as a major progressive city. Having worked for years as a consultant to Exxon-Mobil, headquartered in Dallas, I offered to arrange a lunch there for us to tell the story and ask for support. ExxonMobil generously contributes many millions to philanthropies worldwide. Ruth agreed that would be a good thing.

I remember pacing in front of the ultra-architectural, sleek Exxon-Mobil headquarters in Las Colinas, waiting for Aunt Ruth to arrive in the driveway lined with fountains and landscaped prairie grasses. She was such a trooper. At age 88 she carried herself with great dignity of occasion and purpose when she arrived at the headquarters and said with a wry laugh, "Well, let's go, Charles. You got me into this."

We walked into the great hall of the imposing corporate headquarters to make the case for Dallas, and the kind of city Dallas had
become, not the nightmare City of Hate described by Jack Ruby's
attorney Melvin Belli. She spoke eloquently that day in the silent
corporate dining room about the need for all of Dallas to unite behind
this effort, not to erase the tragedy, but to mark it with a dignified
ceremony and a forward-looking message of hope. She had called her
friend, historian David McCullough, to speak, and she'd asked former
Dallas Cowboys quarterback Roger Staubach to reach out to his alma
mater, the US Naval Academy and its glee club. Staubach was a Naval
Academy Heisman Trophy winner and had remembered JFK in an
ESPN interview: "He was at the '62 game . . . and he was going to be
at the '63 game."[27]

She asked ExxonMobil for $50,000, explaining that her goal was
that the $3 million needed to pay for it all would be paid for by private
donations. The ceremony was needed "to grieve as well as to reflect
upon what Dallas has become . . . I am tired of the City of Hate and all
that junk," she said. I suppose we should not have been surprised when
no one at ExxonMobil, with then chairman and CEO Rex Tillerson,
ever got back to her. I had to push and push, and then the response
came, a cold "No." No to Ruth and no to Dallas history. I could only
blame myself. Most American companies are mistakenly all-in for
politics, not history. History is soul. Corporations do not have one.
Nor do global corporations have hometowns. They have headquarters. ExxonMobil later moved to Houston, and Tillerson joined the
Trump administration. For the companies that dodge history, this scale
of erasure is a grave one. Will cities without honest history, immersed
in political division, support the "ism," as Grandmother Francis would
say, of capitalism?

Looking back at the memorial, Mike Rawlings said it was not the
companies that came through; it was individual Dallasites like the
iconoclastic Ross Perot and Ruth Altshuler. Ruth used her perfected
technique of personal, handwritten notes to raise the money for Dallas
to remember, and she was unphased by those who would not step up

or those who criticized the project altogether. "Ruth," they would say, "why on *earth* are you doing this?"

She arrived November 22, 2013, at the podium in Dealey Plaza with a cough that would never completely go away, wearing her earmuffs in the cold drizzle. Mayor Rawlings spoke powerfully, and plainly for all who—like Ruth—were there in 1963 at the Dallas Trade Mart luncheon waiting for the slain president who would never arrive. "The past is never in the past," he said.

Rawlings and others remembered the words of Dallas Rabbi Levi Olan from Temple Emanu-El who spoke eloquently about the tragedy on its first anniversary in 1964. "The most threatening danger to our existence," Rabbi Olan said on his KRLD radio program, "is the poison of hate which had been coursing in our national veins . . . Epithets of treason and traitor were hurled recklessly and crudely in passion and bitterness." He continued almost prophetically, "A group openly organized and dared to call itself the American Nazi Party, hoping to transform our nation. On that day we became aware of the poison." The commemoration reminded us the poison is still with us.

It was a somber, dignified ceremony marked by scores of church bells pealing precisely at 12:30 p.m. all across Dallas. No longer the light-hearted big D, little A, double L, A, S, Dallas did remember that day, and, thanks to Rawlings and Ruth, Dallas could let go of Paul Crume's "ghosts of old hopes and dead dreams."[28]

The morning after, Mike Rawlings hand delivered the *Dallas Morning News* to Ruth on her front porch. "Looking like a movie star in a flowered Japanese-style dressing gown," Rawlings remembers her that morning when he held up the page one headline: "Dallas Struck Pitch-Perfect Note in First Observance of JFK Assassination Anniversary."[29] "Pitch perfect. At that moment, Ruth looked like the happiest woman on earth," he said.

Dallas and I are forever linked in a weave of nonlinear time flying from a hospital oxygen tent through this young city's history, neither forgotten nor fully reckoned with. As ridiculous as it may sound,

Ruth Altshuler challenged Dallas to remember. Photo by Charles Francis.

I began my reckoning with Dallas when, like an emigrant of sorts, I escaped its gravity to attend Thomas Jefferson's University of Virginia. At age eighteen, I was a Texan first. That was my identity, both callow and cool (I thought). Then I was turned, as spymasters say, at the University, which is what many Virginians still call UVA. Turned from a Texan to a Virginian? No, but a Texan transformed into an *American* youth my mother would later laughingly say she no longer recognized. The squeaky student council president? Gone. The Transformer now at her front door had been exposed to the sixties, fused with the ideas of Jefferson and his failings, too, while the country was mired in Vietnam.

Turned and "turned on," as people once said, I became co-chairman of the University's concert production organization that in 1972 brought Chuck Berry to Charlottesville for one of the University's so-called Big Weekends. I did not know whether to call him Chuck or Mr. Berry, I was so unnerved when he arrived after 9:30 p.m. Berry the legend was real high and real late, with one thing on his mind—getting paid. I can still hear the wall of boos that exploded into a roar when Chuck Berry, styling a shiny white suit and gold chains, duck-walked into the spotlight. "Roll over, Beethoven," he rocked.

On the academic side of life (there was one) I had the opportunity to study at UVA's Department of English a fabulous survey of American literature that introduced me to America's poet laureate Walt Whitman. It was the exact right moment in my life to connect with Whitman. A gay youth looking for new moorings, I immersed myself in Whitman's writings and ideas, which changed me. "In Paths Untrodden" became my path and a light in the years to come. "In paths untrodden," he wrote, "In the growth by margins of pond-waters . . . I proceed, for all who are, or have been, young men, / To tell the secret of my nights and days, / To celebrate the need of comrades."[30] That need of comrades drove me onward.

I walked that path far from Dallas. With the burr in my saddle of being gay, an identity of difference and talents yet to be explored, it was time for a new life elsewhere.

Chapter 2

TVTV to USC

A fter leaving Texas, I thought forever, and graduating from UVA, my goal in moving to Los Angeles was to join a self-described guerilla video commune born in the San Francisco Bay Area by the name of TVTV (Top Value Television). I had not lost my mind. In 1976 I had fallen in love with something called a Sony Portapak. Of course, underlying it all, the mission was to become a whole, not a half, human being who could love whomever I wanted. I could not find that in Dallas.

The Portapak was a Sony half-inch video camera and reel-to-reel recorder that you could strap onto your back and produce documentaries with a half-hour battery. It was that long ago. No longer would documentary production be the sole province of networks or major production companies. The Portapak was a revolutionary tool, mastered by TVTV. "At the time, no one had ever seen a portable camera stuck in their face, let alone one held with what *Newsweek* called 'braless, blue-jeaned, video freaks.' . . . TVTV used it to make format-bending satirical shows about whatever interested them."[1] For the first independent video documentary shown on national public television, made with Portapaks, the TVTV guerillas went to Houston to produce *Lord of the Universe*—a hilarious documentary that unfolded at the Astrodome.[2] The Guru Maharaj Ji promised to *levitate* the Astrodome in a three-day "happening" for the lost and crazed. This Texas scam spokesman for the Divine Light Mission was the antiwar Chicago Seven activist Rennie Davis.

Back in Dallas, before moving to LA, I must have watched this documentary a dozen times in laughter and awe, far away from the Divine Light Mission, in Dallas, on a 16 mm projector borrowed from the St. Marks School of Texas. This was how life was before the internet. After seeing what TVTV had accomplished at the Astrodome, I had to have a Sony Portapak. Where to focus it but on the Southwestern Exposition and Livestock Show in Fort Worth? Hot cowboys, spangled cowgirls, a pair of conjoined teenage twins, and pure Texana in the key of Bob Wills and His Texas Playboys made this rodeo Portapak perfect. My friend and Portapak partner, Mike Langley from Midland (who later joined CBS Theatrical Films in New York), loved Bob Wills and introduced me to the Texas Playboys' western swing hit "Big Balls in Cowtown." I never could quite figure out that title, but we included it in the video. Our next subject was Dallas's "rasslin'" promoter Jack Adkisson, a former SMU football player whose villainous ring name was Fritz von Erich. Mike and I focused our Portapak on Fritz's ghastly Texas Death Matches held inside a barbed wire cage at Dallas's Sportatorium while longing to acquire his collection of old Kinescope 16 mm films of Texas wrestling stars of the fifties and sixties.

Among those stars was Duke Keomuka, a former Texas heavyweight champion. His real name was Martin Hisao Tanaka, and he was a Japanese American from California. Unknown to the Dallas fans, Keomuka/Tanaka had been incarcerated during World War II at Manzanar, California, the internment camp for Japanese American citizens stripped of their constitutional rights. Now a national historic site, the Manzanar camp held at its peak some ten thousand Japanese Americans behind barbed wire without charge or trial. Somehow

Keomuka/Tanaka found a way to fuse anger, cynicism, and financial need into the role of a Japanese karate and "claw" master who destroyed his American opponents. Maybe he loved the revenge at some level: if you cannot get even, get rich.

The Sportatorium, a corrugated-metal auditorium on the corner of Cadiz and Industrial in downtown Dallas, hosted the Fritz von Erich world of reenacted violence of Germans, Japanese, and masked Mexican heroes and bad guys. These kinds of slightly twisted subjects and my hoity-toity background as an English major became my ticket to LA; I was accepted to the University of Southern California School of Cinematic Arts in Los Angeles. Somehow I explained it all to the folks at USC and TVTV.

The video guerillas at TVTV, relocated from the Bay Area to Robertson Boulevard in West Hollywood, were nonplussed when this young man from Texas knocked on their commune door. But they were impressed I knew so much about *Lord of the Universe*. I understood what they were trying to accomplish with their half-dozen Portapaks lying around on counters, so the founders, Michael and Megan Shamberg, and their team let me volunteer as a student from USC. I was a Texas refugee who suited their counter-industry style. Michael Shamberg called the networks "beast television." How cool to became a TVTV gofer. I happily painted their walls. I dropped off gear and tapes to Bob at his Malibu home (that'd be Bob Dylan). I met Bill Murray at the TVTV house on Robertson, working on the next TVTV guerilla video, *TVTV Goes to the Oscars*, a deadpan comedy look at the Oscars built around a fictional character played by Lily Tomlin.

TVTV productions, I recollect, were shot on half-inch and edited on three-fourths-inch magnetic tape with no computers—a generational and technological leap for documentary production. I was inspired to witness this countercultural video frontier. TVTV was located in the heart of gay, big-time decorator Hollywood, across the street from the massive disco Studio One, described as a "temple of excess."[3] Soon enough I found it to be just that. Bill Murray joined the new *Saturday Night Live* (SNL) the next year, and TVTV got a deal with NBC. I received

TVTV
PO Box 48-455 Los Angeles CA 90048

14 December 1976

Mr. Charles Francis
3789 S. Menlo
Los Angeles, California 90007

Dear Charlie:

Now that NBC has moved TVTV out of the short lived phenomena
catagory, it is more important than ever that we keep in touch
with our former peers.

My "Dear Charlie" letter from TVTV. Loved their logo.

a nice note, despite my lowly status: It looks like we are moving out
of the short-lived phenomena category, so please keep in touch. I did
keep in touch—with the big idea I took from Robertson Boulevard: one
could independently originate research and create ideas and materials
with a new voice for national distribution. Long before there was
an internet, there was TVTV, with a new generation's approach to
television production and comedy, adopted by SNL. It was all there
within reach, I knew now, thanks to TVTV.

USC Cinema, where I enrolled in graduate studies in 1976, was
the anti-TVTV. I entered a world of traditional Hollywood industry
storytelling, learning the history of movies and moviemakers.
This seems prehistoric today now that USC School of Cinematic Arts
has a new George Lucas building, named for the school's most famous
graduate. Across the street from USC Cinema in Los Angeles's
Exposition Park is the spectacular Lucas Museum of Narrative Art,
a three-hundred-thousand-square-foot intergalactic, eye-popping

building set to become the leading visual narrative cinematic museum in the United States. It is a wonderful contrast with USC Cinema's open quadrangle of sheds in the seventies and the day we screened the 1951 classic Hollywood musical *Singin' in the Rain*, starring Gene Kelly and Debbie Reynolds. So far from Lucas, we endured a nearly shot-by-shot analysis taught by my professor who was *the* authority on the musicals of Kelly and his codirector Stanley Donen. This was old-school Hollywood, only at USC Cinema. But no matter the era, we were well taught the fundamental vocabulary with super 8 mm and 16 mm student film projects.

I learned to think for the first time about the power of images themselves to move audiences, from the theories of Russian filmmaker Serge Eisenstein's Odessa steps sequence to the French documentary *Night and Fog* (1956), a devastating exploration of Auschwitz and its meanings, produced when the Holocaust was often depicted as a Jewish side issue to World War II. USC Cinema would screen three and four films a day for us, a Hollywood immersion with discussions by colorful experts like A. D. Murphy, a *Daily Variety* box office analyst. "Domestic B. O. Sizzles in Record July," was the argot of this chain-smoking, seen-it-all reporter with a Hollywood leather bar look. George Lucas he was not.

At USC I learned about myself apart from Dallas and Charlottesville in a wholly different way. For the first time in my life, I was anonymous. As E. B. White wrote about New York, LA bestowed upon me "the gift of loneliness and the gift of privacy."[4] This was my golden opportunity for growth. All of my networks were erased. It felt good, but at times that feeling came along with the anxiety of free-falling—to where I did not know. I joined my first gay family, a chosen family of dear queer friends, an essential step in "coming out" with any semblance of mental health. Until then I had been a solo operator. But coming out is not a solo act.

We met at the ersatz Spanish Casa Loma apartments almost beneath the Harbor Freeway in the heart of downtown LA. At Casa Loma we were exploring our own personal stories entwined with living through

LGBTQ history. Only three years earlier had homosexuality been delisted as a mental illness by the American Psychiatric Association. We were characterized as insane by our enemies while we were loving our LGBTQ edges. We would screen for each other our super 8 films and read some excellent screenwriting. Greg would explain communications theory, as taught at the Annenberg School of Communications. Daryl from Burleson, Texas, would hilariously interpret Vivien Leigh and Los Angeles faith healer Kathryn Kuhlman. Karl from Girard, Ohio, schooled us on playwright Harold Pinter and British cinema. And there was John, the one true filmmaker among us. He could write, shoot, and cut the old footage, solve the film's problems, and create the magic. I thought it exciting when John went to work as an editor for Alan Landsburg Productions, a grinding television factory that produced an early reality television series titled *In Search of . . .* on thoughtful subjects like the paranormal, Bigfoot, and the Loch Ness monster. This was the real world in LA, but we all knew John would go far beyond Bigfoot. Until he fell ill with something dreadful and deadly, before there were words or meds. Before we knew anything about the breaking epidemic coming our way. We will always be "in search of" John and his lost brilliance.

In Los Angeles I collaborated with a brilliant friend from Jefferson City, Missouri, on a screenplay entitled *Western Swing*. It was about Delmonico "Del" Jones who sold steaks out of his cow van, became a cattle rustler, and fought for justice to get a life in Kilgore, Texas, with a Kilgore Rangerette at his side. (The Rangerettes are an East Texas collegiate drill team.) Without an agent, with no connections or family networks in LA, we worked hard to have our screenplay read and optioned by a studio. The rejections were painful and a first for me. I was conditioned to believe I would always succeed, even when that belief made no sense. The executive editor of Walt Disney Productions wrote me, "While you are to be commended for a well-written script, the subject is too controversial for the audience we are trying to reach. We question whether or not a cattle rustler as a hero would have wide appeal." So funny, and back then painful, because our cattle rustler was a young man, not unlike me and my Missouri partner, who believed passionately in the future. I see now that I was looking for a rustler of my own. I was starved to meet a fellow young Texan (I still missed the breed), someone who could relate to me as gay man and be interested in filmmaking and storytelling . . . and who believed everything was possible. Oh, and he needed to be gorgeous and cool. Thanks to the fates of Hollywood, that would be the actor and Fort Worth native Bill Paxton.

I met Bill in 1976 on a set at the landmark Western movie theatre not far from USC. He was acting in a student film project and reminded me then of a silent screen idol. He was in love with his image, in a healthy way, instinctively knowing that the way forward for him was the camera . . . and his face. I was there to watch and help out, if I could, as part of the student filmmaking crowd always on the lookout for actors and actresses who would work for free in our productions in exchange for a copy of the film.

We had Dallas–Fort Worth and film in common and hit it off. Bill told me he had been in LA since he was eighteen, beginning with set design and production with Roger Corman, a legendary low-budget horror film producer, and Sissy Spacek and her husband Jack Fisk helping out on various production design projects. I was so impressed with Bill's ability to survive and thrive in this world—and to escape Fort Worth. There was a fuzzy line between crushing on him and being a buddy. His wide grin and Fort Worth accent dazzled me, as did the real possibility of his future total stardom. So I preferred crushing and being with him whenever I could catch up. To his credit, he could be in like while I could be in love, and he fended me off while making it all so pleasant. Bill Paxton had a lot of experience with that.

The thing about Bill I loved so much, beginning years before his first break, was his earnest interest in acting, not just in stardom or working. For his entire life that interest was anchored in an appreciation of history itself—art history, film history, and Texas history. When we would talk about him and his acting, which was fine with me, we'd wind up talking about Buster Keaton's close-ups or Harold Lloyd in the silent classic *Safety Last*, hanging from the hands of a huge clock on the side of a building. Then Bill's facade would crack and reveal a young actor's fear that it would all go absolutely nowhere under the white-hot LA sky. Like so many others, I am sure, I would rush to Bill's side. The whole process of endurance is murder for stunning Hollywood nobodies. My one idea, and it turned out to be a good one, was to present Bill with a copy of an essay that had meant so much to me (and still does) as an openly gay newbie in search of a career. Titled "On Self Reliance," by Ralph Waldo Emerson, the essay struck a resonant chord with Bill. "There comes a time in every man's education," Emerson wrote, "when he arrives at the conviction that envy is ignorance; that imitation is suicide; that he must take himself for better or for worse as his portion. . . . Trust thyself, every heart vibrates to that iron string. . . . Your conformity explains nothing."[5]

Bill and I talked a lot about Emerson's nineteenth-century set of ideas. Decades later, after *Titanic*, *Apollo 11*, *Twister*, *True Lies*, and so many other films, he wrote me a handwritten letter about us in that time: "I still have the R. W. Emerson tome on 'Self-Reliance' you armed me with when I ventured to NYC . . . It has served me well," Bill wrote. I *armed* him with it; I teared up. Nostalgically, he reminded me about the day I handed him the key to my wonderful, old Hollywood-style bungalow called the Cha Court. It once was the Chalet Court, but the "let" disintegrated in the salty fog near Santa Monica beach. So that he could get out of Hollywood, I bequeathed him the Cha Court. "I was down by USC and thought of your apartment back in the day," he said. How could we ever forget?

Over the years it was so much fun to see how Bill's fans loved him and his roles, thanks in large part to his best friend and agent who guided his career, Brian Swardstrom. At a reception in Dallas in 2015, my husband, Stephen, and our baby boy, Thomas, were with Bill and a group of people who loved Western art, including a number of folks from Utah who were raised in the Mormon faith. The History Channel's miniseries *Texas Rising*, starring Bill as Sam Houston, was about to premier. ("The citizens of Texas must rally

Catching up on old times in Santa Monica with Bill Paxton (1955–2017).

to the aid of our army, or it will perish."[6]) Suddenly there was a stir when three ladies introduced themselves to Bill and began laughing, playfully flirting with and teasing him. They then dropped to their knees in mock adulation. Bill cracked up, and it hit me. He was no longer Bill Paxton, or Sam Houston, but the polygamist he had played for five seasons—Bill Henrickson from the hit HBO series, *Big Love*.

"Oh no, ladies, please," he laughed, and they all hugged each other like he was their *Big Love* patriarch with three sister wives. This was head spinning, pure joy, I thought.

My favorite buddy and patriarch, Bill, and I remained friends for life, until his passing at age 61 in 2017.

I was probably the only person in the seventies who thought of Bill as Capraesque, film school speak for the virtuous Everyman created by director Frank Capra in films like *Mr. Smith Goes to Washington* (1939). Bill was a Texan Mr. Smith, I thought. I was searching for ideas to write about, or to discover—this kind of innocent, brave hero in the America of the 1970s, men or women who believe in their personal agency to make things better, and they were out there, I knew. They still are.

Oddly enough, I found them in the debates surrounding the national debt. The seventies go-round of controversy over the size of the national debt was giving the country migraines, and still is with our fierce debt ceiling debates. However, for some few it inspired them to help their country in charming, quixotic, and selfless ways. I had read and heard about this and came up with the idea to take advantage of the new Freedom of Information Act to put a human face on citizen concern about our debt. I wrote the Department of the Treasury a FOIA request: "As you probably know, each year the Treasury Department receives voluntary payments from private citizens who are concerned about the ever-increasing national debt. May I have the names and addresses of these 'national debt donors' or some way of contacting them so that those who would like to appear in a documentary may do so?" The Treasury Department went into action, contacting the donors about the project and forwarding them my address in Santa Monica. I still cannot believe this happened, but it was a simpler, more func-tional, certainly more trusting time.

This first time I hit FOIA paydirt was thrilling for me. I received a letter written by a widow from Seabrook, Texas.

"Dear Mr. Francis, Last year my husband made a sizeable payment to the Department of Treasury as a donation to decrease the national debt," a handwritten letter reads. The donation was requested in his will to reflect "his share of the national debt . . . by dividing the total national debt on 12/26/75 by the total population, the per capital debt was $2,656.15 and this is the amount my husband paid to the Bureau of Government Finan-cial Operations." Another wrote me, "I have been giving to the Treasurer a dollar for each year I have been privileged to be part of our great country for a long time . . . in itself it amounts to nothing. All it does of course is make me feel a little better that I have done what I can to the solution of one of our most important problems." And there was one about "my dearest little friend, my Airedale Scotty . . . I have been wondering how I can honor her memory."

I pulled all of these letters together and, rather than track the writers down with a Portapak (hat tip to TVTV), pitched the concept to a senior producer at CBS's *Sixty Minutes* in New York. I wrote him, "Some viewers would consider the 'national debt donors' as sad, stupid or just plain brainwashed . . . whatever your beliefs, there is something touching, heartwarming and, at the same time, quite serious going on here." The letter hit its mark. Without completing my degree program, I loaded up the car for the five-day drive to New York City. In 1979 *Sixty Minutes* produced it in a segment titled "Dear Uncle Sam," brought to life in the perfect tone by Morley Safer, and thanks to the decency of veteran CBS producer Joe Wershba, the show granted me the credit I craved to get a start in New York. Just meeting Joe was a thrill. His manual typewriter letters, complete with strikeouts and little notes, would close with "Yr Obdt etc joe." "joe" was the deputy to legendary CBS newsman Edward R. Murrow in the 1950s, and created investigations for *Sixty Minutes* for two decades. He was forever asked about Murrow and how he played a key role in Murrow's 1954 showdown with Senator Joseph McCarthy over the accusation of Communist and homosexual infiltration of government—"nests" of them. "joe," true to form, would play the whole thing down because it was simply so huge.

In 1953 President Dwight Eisenhower had signed the infamous Executive Order 10450, declaring so-called perverts a threat to the nation's security, banning homosexuals from government service and dooming us all to investigations, firings, and discharges for decades to come. Wershba, in the day, was part of that fight—by helping end McCarthy.

I still kiss the sidewalks of New York City for all of this. In the typewriter style of "joe wershba," charles f. moved to nyc.

Chapter 3

Chase Manhattan Rockefeller

I first met David Rockefeller on a loading dock.
I thought I recognized him. Bespoke wool pinstripes, that was he. I was waiting in the bowels of One Chase Manhattan Plaza in lower Manhattan for the bank's car. In 1980 I was a new hire in the bank's public relations and corporate communications division with the assignment to write remarks for the bank's management and to help field the scores of press inquiries that would pour weekly into the bank. After having conceived and researched that segment of *Sixty Minutes*, I applied for a job at Chase with a writing sample of remarks on the stultifying subject of "Improving the Nation's Productivity." The vice president of public relations, Fraser Seitel, held up a giant stack of resumes, laughing, and said, "Let's see what you can do." A chance, I thought, and went for this opportunity as though I had just landed at the Port Authority Bus Terminal on Forty-Second Street. It takes that mixture of panic and optimism to launch in New York. My first assignment, thankfully, was nothing about productivity. It was to draft Chairman David Rockefeller's remarks for a check presentation to purchase horses for the Central Park Rangers.

The key to working for David Rockefeller: treat him like a thing, maybe a luxury watch, I learned. He did not know how to be a boss or one of the fellows. Raised during the 1920s in Manhattan baronial style, the grandson of John D. Rockefeller Sr., he was neither arrogant nor overbearing in any way, only understated to a degree almost startling to a Texan like me raised around the vivid and loud. (Think "Namath. Namath.") Mr. Rockefeller's work schedule was in fifteen-minute meetings and moments. From me he needed one thing: words and more words. I did my best to deliver them by mining his memories and ideas. I poured myself into our first set of remarks: "I am delighted to present this check for $50,000—and I hear one of the horses is already named Chase." The remarks are so silly, and yet I have them framed on my wall. I took the remarks on cards to the loading dock, where I was told to meet Mr. Rockefeller and ride with him uptown to Central Park, in his limo driven by his longtime bodyguard.

"Hello, Mr. Rockefeller, I am Charles Francis from Public Relations."

"Oh, hello"—he was super distracted, not focused on the loading dock—"now where are we going?"

I almost thought he seemed confused. I had never been around an overscheduled CEO before, so what did I know? What I did know was to throw myself into this ride uptown and brief him on the all-important check presentation—the park rangers, the horses, and Elizabeth "Betsy" Barlow, the visionary new Central Park administrator from San Antonio who had the idea to create a public-private partnership to save the park from total destruction. He listened patiently, shuffled through some papers, and pocketed the remarks, never to touch them again.

He needed no preparation. He had been speaking to groups and making presentations, receiving every award imaginable for decades. He later recounted for me how he once spoke to the Hobo College in Chicago during the Depression. I learned the Hobo College was an organization to benefit teenage migrant workers and men of the road and rails to uplift them during the Depression with lectures about politics, history, and personal hygiene. I loved how he spoke with sincerity about Central Park itself, recognizing it as a powerful expression of American democracy and, later, posing with park rangers, horses, and a mock check for the *Daily News*. For him this was a nano-moment in a busy day. For Betsy Barlow it was an important endorsement of her work to save Central Park, then teetering on the brink of collapse. For me it was like Robert Lawson's children's story *Ben and Me* (1923), a mouse-eye view of Benjamin Franklin. I was the newbie getting a glimpse of this towering public figure.

David Rockefeller (DR) making a donation to the Central Park rangers was my introduction to his role as the preeminent corporate statesman of the era—the founder of the New York City Partnership, which includes three hundred CEOs; chairman of the Museum of Modern Art; and on and on for the youngest grandson of John D. Rockefeller. For the first time, I witnessed how power and civic engagement can work for the public welfare. Decades later at his memorial service celebrating his 101 years, attended by thousands, Mike Bloomberg described him perfectly: "No individual has contributed more to the community and civic life of New York City over a longer period of time than David Rockefeller. . . . [it was a] spirit of civic responsibility that defined his career."[1]

Heading back to the bank from Central Park, he and I rode together in the back seat and became snarled in traffic. There were no phones, not even those phone bricks that would come later. So the corporate statesman, poor guy, was stuck with me for nearly an hour. We cruised past the Council on Foreign Relations, the international think tank where he had been serving as chairman since 1970. We had nothing but time, so he told me about the council and how he and Henry Kissinger had been associated there since the fifties. Somehow I was able to parry those memories by bringing up a new controversial book by William Shawcross, *Sideshow: Kissinger, Nixon, and the Destruction of Cambodia* (1979). In it Shawcross savaged Kissinger. DR's reaction was swift—"outrageous, inaccurate, and unfair to Henry," defending Nixon and Kissinger's war strategy that had rocked the

country. I strongly disagreed but listened intently. Our snail's pace
limousine tour continued.

"There, that mansion next door to the council, is the headquarters of the Americas Society / Council of the Americas." It was given
by "my Cousin Margaret de Cuevas," arranged by DR since he had
founded the Council of the Americas. Head-spinning stuff, it was like
that all the way back to the loading dock, where my career in corporate communications begins. The next day I received a note from my
boss: "Just wanted to report that Mr. Rockefeller was very impressed
with your performance at the equestrian ceremony in Central Park.
Well done."[2]

I had done nothing but listen.

As a walk-on into the ether of Rockefeller's world, I was punching
so far above my weight that a reality check was long overdue. It came
with a bank robbery. When one thinks about Rockefeller and a global
financial powerhouse like Chase (now JP Morgan Chase), the idea
of a heist seems impossible. I found out differently when I was told
to report to the same loading dock and pile into a bank car waiting to
speed me to a branch in Roslyn, Long Island. I learned on the ride to
the branch the police said this was a "professional, sophisticated job."
Long Island's *Newsday* reported a trio of burglars had used a blow-
torch and a "$4,000 drill to cut through the six-inch-thick steel and
concrete sides of vault."[3] That vault was a huge safe deposit box, I was
told without further detail. My job was to witness the scene, advise the
branch manager on how to respond, and get back to One Chase Plaza
and start drafting our statement and responding to the city tabloids that
were going wild.

Like a PTSD flash, I can still see the inside of that vault with scores
of safe deposit boxes drilled and ripped open, cascades of documents,
cash, destroyed jewel boxes, and pearls scattered on the vault floor.
When I saw a lock of baby hair, I gasped. I was quoted in the same
Newsday piece as the bank's information officer, calmly saying, "We
have started an inventory asking all box holders to provide a list of
what might have been taken."[4] I still shiver at the temerity of that

statement. What might have been taken? At that point my main goal was to squeeze through the branch's locked doors without experiencing the physical wrath of Long Island customers—and return to headquarters. The memory of that crazy-world, breached vault reminds me of revelations to come.

The writing assignments kept rolling in: Pusan lunch with government officials and customers, DR Seoul breakfast with Chase officers, DR Hong Kong dinner hosted by Hong Kong and Shanghai Bank. DR was ever gracious as I sometimes struggled to keep up with him and his amazing life. I was assigned remarks he was to make at the Asia Society's new headquarters on Park Avenue. In preparation I interviewed him at the Rockefeller family office, called simply Room 5600, the fifty-sixth floor of 30 Rock, to extract stories and facts that only he would know. DR's late brother John and his wife Blanchette played the leading role in the formation of the Asia Society and its art collection.

"So, let's talk about Blanch-ette," I said, mangling her name, Texas- style. "Blanch-ette" like Rockette.

Without missing a beat, he responded, "Umm, Blanchette," as pronounced properly in French.

Later I was asked to staff DR on the US Business Committee on Jamaica, an effort requested by newly elected president Ronald Reagan, who had invited Jamaican prime minister Edward Seaga as the first foreign PM to meet with him at the White House. "Why Seaga?" I asked.

"He won election against a pro-Cuban Marxist predecessor."

Oh, I see.

And then there was the so-called prime rate of interest. It had already hit a record 21 percent. Under fire I would say the prime was "our response to current market conditions . . . the raw material of banks is money,"[5] a deliberately anodyne response to sharp inquiries as the Reagan anti-inflation policies took hold.

Back at One Chase Plaza, I walked past the bank's looming, child-like sculpture by Jean Dubuffet, *Group of Four Trees*, commissioned

Sitting in on an interview with DR, Chase Manhattan Bank Chairman
David Rockefeller (1981). Charles Francis collection.

by DR in 1969. It is a fun, fantastical contrast to the financial institution
towering above it. I was taken aback by the stark contrast of the bank's
Dubuffet encircled by enraged Iranian students shouting and chanting
about Rockefeller, the Great Satan, and the exiled shah, Mohammad
Reza Pahlavi. We were not in Central Park anymore. By 1979 the world
knew how David Rockefeller and his team—led by his chief of staff
Joseph Reed—had played a major role in bringing the exiled Pahlavis
into the United States for medical treatment. We were constantly field-
ing questions in our public relations unit about his relationship to the
shah and the role he played with respect to the government's decision to
admit the shah to the United States, which triggered the Iranian hostage
crisis that would bring down the Carter presidency. All of us in Corporate Communications would constantly restate that helping the shah
was done not only for friendly reasons but also for strong humanitarian
reasons. Reflecting on those questions and answers, I am reminded of

a photograph of DR and me in his office, him being interviewed on the occasion of his retirement. We look like older/younger "Mad Men" discussing a brand—his brand.

Decades later, in 2017, after Joseph and DR had passed, I discovered a secret history of Chase's relationship with the shah in exile. This history was in an archive created by Reed and donated to the Beinecke Rare Book and Manuscript Library at Yale, restricted until after his death.[6] Joseph had alerted me to its existence. I traveled to New Haven as soon as the Yale librarian gave me the green light. The contents of the Reed/shah files were revelatory. David Kirkpatrick, reporting for *The New York Times*, wrote "How a Chase Chairman Helped the Deposed Shah of Iran Enter the US."[7] Kirkpatrick reported it all began when the shah fled the 1979 Islamic Revolution and was not admitted into the United States, so he appealed for help to DR and Reed. The shah was one of the bank's most profitable clients, so Chase launched a full-court lobbying effort to gain his admittance to the United States. They succeeded, triggering Iranian students' takeover of the American embassy in Tehran. Reed dubbed their effort "Project Eagle" and locked it up in his papers. The Project Eagle archive confirmed what we were saying during the Carter years was neither a lie nor wholly true. Discovering Project Eagle, I was reminded of that blow-torched Chase bank vault—our secure world, all that we thought we knew, dumped all over the floor.

I did not know then the extent of the bank's involvement in an ultra-sophisticated lobbying campaign led by Henry Kissinger to bring the shah into the United States. I felt it important that I, having spoken for the bank about this,[8] bring the archival truth to the *Times*. "Now a newly disclosed secret history from the office of David Rockefeller shows in vivid detail how the Chase Manhattan Bank and its well-connected chairman worked behind the scenes to persuade the Carter Administration to admit the Shah, one of the bank's most profitable clients," Kirkpatrick wrote. "Charles Francis, a veteran of corporate public affairs who worked for Chase at the time, brought the documents to the *Times* attention."[9]

After the story was published in 2019, so many years after I had worked for Chase, I was sorry to hear a Rockefeller family insider felt Kirkpatrick's article was a malicious hit piece. Of course he would. But it was not. The article was an accurate report on the Reed archive that contained all of the evidentiary history, from handwritten letters (including the shah and his wife) to confidential memos describing the Rockefeller/Kissinger/Chase operation in real time. Discovering erased history like this, "documented by those who perpetrate it,"[10] is the passion of Archive Activists. The rescue of forgotten, often sealed, history is the mission for citizen Archive Activism. This is especially the case due to slashed media budgets and inattention to topics like LGBTQ history and long-forgotten stories such as the shah's efforts to find a safe haven.

***

"As the curtain falls on the Rockefeller Era at Chase," Joseph Reed wrote me in a memo, "I wanted to take this opportunity to express my full appreciation for your efforts with the finale at the Cloisters."[11] DR's retirement dinner was held at the Cloisters, a medieval art museum built by his father in Fort Tryon Park. I was excited to be part of the writing team for that dinner, marking the end of his chairmanship of "The Chase." Joseph concluded in his uniquely bright and flamboyant style, "Thank you! Bravo! Aloha!" The curtain did fall on this special time in our lives, which was going to play on for DR for another forty years. DR and I maintained our friendship even as I had become openly gay and started agitating the Republican Party of old that he embodied. He never flinched; more so, he stood with me. "Call me David," he said well into his nineties.

For Joseph there would be many subsequent acts, including his being named by President Reagan as ambassador to the Kingdom of Morocco; asked to serve as chief of protocol by his friend President H. W. Bush; and appointed under-secretary-general of the United Nations. "The dogs bark, but the caravan moves on," was one of Joseph's favorite sayings . But for me Rockefeller's curtain was my cue. I would soon learn about a new-style public relations / public affairs company in Washington, a company built upon a bipartisan notion of lobbying and PR star power. This firm was going public on the NASDAQ stock exchange and was located in an old Georgetown electricity plant overlooking the Potomac. It was called the Power House.

Chapter 4

Kings Can Never Be Wrong

"**D**ear Mr. Gray," I wrote Bob Gray cold in 1984. "I hail from an old Texas family of which I am proud. My step-grandfather lived to be 103 years old; and I remember him crying when he watched Neil Armstrong walk on the moon." This was definitely not the usual open for a job inquiry but I figured there might be something different about Robert K. Gray, Republican Super Lobbyist in Washington, DC. The man was an old-school Eisenhower Republican, a hurricane of energy, contradictions, and creativity—and gay. I was an avid reader of the market weekly *Barron's*, which had published a story about Gray & Company, a public affairs consultancy in Washington, DC, that was going public with a stock offering on the NASDAQ. Gray & Company's assets? Nothing real at all—except its sky-high hourly billing rates and its "stars"—presidential advisors and campaign veterans, media personalities and Washington power players, like Robert K. Gray, former secretary of President Eisenhower's cabinet and recent cochair of the Reagan inauguration; Frank Mankiewicz, former head of National Public Radio; House Speaker Tip O'Neil's chief of staff Gary Hymel; Kennedy insider and former trustee of the

Kennedy Center Joan Braden; and board members like Bryce Harlow, former assistant to the president for Presidents Nixon and Eisenhower; and Ambassador Clare Boothe Luce, author of the hit 1936 play *The Women*. Gray & Company was a big new idea: a bipartisan, high-profile firm that combined public relations and lobbying practices, all branded with the panache and style of Gray and the young people he would drive to propel it all. "Robert Gray: Capital's King of Clout,"[1] was one of many such headlines in the year I met Bob.

When I walked into the Power House, a 6,400-square-foot converted red-brick, nineteenth-century power plant, I could only think how far away this was from the East Coast establishment of David Rockefeller. Inside an open atrium of glass, three US time zone clocks (can you believe?) and wire service printers were spewing roles of ticker paper. Escorted up to Mr. Gray's glass office overlooking his public affairs hive, I climbed the stairwell past the first "Me Wall" (a Washington fixture of yesteryear) I had ever seen. There were a score of beautifully framed photographs and mementos of presidents, senators, media stars, and swells all signed in various permutations of "Dear Bob, you are the greatest, love forever." Nixon's secretary Rosemary Woods. Dick Nixon. Barbara Bush. Ike. Pat Nixon. Margaret Chase Smith. Ronald Reagan. And there was Robert Keith Gray himself—not on his Me Wall, but in real life, this tightly wound, dashing, Hermes-tie-type CEO.

My letter to Gray was on his desk, surrounded by statues, gold and Steuben glass, of Republican elephants and eagles. He began without small talk. "I circulated your letter. Our people need to see great letters." Shifting gears, he said, "Maybe I should write a book one day on how to get a job. Welcome, Chas." Chas? It wasn't what I said in my letter, but how I said it, I realized. His focus that day and forever was on the shares in Gray & Company Public Communications Worldwide (GRCM) that had been sold in the IPO covered by *Barron's*. He owned 75 percent of the common stock priced in the IPO at $7.50. The investment bank that did the underwriting was Washington's Johnston, Lemon and Company, and Bob wanted someone with a background in financial PR to work with the firm's savvy and slick investment bankers. Reaching out to investors, analysts, and financial media, the game was to sell, sell, sell Gray & Company and Bob Gray to investors, and I was ready and able to do that, I told him. So we began in the Power House.

Starting with the usual annual reports, analyst calls, and one-on-one briefings with brokers and market makers, we shifted to promoting our activities worldwide so that investors could read about our adventures and clients. Feature stories in the *Washington Post*, *New York Times*, and *Wall Street Journal* propelled our investor relations program forward—until gravity grounded this flying machine. Gray was the kind of leader who would encourage chaos in order to achieve his goals, often unrealistic and sketchy ones, dividing the firm. It was not long before "Mr. Market" figured all of this out and SOLD. I can still hear a broker by the name of Alexander Lanyi screaming with his thick Hungarian accent into the phone about Gray's latest government relations catastrophe in Spain of all places: "He lied. He lied." The SEC conducted an investigation. GRCM shares cratered, never to recover. Gray himself continued on, above it all, for decades to come. He had a gift for that.

A Gay Door into Washington

After my first few weeks at the Power House, I was invited to Bob's house in a wooded glen in Arlington, Virginia, for drinks and dinner with my new colleagues. The atmosphere was warm and casual, like family, and largely gay. In those days this was a big deal. Gay and lesbian players, both Democrats and Republicans, even in the 1980s, lived double lives with two or more telephone hardlines in their homes and opaque life stories, ever aware of how precarious their position no matter their titles. Do you want to keep that security clearance? At Bob's with his partner, Billy Austin, there was only one life—our lives as openly gay team members of a gay-owned company (with straight colleagues, too), operating at the highest levels of Washington consulting. This was an epic first for me. Even at Chase there had to be two, not one, Charles Francises. Living one fully integrated life together at Gray & Company allowed us to forge a fabulous team and lifelong friendships with gay and straight leaders like Jeff Trammell, Bob Witeck, Lauri Fitz-Pegado, Jill Schuker, Ronna Freiberg, and Mark Grayson. Jeff chaired the LGBTQ outreach of both the Gore and Kerry campaigns for president. Bob practically invented the specialty of LGBTQ marketing communications consulting for such clients as Walmart and Marriott. Lauri served as Assistant Secretary of Commerce and Director General of the Foreign Commercial Service working with Bill Clinton's secretary of commerce, Ron Brown. Jill went on to become a special assistant to President Clinton for National Security Affairs. We still gather together with much laughter at our skirmishes, crises, and insane clients and have some tears at what it cost us along the way. For example, how we could endure Gray's— and our—proximity to a Reagan administration that would not even mention the word *AIDS* for seven agonizing years into the epidemic? That still haunts and angers me.

Amid the shadows doors close and open. Not long after Mr. Lanyi liquidated his position in Gray & Company, in August 1984, I heard from my friend Joseph Reed, now our ambassador to the Kingdom of Morocco. "Mr. Ambassador," I shouted into the crackling phone connection with our embassy in Rabat, Villa America. On my way out of the door at Chase, I had responded to media inquiries about "the shah's former banker" being considered for this ambassadorial post. It was always, and forever, exciting to be in touch or work with Joseph. Raised by family caretakers on a 125-acre estate in Greenwich, Connecticut, Joseph was a definite Yankee blue blood. Normally this would work against a kid who had it all. But Joseph was hungry for earned success and recognition and could disarm and charm anyone he targeted with his creative energy.

"Joseph, how can I help you?," I asked. He responded cryptically with a whistle into the phone, a whistle he had perfected that sounded something like an incoming missile.

"Lunch in Washington at the Metropolitan Club. Date to follow." Click. My mind reeled, although I grinned at the same time, knowing that whatever news was breaking, Joseph could easily light up the Power House.

I hit the Me Wall stairs to Bob's office with the intriguing news from Ambassador Reed about some kind of incoming disaster, I knew not what, from Morocco. Gray pondered the riddle, What's up with Morocco? He had an idea. From his bookshelf he pulled a copy of *Eighteen Acres under Glass: Life in Washington as Seen by the Former Secretary of the Cabinet*, by Robert Keith Gray. The first White House tell-all by an insider, written in 1962 about the Eisenhower White House, *Eighteen Acres* is so trivial and boring it is almost unreadable today, but when it was first published, it caused a stir. What former official would dare write an unauthorized, inside look at life in the White House? Gray, of course.

He opened his book to a black-and-white photograph of a young Bob Gray greeting, in 1957, the king of Morocco at the front door of the White House. It is a picture of His Majesty Mohammed V wearing a traditional Moroccan djellaba, alongside his dashing eldest young son, Prince Moulay Abdullah, who would become King Hassan II. He explained, "Eisenhower had this 'slight' stroke. I was asked to be the official greeter as his appointments secretary to welcome the king." How is it, I wondered, that this photograph had escaped Bob's Me Wall? Since those days, the king and his son had become one of America's closest allies in the Arab world. So there was this bond in 1957 at the Eisenhower White House—the day Bob Gray greeted the king.

"A Moroccan Libyan 'Union' Jolts U.S." was the *New York Times* page-one headline cresting through Washington the day Reed and I met for lunch in a corner of the Metropolitan Club, as quiet as proctored study hall.[2]

"Have you ever dealt with a king?" he asked me seriously. "Charles, His Majesty can make no misjudgments. Impossible, in his mind. He is one of the last divine-right kings. He claims direct descent through centuries from the Prophet. Our team, you and Mr. Gray, we all have to help our ally and friend, this king, find a royal off-ramp." In what he thought was a brilliant diplomatic idea, King Hassan created a treaty of union with Libyan dictator Muammar Gaddhafi that no one in Washington expected or understood. Reed explained royal irony to me: a possible misjudgment that is considered brilliance. It was the king's perfect judgment that this union would allow him to isolate neighboring Algeria and complete Morocco's destiny of reunification with the Western Sahara territory claimed by desert Polisario guerillas. "This is a disaster that may just work," Reed said with flair, with a request for a proposal from Gray & Company to provide our services to His Majesty.

Within weeks Bob and I were waiting and waiting at the storied Hotel La Mamounia, adjacent to the Square of the Dead in Marrakech. Reed simply told us to arrive at the hotel and we would be summoned for our audience with Sa Majesté. Days went by. Already a wired and impatient alpha personality, Gray was crawling the Mamounia's garden walls wondering if the king even knew he, Bob Gray, was waiting. We learned soon enough that this is the way of the palace. Wherever, whenever. Only then will you have your audience with the king. We did know that our meeting would be at the royal palace in Marrakech, one of seven such grand, restored palaces across the kingdom. Depending upon the palace where the king is in residence, that is where the head of state is—and where we would make our pitch.

It was critical to shift gears into Moroccan time and ways. For me this began at Villa Taylor, the home of La Comtesse de Breteuil. A ravishing Moorish garden oasis, cultivated for decades in the medina, the comtesse's villa was also known in Marrakech as the American Villa because it was the American headquarters during World War II. A deep river of Moroccan, French Colonial, and American history ran through the house. Ambassador Reed had made the arrangements for us to meet Breteuil and have tea in her Moroccan garden of palm trees, roses, oranges, jasmine, and water lilies around a sapphire-colored swimming pool. Reed was in his French element, conversing fluently with Breteuil in both a language and style he so well understood. As a young boy, Reed had lived in Nice with his father and a governess at the historic Hotel Negresco. Joseph was a great match with la Comtesse Madeline, who had been photographed for *Vogue* magazine in the thirties. En Francais, he told her about our office in Washington, DC, the Power House, "La Maison de Pouvoir," he laughed. He explained we were here on a mission to meet with His Majesty to advocate for the kingdom back in the United States. Of course that lit her up, and we tried our best to listen closely and learn anything she might share.

The countess's deceased husband had owned the largest chain of French newspapers published in the French Maghreb (Morocco, Algeria, and Tunisia). Breteuil explained how the villa had been built in the mid-twenties by a granddaughter of Ulysses Grant and over the years had enjoyed visitors like President Roosevelt and Winston Churchill. In the villa hangs an Atlas Mountains landscape with orange groves painted by Churchill.

"So, when will you have your audience with His Majesty?" she asked in a studied, off-hand way.

"Insha'Allah," Reed responded, literally meaning "God willing" or "who the heck knows?" Gray, dazzled by Breteuil and her villa, asked if His Majesty had ever visited Villa Taylor.

"Oh, indeed yes, after the war many times. He admires it greatly." Reed flashed me a look to bookmark that, and I did. It was reported in later years that la comtesse had indeed "sold" Villa Taylor to His Majesty, who graciously allowed Breteuil a lifetime use of the villa until her death. Have you ever dealt with a king?

Summoned

We finally got the message that His Majesty would see us immediately at the royal palace. We dove into the vans and prepared to meet our royal fate. We were told to carry no papers or proposals.

"Charles, do not dare extend your hand to the king," Reed cautioned. To this day the palace remains closed to visitors. If it were ever opened, a visit there would become an international sensation. I can only think of a wing of the Louvre or the Forbidden City.

We were ushered into an Alhambra-like great hall the size of a football field, a Moorish architectural and design wonderland of honeycombed vaulting, filigree walls, marble arches, and dazzling shades of cobalt blue, bright reds, and emerald green, the color of Islam. It remains a showcase of traditional Islamic craft, wisely supported by King Hassan II to ensure that none of this artistry could ever die in the kingdom of Morocco. Our heads were spinning, which was certainly the desired effect, when we were asked to be seated in a cluster of golden silk chairs. This was no palace museum; it was a working palais royale where people conducted business with the nation and its sovereign.

Seated in an adjacent grouping was a young Moroccan pilot wait- ing for an audience with the king or his ministers. He told me he had been trained in the United States at an air force base in San Antonio, which punched all of my Texas buttons, so we became instant allies in this totally unreal setting. Bob, Ambassador Reed, and I waited a good while, as we had learned to expect; then from nowhere and everywhere began a kind of chanting in Arabic, almost a call to prayers, louder and louder. Sacred and dynastic, sometimes guttural, then soaring higher and higher. Now the Moroccan Royal Guard was on walkways above us, wearing red fez hats, white uniforms, scimitars, and gold Moorish shoes. It was a dreamlike experience. I urgently whispered to my new friend the pilot, "What are they saying?"

He interpreted quietly into my ear: "Our king is the king of all kings. He is greater than your king," he said. "God is the greatest. Long live the commander of the faithful."

Suddenly all was quiet. And through an elegant door emerged King Hassan II, with his chief of staff, Minister Abdelfattah Frej, trail- ing behind him. His Majesty seemed almost European for a moment, dapper, wearing a stylish suit. In a friendly, low-key way, he welcomed us in a personal manner.

"Bonjour, Messrs. Ambassadeur. Welcome, Mr. Gray, Messrs. Francis. Welcome to Morocco. Please," he gestured us into his throne room. It was not a glittering throne, although I am sure he has several. This was a large, formal chair with a desk and gorgeous brass tables. We were seated before him.

King Hassan began, "We are pleased that you are here. The nation's destiny lies before us as we seek to reunify and strengthen our kingdom. You may know of the Marche Verte, our historic Green March, where 350,000 of our people marched unarmed into the Western Sahara to touch sand that is our sand. Mr. Gray, I prayed in the sand with them." We listened and did not doubt his deep sincerity. His Majesty rolled on with his reasons for this new Union with Muammar Gaddhafi.

"But first . . ." He lightly clapped his hands. With that a royal servant entered with a large brass tray of juices, milk, nectar, and mint tea. In another beat a huge tray of cigarettes was offered to all of us. There must have been twenty new packs of cigarettes, each opened just so with two or three cigarettes at the ready: Gauloises, Marlboro, Camels, Maghreb, Dunhill—every brand imaginable. The king selected one for his enjoyment. We three declined. I thought, Dear God, please don't make me smoke cigarettes with sweet juice and milk with a king.

Ambassador Reed, Bob Gray, and I each made our points about the importance of targeting key American audiences—from the Reagan administration to the Congress, the business community and the American people themselves—about the historic US-Moroccan friendship and the overriding importance of our alliance. Joseph reminded the king how His Majesty rode into a liberated French Vichy Casablanca on a tank with General Vernon Walters. He never forgot that, and his foreign policies remained generally aligned with the United States. We talked at length about reaching out to key constituencies with traditional Moroccan loyalties—including the American Jewish community and Moroccan Americans. The king listened intently, especially when we raised the need to open the palace door just a bit to allow more daylight in upon the magic and help people to better understand his diplomacy. This part did not sit so well, I could see. The royal attention span flickered. The king's chief of staff, Minister Frej, jumped into the discussion. All of these ideas will be taken into consideration for a future decision, Frej said. At that I almost could see smoke coming out of Bob Gray's ears. I knew Gray could never settle for this moment to go sideways.

For Charles Francis
Patriot and special friend.
With all good wishes

VILLA AMERICA 1983

Josyl Verner Reed
Ambassador

Ambassador Reed in his bespoke djellaba (*left*) at our embassy Villa
America in Rabat, Morocco. Charles Francis collection.

"Your Majesty, if I may?" Gray stood. The king paused. Stepping
forward, Gray materialized from nowhere a copy of *Eighteen Acres under
Glass*. I thought, oh no. Where is this going?

"Your Majesty," said Bob, "may I present you with this copy of my
book about life in the White House working for President Eisenhower?"
King Hassan rose from his throne. Gray opened the book to the page
with the photograph of the young king and his father being greeted at the
White House by young Bob Gray. The king lost his breath, as if punched
in the solar plexus, and took a step back. I think somewhere deep in his
soul he was moved. Gray closed in.

"Your Majesty, there is too much at stake. Your friendship must
be communicated and our historic alliance must be strengthened
at once. We stand ready to do that." King Hassan recovered and
accepted—almost cradled—Bob's book in his arms. Eisenhower.

His father. His youth. And now at this moment, his core. His Majesty straightened to full royal posture and then pronounced: "Messrs. Gray, *go*." He paused for effect. "Tell the American people about their friends in Morocco."

Ambassador Reed knew this was the precise moment to take our leave, say good-bye to Minister Frej, and pledge ourselves to the journey ahead. We beat our exit down the great hall of the palace with the chanting of the royal guard lifting us as high as we would ever be again in Morocco.

I can still hear the call to prayer from the Koutoubia Mosque at dawn, roosters crowing in the distance, overlooking the orange grove of the Mamounia. It hit me that Charles Francis was learning at the feet of two masters—Bob Gray and Joseph Verner Reed—now serving a wise king who had made a mistake that could be corrected. Where would this lead?

"You Cannot Conceive What It Was Like"

Gray played his fifties Eisenhower card so deftly with King Hassan, and I wanted to know how he had managed to survive as a gay secretary of the cabinet inside the Eisenhower administration. How had he, as a homosexual in the White House, avoided detection by J. Edgar Hoover himself? It was President Eisenhower who in 1953 signed the notorious executive order that branded homosexuals as "perverts" and security risks. In 2012, finally letting his guard down at age 90, Gray allowed me to interview him.[3]

"It took six weeks to get a clearance," he said. "I remember how relieved I was when the Naval Department said, you got your security clearance. I tried to act as nonchalant as I could, even though my heart was pounding. I was still trying to make myself straight, dating women . . . I had no personal life." But what was it like to be gay in the 1956 White House? "You cannot conceive what it was like. Eisenhower was a fair guy, but the law was the law. There would be no reason anyone would know my story. I knew I was different. . . . It is so hard to appreciate how far we have come," Gray said, trailing off.

I pressed him on this, the whole issue of being undercover, underground, and always hiding. He snapped, "Hey, I don't want to be known as the 'gay guy' who worked at the White House. Being gay is a miniscule part of who I am, not my whole being; nor am I a standard bearer. I was not hired because of it, nor was I hired because I was heterosexual."

By the time of our interview, no one expected a whole lot from Bob Gray anymore. He had become so strident in his partisanship—and somewhat cranky in tone—that he'd lost much of his credibility. Having worked with him throughout the eighties, I was disappointed to see him drift further and further into irrelevance, immersed in the gay high-roller Miami Beach scene and angry writings about Barack Obama. He became, finally, only a "standard bearer" for himself. The king who could never be wrong. The old Bob Gray might have stood for something noble—a Washington he helped invent where people could deal with one another in a bipartisan way, even if socially or after hours in unusual combinations and settings, enjoying unique relationships in service to the country—but that was now gone.

When I was working for Bob Gray and a king, I had no idea of the meaning of historiography, how first drafts of history are written, how history itself takes enterprise to see it happening and record it. "There is no period so remote as the recent past," wrote Alan Bennett in *The History Boys*.[4] Sitting Bob down for an interview, even a brief oral history, gave me important insight into the LGBTQ world of mirrors, queer hiding, and politics inside the Eisenhower White House.

***

In Morocco, I learned a king can never be wrong or in error, so it is of critical importance to give the sovereign a way to correct course.

I heard that without a king, society is "ingouvernable," as some would say in Morocco. A king can admire one's golf trousers, and that slight compliment may oblige you to present your pants as a gift. Ambassador Reed did just that. The king can like your villa a great deal, and you just might think about selling. A king's prayer may bring rain. A king may bring earthly problems your way, or His Majesty can make your life brilliantly pleasant. Which will it be?

For nearly two years we told the story of this king and his creative, albeit misunderstood, diplomacy to one and all. It was all true. We admired him a great deal for keeping Morocco on track as a strong ally; it was, after all, the first country in the world to recognize the American revolution. Our goal was simply to help Morocco, and we had to find a way to make this possible. I was joined in this effort by my colleague, the young Robin Roosevelt. Yes, Robin was a Roosevelt, and he adored his late cousin, Teddy Roosevelt's eldest daughter, Alice Roosevelt Longworth (1884–1980). Alice lived in Georgetown, a few blocks from the Power House, and her dinner parties were a coveted invitation, as Robin would explain it all to me. "If you can't say something good about someone, sit right here by me," she famously said.

Robin was raised to serve or play, as it were, in the postwar Arab world. He spoke fluently both French and Arabic and had a life-long love of Morocco, with a Moroccan boyfriend in Tangier. Often, because of people like Robin, the Gray team succeeded in telling Morocco's story and bringing American business delegations to the kingdom; and sometimes we derailed in ways both funny and serious. How can I forget when we assured the palace that Prince Rainier of Monaco would attend the king's annual Fête du Trône to celebrate King Hassan's reign? Unexpectedly, Rainier declined the royal invitation. I thought, Okay, Robin, let's simply tell the palace that Rainier can't make it. We soon learned there was both embarrassment and dismay inside the palace that the royal invitation had been spurned. Have you ever dealt with a king? While a king can never be wrong, we certainly could be. So we received thanks for our efforts and gradually eased out of the country.

King Hassan II was able to find his "off-ramp" from a union with Libya. His reason was Gaddhafi's personal attacks on him for hosting an Israeli delegation. For this the king expressed great bitterness at Gaddhafi. We had worked hard to tell the story of Morocco's relationship with its historic Jewish community. As for Joseph Reed, he came through this experience decorated by King Hassan with Morocco's highest civilian and military honor, the Order of the Commander of the Throne, the first foreigner in Moroccan history to be so honored. And we got paid, which seemed the point back then. But it was Reed's greatest gift to me that I treasure—the memory of his élan in foreign lands among strangers. In thanks he gave me a first edition of T. E. Lawrence's *Seven Pillars of Wisdom*—the epic war memoir (on which the movie *Lawrence of Arabia* was based) about the man "who gives himself to be a possession of aliens . . . who is not of them." As if describing us, Lawrence wrote, "We lived for the day and died for it."[5]

Chapter 5

Teach It Flat or
Teach It Round

"So you are Ted Kheel's press agent?" poked William Safire, the *New York Times* columnist and author in 1999 when I got him on the phone.

"Press agent? No," I laughed in order to keep pitching the old Nixon speechwriter, a genius on language and words. "I am a friend of Ted's who is helping him reach out on his latest passion. Something called 'distance learning,' an Internet thing." I wondered if he would care. At least "distance learning" might be a new way of learning with technology for Safire to unpack in one of his On Language columns. "We'd love to come by," I said in that informal, studied way. Safire did not care about the new phrase but obviously loved Ted. At this moment, I did not know why.

"So how is Ted? Yes, Mr. Francis, please bring him over for a chat." Click.

"Ted, we're on."

Boom. This is the long and short of public affairs consulting, a career I enjoyed for decades in Washington. As Ted once schooled me, it was all an art form of "know how" and "know who," mediating issues and policy options with people and moments.[1] I loved this, and learned watching masters like Kheel.

Theodore Woodrow Kheel, a storied labor mediator and lawyer, was born 1914 in Brooklyn and named for Teddy Roosevelt and Woodrow Wilson. It was my good luck Ted and I met in New York, where he let me have a desk at his East Side labor think tank townhouse that he had christened the Automation House. Outside of his office door, I would hear the passionate eruptions from his labor mediation practice: "If you think we are starting our trucks at 6:00 a.m. . . . ." I understood then why he was once described as "the master locksmith of deadlock bargaining."[2] Now my firm was representing AT&T, and Ted was one of the allies I had recruited to help us build awareness and union support for various telecom issues.

Safire warmly welcomed Ted and me to his sanctum at the *Times*, where we spent five minutes on the issues before they plumbed their memories for events from thirty-five years before. "Remember the Lawyers' Committee for Civil Rights?" Ted asked Safire.

Well, there goes distance learning, I thought. But it got so much better. Bill Safire told the story, describing his 1963 self as a "hotshot press agent"[3] working for a Tex (not Camp Longhorn's Tex). This Tex was the public relations maestro and popular radio personality Tex McCrary. McCrary was born in 1910 in Calvert, Texas—Brazos River country. He attended the Phillips Exeter Academy prep school in New Hampshire and often explained, "Anybody from Texas who went to Exeter got called Tex."

Ted had been part of the Lawyers' Committee for Civil Rights to represent civil rights activists and organizers under fire in the South and asked McCrary, a staunch Eisenhower Republican, if his young employee Bill Safire might provide the committee some help pro bono. This idea was vintage Ted Kheel. The "Tenth Commandment of Mediation," according to Ted, was "at all times you are the friend of contesting adversaries. Give them no reason to share you as an enemy." Kheel was a mediation and conflict resolution master. He brought that inspiration into every possible arena. Ted hungered for press coverage of the coming meeting with the civil rights activists. Safire and Tex McCrary could deliver publicity like oxygen. To entice young Safire to work for free, Ted set the bait. "You'll make some new contacts."

Safire mentioned how Roy Cohn had warned him about the Communists behind these activists, but he was undeterred and attended the meeting at Ted's office. There, Safire later wrote, one of the civil rights activists "put forward a low-key, businesslike, cogent summation of his problems." That leader in the meeting room was Martin Luther King Jr.

"I still think of him as Martin," Safire told Ted.[4]

I was too young in 1964 to fully appreciate "Martin" and how he faced the evil of Southern police states enforcing Jim Crow. Decades later, as a gay Archive Activist, I learned how the Mississippi State Sovereignty Commission attempted to crush the Civil Rights Movement with state police targeting "perverts" who were organizing voters. I thought of Ted Kheel and Bill Safire's meeting with Dr. King when we discovered this memo at the University of Southern Mississippi in Hattiesburg: "What To Do during Registration Drives." The police investigator writes,

> The best methods which have been used during Negro voter registration drives. . . . No. 1, they should be told at their congregating place such as church, school, or wherever they met that they will not be permitted to march in mass groups to the courthouse, and if they attempt to go in a mass group they will be arrested. No. 2, they should be advised to go in groups of not more than three, spaced from 75' to 100' apart. If, and when, they arrive at the courthouse, they should be lined up in an orderly group and the name and address of each one ascertained by the sheriff . . . they should be told to remain in line until such time as the clerk can get to them to give them the voter registration test.[5]

So here we were at the *Times*'s Washington bureau. Ted Kheel, labor lawyer Democrat, joined with Bill Safire, libertarian conservative and former Nixon/Agnew speechwriter—both fused at an intersection of

NOTICE!

ARE YOU ONE OF THE MORE THAN 230,000 WHITES IN MISSISSIPPI WHO ARE ELIGIBLE TO VOTE BUT NOT REGISTERED?

YOU DO NOT NEED A POLL TAX RECEIPT TO VOTE IN THIS NOVEMBER 3 PRESIDENTIAL ELECTION.

DEADLINE:

YOU MUST REGISTER BEFORE THIS JULY 3

TO BE ABLE TO VOTE YOU MUST:

1. Be at least 21 years of age prior to November 3, 1964.
2. Have been a state resident since November 5, 1962.
3. Have been a resident of the county in which you wish to register since November 5, 1963.

AS A PATRIOTIC AMERICAN CONSIDER IT YOUR DUTY AND PRIVILEGE TO PASS THIS MESSAGE ON -- AND VOTE THIS NO-VEMBER 3.

If more information is needed or desired contact
UNITED FRONT, INC.
P. O. Box 10025
Jackson, Mississippi

"Hey, all you white voters!" A naked appeal. From of the Paul B. Johnson Family Papers, 1960–1964, courtesy McCain Library and Archives, University of Southern Mississippi, Hattiesburg, MS.

history and a memory with a young Martin on one of the most difficult struggles of our time: voting rights. Safire finished the story: A year before the passage of the Civil Rights Act of 1964, it was agreed in Ted's office to get Dr. King the money he needed.

Mankiewicz

Frank Mankiewicz would hate it but laugh if I ever compared him to Tex McCrary. But Frank was the only public relations master steeped in radio that I ever knew or had the luck to work for. Frank was raised a Mankiewicz in Hollywood. A chapter in Frank's memoir, *So As I Was Saying*, is titled "In Which I Watch Orson Welles Rehearse Live Radio Broadcasts and Develop a Love for Radio That Later Shapes Much of Today's NPR."[6] It's a crazy long chapter title, but he grew up in that world. I considered him a mentor. I met Frank when he headed Gray's Public Relations Division, but that was only a sliver of his incredible working life. Having studied film in Los Angeles, my first mental connection to Frank was through the iconic name: his father, Herman Mankiewicz, Hollywood royalty who wrote the screenplay for *Citizen Kane*. When I met Frank, I thought, holy cow "Rosebud," the film's iconic sled. Later I learned how his judgment and wit were hard-earned in a serious life.

Frank would often ask, "Is _____ a 'serious' person?" Frank certainly had the depth of character and range of experience he meant by "serious." Fluent in Spanish with a law degree from UCLA, he served as a South American regional Peace Corps director, as Senator Bobby Kennedy's press secretary (who had to famously and awfully announce Kennedy's death while campaigning), as George McGovern's campaign manager, and as president of National Public Radio. We could always rely upon Frank's balance and understanding even in the most difficult circumstances working in a firm like Gray & Company. Our clients were a cavalcade of crisis and controversy. That's why they had come to us, often only for time with Frank to sift through the tangles of their predicaments. Frank's mental process was a mixture of experience tempered with irony that most always solved real client problems—or helped clients cope. Of course, we also learned how to take incoming criticism and attacks because we found ourselves so often in the Washington center arena.

Bob Gray (*left*) and Frank Mankiewicz at the last Gray and Company Public
Affairs reunion (2014) at the Power House in Georgetown.
Photo by Charles Francis.

The stock criticism was that Washington government affairs and
public relations consultants had no moral compass or had lost it long ago.
Believing that clients have the right to be heard, especially on matters
of national importance, we would dutifully respond to that charge or
simply not take a particular client. "Everybody has a constitutional right
to be heard," we would say, comparing free speech to the right to counsel
in a court of law. When our parent company, Hill & Knowlton, did take
such clients, the results could be controversial, like the time we represented Citizens for a Free Kuwait. This was a group of Kuwaitis in exile
who funded Hill & Knowlton's prowar public education campaign after
Iraq invaded Kuwait without warning in 1991, before the US Congress
voted for Operation Desert Storm under President H. W. Bush.

All of us were proud to defend the principle that countries do
not invade each other or annex each other, period. And Iraq had

invaded Kuwait. We understood the stakes were higher than oil supply. It was about people in a country unfamiliar to the majority of Americans. We believed it an honor to carry that message. However, we soon found ourselves working in a hall of mirrors, with incomplete disclosures from Kuwait, the Citizens for a Free Kuwait themselves, and our own government. It was truly a PR fog of war for which we took a ton of criticism, some of it deserved. At that time Craig Fuller, H. W. Bush's chief of staff from when he was vice president, had been named president and chief operating officer of Hill & Knowlton Public Affairs Worldwide. We used every tool of public communications we had back then in support of the restoration of Kuwait's sovereignty. My focus was on the New York financial community, which had many personal and institutional ties to the Kuwaitis, and we persuaded them to join our effort. None of us in the firm were required to work for any client with whom we did not agree. I supported that approach and wholeheartedly worked to support the Kuwaitis who were, like Ukrainians today, defending their national sovereignty against an unprincipled invader who flouted international law.

When to play and when to pass on representing clients who came in the door? Frank—bemused and always entertaining—would answer this with a story about the unemployed geography teacher who was desperate to land a teaching position. Concluding his interview, the teacher spoke plainly: "Look, I can teach it flat. I can teach it round. Just give me the job." We'd laugh with a chill at that one. Of course, "teach it flat or teach it round" is the credo of compromise, which we certainly knew how to do. By accepting a particular client, were we compromising fundamental principles of honesty or ethical judgement? For example, whether or not to work for the Independent Bankers Association or the national banks was "teach it flat or teach it round." One could go either way, and we went to work. But over time my young colleagues and I learned that that philosophy, even within boundaries, was soul killing.

Mr. Clifford, Teaching It Flat

"Frank, thanks for coming over. Mr. Clifford is expecting you," said his secretary as she motioned Frank and me toward the long office hallway. Through the closed door, we heard the old man's tremulous baritone.

"Frank, come in, please." It was Clark Clifford himself, then 84, the revered Democratic senior counselor, President Johnson's secretary of defense, and counsel to presidents and CEOs for decades. I had heard the stories of him as the Hollywood-handsome naval aide to President Harry Truman, playing poker with the president at the Little White House in Key West, Florida. That young man at the Key West poker table now was face down on his desk with the heavy drapes closed. I heard he had issues with bright light, but this scene was almost eerie. It was so sad to meet a legend this way.

He raised himself, rubbing his large hands over a face transformed, no longer the face of a dashing attorney. The French have an expression for this kind of dramatic transformation. They call it a *coup de vieux*, a coup of old age that comes upon one suddenly as the result of great grief or a broken heart. It was as if that switch had flipped for Clark Clifford, who had stayed at the table far too long.

Frank and I were taken aback.

Clifford, on the ropes in the worst controversy of his long career, had called upon Frank—as one Democratic Wise Man in the club to another insider—for an immediate, tactical solution to an intractable problem. The Bank of Credit and Commerce International (BCCI), a nefarious, alleged drug-money-laundering Middle Eastern institution, had allegedly acquired Clark Clifford's Washington, DC, bank, First American Bancshares. It was later admitted by the new management at BCCI.

Throughout the eighties, Clifford had been chairman of First American as well as his law firm, serving as its attorney. People wanted to know how BCCI could obtain control without Clifford or his firm even suspecting, investigating, or knowing. He was either being fooled by the mysterious Middle Eastern investors or was in a conspiracy with them. Was he a dunce or a crook?

"Frank, where are my friends?" he said in dismay to challenge Frank, who knew them all, the editors and columnists who had covered Clifford for years. Clifford believed the aggressive, often hostile, reporting by the media was grossly unfair, sensationalized, and misleading. "Why aren't they coming to my defense? I have helped them in their hour of need."

Frank and I listened for hours on end to his perfectly memorized and delivered chronology of events surrounding First American and BCCI. I could see Clifford and his partner, Robert Altman, were schooling us on how to deliver their story—as though Frank was a "dumb pipe" to carry this story to members of Congress and the press, with a particular focus on the *Washington Post*. The *Post* coverage of the First American / BCCI story had been relentless, moving from the business section to page one, including a brilliant and brutal, ten-thousand-word Style section feature by Marjorie Williams, all of which upended Clifford's carefully groomed and managed reputation. Then came the request, where Mr. Clifford had been going all along.

"Frank, how do we deal with Kay?" he cut to the chase. "Should we reach out to her? We are at that point," he said. "Kay" was Katharine Graham, then the publisher of the *Post* with whom Clifford enjoyed a decades-long relationship, on more levels than either Frank or I knew at the time. I could see Frank flinch for a half second.

"Kay owes me one, Frank. When Phil had his breakdown in Arizona, it was I who managed the situation for Kay to bring him back to Washington. It was a terrible situation requiring great delicacy and the utmost confidentiality." Mr. Clifford was referring to Kay's husband, Philip, who had suffered from bipolar disorder with manic episodes. This particular episode involved a mistress and a total meltdown by Phil in 1963 in Arizona, requiring immediate action. Phil was hospitalized in Washington and ultimately took his own life.

Frank responded tactfully to Clifford's suggestion with a firm "No. That will neither work nor be helpful." He shut it down. There could be no old-school fix with a Kennedy insider like Frank. It was a new era in Washington, not the old days when a handful of players could tamp down controversy.

In 2019 the *Post's* Style section commemorated its fiftieth anniversary by republishing a number of its most high-impact pieces, including the 1991 Clifford profile by Marjorie Williams. "This one knocked Washington off its axis," the *Post* crowed. With her piece "Clark Clifford: The Rise of a Reputation" and part 2, "The Man Who Banked on His Good Name," Williams "trained her near-clairvoyant mind on a paragon of respectability and found instead a mere mortal betrayed by his own reputation," wrote the *Post* in an introduction.[7]

Williams's piece was a near-fatal blow to the reputation of Clark Clifford, now a mere mortal, and of his driving, ambitious young partner, Robert Altman. On August 22, 1991, Clifford inscribed his memoir, *Counsel to the President*, "To Charles Francis, with best wishes and appreciation for his fine advice and splendid assistance." I can only imagine how Altman would have inscribed it. "To Charles Francis, if I ever see you again it will be too soon. Why couldn't you and Frank make this go away?"

On August 29 we were terminated by the new leadership at First American Bank Bancshares. This was a good thing. Ultimately, Clifford and Altman were absolved of any criminal wrongdoing in federal court in New York. They had been deceived, the defense argued, and prevailed. Despite this sad vindication, Clifford lost his law firm, his bank, and his most valuable asset, his good name. If Mr. Clifford seriously wanted to know if he was being used, he might have avoided his fate. The reputation never recovered.

***

"I can teach it flat. I can teach it round," once underlay the whole edifice for lawyer-lobbyists like Clifford and the industry they invented. For me, Mr. Clifford's defense from his darkened office remained forever as a warning. The simple takeaway was the danger of being a workaholic or being involved with one—those who have such impoverished interior lives they cannot retire or imagine life without work, even if their reputation is mauled. The darkest connection I make from the Clifford and Altman wreckage is the straight line from "teach it flat / teach it round" to self-deception. From there it is not far to invented alternative realities hoisted into the public square. All have so poisoned our politics and lives. I worked with that "teach it flat or teach it round" worldview for way too long.

Frank and I were honest with Clifford and Altman, gave them our best counsel, and moved on.

Chapter 6

The Governor Meets with the Gays

"I will meet with you!"

This pledge by presidential candidate Governor George W. Bush to a gay Republican—leaving the young man thrilled and agog—at a fundraising event in 2000 rocked the small world of libertarian conservatives and gay Republicans. It is hard to fathom today that a pledge simply to meet could mean so much. It reminds me now of the popular book title in the sixties, *Been Down So Long It Looks Like Up to Me*.[1] This looked like up to us. How beleaguered we were. For years gays and lesbians had been making attempts to moderate the Republican Party but never gained the trust of Governor Bush or obtained a meeting with the party's final nominee for president. This seemed to be a moment of change, so I reached out in a personal way to this family friend.[2]

"Charles, I always knew you were gay but didn't know how to bring it up," Governor Bush warmly put me at ease. He continued like the celebrity governor he had become, cowboy boots on the desk in his Texas governor's office. "I welcome your help and appreciate learning."

I was there because of a bass fishing place our families shared in Athens, Texas, and a letter I had written him confirming my belief in the power of letters in an age when no one writes them. Pen to paper, here goes nothing, I thought.

"Dear Governor, As a strong friend and supporter with family-like kinship, I have thought long and hard about ways I might be of help to you and Laura in the coming year and into 1999. . . . There is one area where I have done much thinking (as well as living it) and that's the whole vexing issue of gay assimilation into the mainstream of American life."

Translated: "I'm openly gay. I believe gays and lesbians are ready to fully participate as equals in civil society and military life, and I'd like to help you achieve your dream." I had helped the governor in the past, but we had not discussed my being gay.

With one of his key advisors, Karen Hughes, joining us, Governor Bush liked the idea of putting together a meeting in Austin with gay and lesbian conservatives and politicos who were ready to support him. If only he would listen and try to learn, we thought—as he had expressed to me with a note.[3] Together with Hughes we brainstormed how such a meeting would play out, especially since this would be the first-ever meeting with gays by a presumptive Republican presidential candidate. Hughes confided to me that she had a gay family member and how important this meeting would be for her family and all of us to move the party forward. The stakes, we knew, were high.

Karl Rove, then largely unknown outside of Austin, and I discussed the contours of such a first-ever group. I emphasized this would represent a new generation ready to make homosexuality a nonissue for the Republican Party. There could be no going back to the Reagan years of psychologically self-tormented, closeted cases like the founder of the National Conservative Political Action Committee (NCPAC), Terry Dolan; or right-wing political consultant Arthur Finkelstein with clients like Jesse Helms; or even my old boss, Bob Gray. Not to mention the gay "invisibles" who already worked for Governor Bush and Rove.

I had already been somewhat helpful. I vouched for Governor Bush to the *New York Times* political reporter Rick Berke in a piece headlined "High in the Polls and Close to Home, Bush Navigates the Center Line."[4] "There's not an intolerant bone in the man's body," I attested and still believe. I reported to the governor and Karen, "I think we may have done ourselves some good."[5]

Rove and I drew up a list and circulated it inside the campaign and among gay and lesbian leaders, authors, and scholars. I had spoken with my friend Jeff Trandahl, clerk of the US House of Representatives. I also called upon friends David Boaz and Walter Olson at mainstream libertarian and conservative think tanks like the Cato Institute and American Enterprise Institute (AEI), the Manhattan Institute, and upon openly gay and lesbian congressional staff. I tried to convey the new thinking of authors and journalists Jonathan Rauch and Andrew Sullivan about emerging gay and lesbian demands to serve in the military and enter legally recognized relationships. We welcomed openly gay members of Congress, like Rep. Steve Gunderson; congressional staff, like Brian Bennett (who worked for "B-1" Bob Dornan); city councilmen, like the passionate David Catania from Washington, DC, and Jim McFarland from Madison, Wisconsin; and Plattsburgh, New York mayor Dan Stewart. New York governor George Pataki introduced us to a charismatic Manhattan real estate developer named Don Capoccia. A Republican board member of the Human Rights Campaign, Carl Schmid; gung-ho, old-school Log Cabin Republicans (who advocate for LGBT rights) like Scott Evertz and Rebecca Maestri (openly lesbian and a staffer for Senator Alphonse D'Amato); and Scott Huch and David Greer all brought fresh gay and lesbian grassroots passion to our group, something Rove and Governor Bush had never welcomed or understood. We were essentially all male and absurdly lily white, but still breaking as much new ground as we knew how in the day.

In April 2000 we decided to call ourselves The Austin Twelve. At their own expense from upstate New York to Orange County, California, the twelve converged upon Austin excited and ready to

With Governor Bush at a Washington, DC, fundraiser, 2000.
Charles Francis collection.

meet with Governor Bush at the campaign headquarters. We twelve
gathered the night before to plan what we were going to say and how
we were going to gauge the success of our historic gathering. All of us
were gay or lesbian—and political—so we well knew Governor Bush
needed us as much as we needed him. There was a mutuality of interests. He had emerged victorious but damaged by his South Carolina
primary campaign against John McCain.

In an interview on Christian radio, candidate Bush was asked
about gays, a subject he usually dodged. This time it was painfully
different: "An openly known homosexual is somebody who probably wouldn't share my philosophy," he said.[6] Going as far to the
right as possible, Governor Bush launched his presidential campaign
at the evangelical Bob Jones University, where interracial dating
was banned at the time. Republican "push-polls" ignited rumors by
asking voters whether they would be "more or less likely to vote for
John McCain . . . if you knew he had fathered an illegitimate Black
child"?[7] After this sullied victory, the Bush campaign calculated it

was time to get back to the middle. A meeting with "the gays" might help with that.

Rehearsing on our own, around the conference table we went, each of us laying down policy demands and venting our anger and frustrations, from the Reagan White House's seven-years-long silence on HIV/AIDS to the Texas sodomy law and the military's continued ban of gay and lesbian service members. Things became heated. We were about to step out onto a national stage, and here we were tying ourselves into policy knots. We desperately needed to find a unified voice and encourage candidate Bush's first steps into empathy. Somehow in that place where there is no turning back, a clear idea occurred to me.

I interrupted, "Let's forget policy. Let's don't start with issues. Remember the description of President Nixon's MEGO response to long policy discussions? ["My eyes glaze over."] Governor Bush will MEGO or default to prebaked positions. Instead," I said, "let's each one of us tell one personal story, one thing about our real lives." The idea caught on. "Choose any story, but it must be personal. It must be about you. Let him feel our humanity." That ought to be enough . . . if his heart was open. I believed it was.

We were moved to hear one another's stories: family fractures over having a gay son in Republican places like Colorado Springs; loved ones tragically lost to AIDS; what's it like to be outed, when this was a huge deal on the floor of the House of Representatives; a lesbian sister and her partner who went through hell to adopt; a lover's suicide; and the real challenge of being a savvy lesbian working for Senator Alphonse D'Amato. There were tears all around, but we knew we had broken the code and might move this celebrity governor. No campaign briefing papers could possibly prepare or inoculate Governor Bush for what he was about to hear.

***

The Austin Twelve did not hold back. By 2000 we had all been through too much as a post-Stonewall gay generation who had survived AIDS and remained engaged in mainstream public affairs and politics. We all took our turn, a kind of queer political version of the Broadway show *Chorus Line*, telling our stories, rooted in experience and struggle, to Governor Bush.

He listened intently and asked, "What have I said that sent the signal I am antigay? What have I done to earn that reputation?" The mood in the room shifted. People began counseling him, in an earnest way, how to earn our confidence and support. It felt real when he agreed to having a gay speaker featured at the coming Republican convention. That speaker was openly gay Vietnam War veteran Congressman Jim Kolbe (R-AZ). Minds were changed when he agreed that sexual orientation would not be a factor in Bush administration hiring decisions and that the Clinton nondiscrimination executive orders would not be jettisoned. He listened, and learned, about AIDS and its ravages, as well as about the need to increase research and global outreach to fight the epidemic. He was moved by the Austin Twelve's sincerity, and the group likewise was impressed with his openness. No reporters were allowed in the room.

He closed the meeting with one emphatic warning: do not discuss our conversation with anyone outside of this room. If you do, our communications and work together will end. "Do you understand that?" He might as well have suggested that famous admonition for illicit encounters: "This didn't happen."

Except it did happen.

Sitting against the wall was Karen Hughes, who was deeply involved in organizing the project. Some years later, when I read Hughes's memoir, I was saddened to see she had erased our historic meeting.[8] It did not happen. And Karl—he was likely fuming during our session that it was all going so well. Peering down a corridor I saw a campaign domestic policy adviser lurking, a 29-year-old Ted Cruz. I loved it that Governor Bush tagged young Cruz with one of Bush's trademark nicknames: "Theodore." Past Theodore, outside the door, was a media wall of reporters, photographers, television cameras, and crews. We filed out in a line behind Governor Bush.

"Hey, Governor," yelled a reporter, "what was it like meeting with 'the gays'?" I cringed when I heard "the gays" shouted, as though we were alien beings. We had done a lot of revealing of ourselves that morning.

With evident conviction, Governor Bush famously responded, "I am a better man for what I heard, today. These are our friends and supporters."[9] The twelve of us could not have been more proud at that moment or more hopeful for a new Republican understanding with our outcast community. By telling our personal stories, we beat the odds. "I welcome gay Americans into my campaign," he said, widely reported in positive stories from Associated Press to the *New York Times* and the *Dallas Morning News*.[10] By any measure our meeting was a huge success. Both Governor Bush and Karl Rove were gracious in their thanks to me in personal notes.[11] I particularly appreciated Governor Bush's note to me about the meeting: "I learned a lot." What better outcome could I have wished for?

Steve Gunderson broke ranks, discussing our meeting with the press. Gunderson, a former member of Congress who had been brutally outed on the floor of the House, was not going to be shy about telling the truth. The next week, on April 24, *Newsweek* magazine published his column, "Behind the Scenes at a Bush 'Sensitivity Session.'"

"I was struck by his (Bush's) lack of familiarity with the issues, as well as by his desire to learn," Gunderson wrote.[12] Gunderson's column chapped Governor Bush and Rove, a sign of the erasure and reverse to come in course. Their idea had been to meet with "the gays" but keep it sealed. It didn't happen.

It would not take long for Rove, along with his friends Jerry Falwell and Focus on the Family's James Dobson, to reverse the Bush course 180 degrees. James Dobson ruled despite the fact that our work had been a resounding success.[13]

One Bush insider pulled me aside. After the ugliness of the South Carolina primary and campaign kickoff at racist Bob Jones University, they were proud of "the boss" and what had transpired. "Congrats, Charles," he said, "You just earned yourself an invitation to Camp

David." In fact, I had just earned myself an invitation to exile, caught in the contradiction of being openly gay, political, and Republican.

Alan Simpson, Our Steadfast Friend from Cody

We were outsiders in a political party that was "not really that into" us, as teens say. No inaugural events were planned or seemed welcoming to our gay and lesbian crowd. Let's say the invites did not come pouring in. The Texas Republican Party remained utterly hostile, as it remains today. I was seated among these Texans at the 2000 convention when they protested the inclusion of Congressman Kolbe by doffing their dumb-looking cowboy hats and praying to their anti-Kolbe god during his remarks on trade policy. Kolbe continued speaking with great dignity. With mixed pride and shame I witnessed this spectacle.

Gay guys and lesbians dancing together at Texas's Black Tie & Boots event sounded like an invitation to a Lone Star brawl. So, following the president-elect's lead as a "compassionate conservative," we were inspired to continue our pioneering work and create our own event: The Republican Unity Coalition, celebrating the inauguration of George W. Bush, an inaugural breakfast with master of ceremonies Wyoming senator Alan K. Simpson. It was our unbelievable good fortune that Al agreed to join us. He is the son of Milward Simpson (1897–1993), a former senator and governor of Wyoming, and his Grandfather Simpson had prosecuted Butch Cassidy and represented William "Buffalo Bill" F. Cody himself in his divorce.

From Western lore to bloody reality, Senator Simpson stood with Congressman Barney Frank in 1998 on the Capitol steps at the candlelight vigil over the murder of Matthew Shephard in Laramie. Shaken by the horror of what had happened in his state, and furious, too, Simpson denounced Shephard's killing as an "ugly, ugly butchering. The people of my state and the University of Wyoming want you to know this is not who we are."[14] Then came the boos and the heckling of Al as a Republican from Wyoming. He told me he never forgot that candlelight booing and resolved to continue fighting for gay equality in the years to come. That moment stayed with him for decades.

Photo of Alan Simpson at the Hotel Irma in Cody, Wyoming, named for
William F. "Buffalo Bill" Cody's daughter, Irma. Photo by Charles Francis.

I believe it is one of the reasons why he participated in our outsider
event and later agreed to serve as chairman of the newly formed
Republican Unity Coalition (RUC), a gay/straight alliance I organized
dedicated "to making homosexuality a non-issue" for the Republican
Party.[15] As if all things were possible in those days.

***

On the eve of the inauguration, I waited in the morning dark snow
flurries outside of the Almas Temple, a former Masonic lodge that
is now a hotel across from Franklin Square in Washington, DC. Our
Austin Twelve team had booked the large event room, raised the
money, and created a great program to feature Alan Simpson and his
barbed-wire wit.

Here he came, walking alone in the dark, windswept DC street to
the Almas Temple. He was not with his wife, Ann, or any staff, all six

feet and seven inches of him, wearing these huge size fifteen Nike running shoes, the retired three-term senator from Cody.

"Senator Simpson, thank you for doing this," I said.

"No, no, it's you I am thanking for stepping into this horseshit. Now, let's get 'er done," he said with a smile one part sneer and one part out-loud laughter.

It was reported that four hundred people attended our event. Senator Simpson, a studied master of wit and politics, had them howling about the "sorry bastards", "zealots and 'phobes" and his repertoire of corny jokes in the style of Will Rogers, his model. Referring to the Republican Party's dark past on gay rights, he said, "We have to look forward, not back, no whining, no 'special rights' [as our foes were calling it], just equality for all of God's children."

I looked around the room, at how Al moved them all with his style and old-school Republican values of live and let live. I did not see, because they weren't there, anyone from the Bush team or campaign—no Bush family, no closeted or invisible gays from the Bush campaign, no Cheneys or anyone from the incoming administration. It would have behooved them. Today I recall what Senator Simpson said decades later, in 2018, at his dear friend President H. W. Bush's memorial service, and it echoes his remarks at our breakfast: "He never hated anyone. He knew what his mother and my mother always knew: hatred corrodes the container it is carried in."

The new RUC thrived as the Bush folks were good as their word in the opening year of the administration. They named Austin Twelver Scott Evertz to be director of the White House Office of National AIDS Policy. There was a general sense that the Republican Party was ready to move out of the ditch on the issue of gays and lesbians openly living our lives, entering the mainstream of American life, and holding high office with all that meant. Al agreed to serve as the RUC's honorary chairman and reached out to his friend President Gerald Ford, who agreed to join our board of advisors. It was a huge thrill to have the first ever former president to join a gay organization. President Ford wrote me,

"I deeply appreciate Senator Simpson's personal comments and his public support" for gay and lesbian equality.[16] My old boss, if he could ever be called that, David Rockefeller, also joined our board of advisors; Mary Cheney joined the RUC because of Al and President Ford's involvement. This was a moment of positive energy for change among such leaders whom we sought to capture. Dick Cheney's communications director Mary Matalin wrote me, "Hey, buddy. Had a long talk with Mary [Cheney] yesterday. . . . She says you are awesome."[17] *TIME* published a feature by John Cloud about our work and others' titled "The New Face of Gay Power." It was so overly positive we should have taken it as a warning: "If you want to understand the future of gay politics, forget Fire Island, New York, and West Hollywood, California. Come instead to Cody, Wyoming, at Yellowstone's doorstep, where a national gay-straight alliance, the Republican Unity Coalition was founded two years ago and counts former President Gerald Ford among its board members."[18]

It was all true, but uh-oh. We were headed for the Yellowstone falls.

The Republican establishment wanted us to succeed in making homosexuality a nonissue for the Republican Party. Instead, it would become *the* issue.

Sodom, Texas

Is there a Sodom, Texas? That would be Dallas–Fort Worth if you asked the screaming protestors we faced at the Texas GOP convention in Fort Worth in 1998. The Texas Log Cabin Republicans were there to demonstrate at the Fort Worth Water Gardens, designed by gay architect Philip Johnson, about being refused a booth and presence at the convention. There was a Log Cabin newspaper ad, paid for by ally Trammell S. Crow, that said, "Sure, it's just a booth. But not long ago, it was just a lunch counter."[19] Insults were flying, like the Texas GOP comparing the Log Cabin Republicans to the KKK and to pedophiles. The so-called protestors were organized by the "venom spouting" Fort Worth area minister Rev. W. N. Otwell, a "former oil field roughneck [and] salvation hustling preacher," as described by Dallas's *D Magazine*.[20] The collision threatened to become violent, so I asked my lifelong friend and neighbor Chip Northrup to come with me to this queer rally in Fort Worth. I told him it was important to me. Chip, a straight ally, was in the mood for a show and, like a brother, understood. He told me he was going to carry a firearm, in case we needed to defend ourselves, which was both troubling and reassuring. I will always trust Chip. Who knew what was about to unfold?

I had kept in touch behind the scenes with Karen Hughes, and I urged Governor Bush to issue a statement to calm matters, faxing him an urgent message about "the heaviest bashing and disinformation I have seen from a political organization calling the Log Cabins a 'hate group.'"[21] Governor Bush issued a statement saying "all individuals deserve to be treated with dignity and respect . . . [and that he did] not condone name calling."[22] Hear that, Rev. Otwell? I was encouraged that Hughes was doing her best to help.[23]

At the rally picket signs like "There's no such thing as a Christian fag"[24] went flying through the air in the face of Log Cabin's national president, Rich Tafel, who bravely stood his ground. Chip was on total alert. The situation was veering out of control, with hundreds of screaming protestors yelling, "Never. Never. Never. Never."

Lory Masters, a leader in the Dallas LGBTQ community (who had formed the first LGBTQ motorcycle club in the South),[25] gave it right back: "I was born right here in Fort Worth, Texas, and we aren't going anywhere."

Dale Carpenter, then president of the Texas Log Cabins, stood on the platform with his grandmother at his side. "It was a tornado of emotion, volatile and dangerous. . . . I was afraid for my own safety and that of others," is how he described the horror show years later.[26] Besides the flying, hateful signs, "Sodomite" was the most common epithet hurled at the speakers. Members of the largest LGBTQ congregation in Dallas, the Cathedral of Hope, and its Rev. Mike Piazza were there to confront the haters with a Christian message. Even in this chaos, one could feel how sodomy law percolates down into the marrow of peoples' lives in a near riot. Chip had never seen anything like this—the cutting edge of hate and homosexuality. Nor had I. We eased to the periphery and made our escape without incident as we heard Lory Masters proclaim again, "We aren't going anywhere!" I will never forget it. Masters stood her ground.

Largely unenforced but used in myriad ways, the Texas sodomy law was supported by Governor Bush on the grounds that Texas is a traditional values state. "Like an unused whip," is how Carpenter, later to become the chairman of constitutional law and Altshuler Distinguished Teaching Professor at the SMU School of Law, characterized the Texas sodomy law.[27] "It worked as a symbolic message of disdain directed toward the people thought to commonly engage in sodomy—homosexuals."[28] As Carpenter documented, there was a huge community effort beginning in 1998 to challenge and appeal the sodomy charge of John Lawrence and Tyron Garner undertaken by gay activists in Houston, the Lambda Legal public interest law firm, and heroic pro bono legal counsel in Washington, DC, including veteran gay Supreme Court advocate Paul Smith. The RUC believed it had a role to play, as a gay conservative organization, in this broad effort. Senator Alan Simpson agreed, and we went to work.

Our idea was to write and submit to the Supreme Court a friend of the court amicus brief for the *Lawrence v. Texas* case in support of the petitioners John Lawrence and Tyron Garner, supposedly caught "in the act" in their private bedroom in 1998—a crime in Texas. We wanted our brief to fill the niche of a more conservative analysis of the case that might resonate with Justice Clarence Thomas or other conservatives on the court like Sandra Day O'Connor. To accomplish this, we brought together Carpenter, then a professor at the University of Minnesota Law School, and Erik Jaffe to be our counsel of record. Jaffe had clerked for Justice Thomas and well knew how to make the conservative constitutional case. Senator Simpson, a lawyer himself, brought his own knowledge of the law and the Constitution to our team.

"The RUC's interest in this litigation is simple: It wants gay Americans to be treated like all other Americans who contribute to the richness and diversity of this Nation. This case is an opportunity to confirm that the constitutional command of equal protection requires that gays be treated as equal to all other citizens under the law, subject to neither special preferences nor special disabilities," our brief stated. We made our position clear that "the statute's inconsistent treatment of identical physical acts by gay and straight couples ["sodomy" was okay for heteros] combined with its context and history, provide ample indicia of animus toward gays as a class, and thus render insufficient the States asserted moral interests for purposes of rational-basis review."[29] This was a legalistic way for the RUC to say Texas's law was rooted in bigotry and animus, period. We were proud of the RUC amicus brief, which was signed by Alan Simpson and our counsel.

Taking another step forward into the national spotlight on gay rights, Al wrote an op-ed, published by the *Wall Street Journal* on the day the Supreme Court heard oral arguments on Lawrence: "Homosexuality should be a non-issue inside the GOP. . . . [sodomy laws] are contrary to American values protecting personal liberty and opposing discrimination. The Supreme Court should declare them unconstitutional."[30]

The Bush Justice Department remained silent on *Lawrence v. Texas*, as did the president. But President Ford wrote me in a private letter that he agreed with what he called "gay equality before the law" and supported the challenge to the Texas law.[31]

There was pure electricity in the court for the oral argument where I was seated with Dale and Erik, who arranged for us to get reserved seats through Justice Thomas.[32] We were on the winning side of that argument, thank goodness, for future generations of LGBTQ men and women who will no longer have to live with that "unused whip." The Court voted 6–3 in favor of Lawrence, with Justice O'Connor, a dear friend of Al's, concurring that Texas's sodomy law violated the Equal Protection Clause, as we had argued in our brief. Justice Thomas? His dissent was an unserious description of the Texas sodomy law as "uncommonly silly." "Silly" or not, Justice Thomas

The Republican Unity Coalition team (RUC) at the Supreme Court as amici
curiae in *Lawrence v. Texas*. *Left to right*: Erik Jaffee, counsel and former clerk
for Justice Clarence Thomas; Charles Francis, RUC president; and Dale
Carpenter, then University of Minnesota professor of law.
Charles Francis collection.

was happy to throw us back into the jaws of a state legislature committed to criminalizing our lives, much as the Virginia legislature had
been committed to banning interracial marriage until the Court inter-
vened.[33] When the *New York Times* asked for my opinion, as one
Texan who had played a small role, I did my best to appeal to a political center that is no more. "I hope the giant middle of our party can
look at this decision not as a threat but as a breakthrough for human
understanding," I said.[34] President Bush's spokesperson Ari Fleischer
pointedly declined to comment.

The Lawrence decision was the final straw as far as the evangelicals were concerned. Then came the fight over same-sex marriage in Massachusetts with the marriage of Julie and Hillary Goodridge.

Protecting Marriage

President Bush reacted to the Goodridge marriage with maximum political hostility. "The law does not protect marriage within any state or city," such as Massachusetts or San Francisco, he said. "For this reason, the defense of marriage requires a constitutional amendment."[35] This was a shock to gay Republicans and conservatives. I received a personal note in 2004 from a gay former Supreme Court clerk that typified the feelings: "Although I have been a strong supporter of President Bush and his administration, I must admit after today that I have made a dreadful mistake. I must acknowledge that I believed the President in 2000 campaign when he said that marriage was an issue for the states to decide." He continued, "I was a fool. The President and many, if not most conservative Republicans do not genuinely care about federalism." The note concluded, "As a gay Republican, I can think of no sadder day in the last three years other than 9/11."

By now most all of the Austin Twelve, including me, were disillusioned and regretted our participation in the project.[36] No on marriage. Civil unions? That could be for the states to decide, but the president would veto that if he were governor. Silence on ending Texas sodomy law. No on open military service. No on employment discrimination protections. No on hate crimes law. There was a definite pattern here. By his second term in office, President Bush and Deputy Chief of Staff Rove would be meeting in the Oval Office with young people, who called themselves ex-gays, from an organization by the name of Exodus International that promoted sexual orientation conversion therapy. The political purpose of this meeting and smiling photos with Rove and ex-gays—like the founder of Exodus, Alan Chambers, and his ex-gay chief lobbyist, Randy Thomas from Arlington, Texas—was to lobby members of Congress to pass the Federal Marriage Amendment. Both Chambers and Thomas have long since admitted they were gay all the time, and Exodus International folded in 2013. Thomas remembers his meeting in the Oval Office, "twenty feet away from the president" and James Dobson, as demeaning: "At the time, I was so proud, I was like, 'Momma, I'm going to the White House.' . . . Now I look back on it, [I ask myself] Why didn't you yell out? Why did you betray your community like that?" Thomas explained, "They felt we gave legitimacy to their [Federal Marriage Amendment] arguments on a relational, personal level."[37]

Thomas goes on to recall with regret his meetings on Capitol Hill promoting the Federal Marriage Amendment. "I went and met with Rick Santorum in his office and gave this big emotional testimony of my story and thanked him for his righteous stand." From betraying the mainstream Austin Twelve to meeting with the deeply troubled Exodus crowd, for President Bush it was a free fall into the wrong side of history.

Years later Bush campaign strategist Stuart Stevens tried to rewrite this sad story. "Rove Says He Didn't Engineer Anti-Gay Marriage Amendments. He Did," was the *Dallas Morning News* headline over the report by Wayne Slater.[38] Discussing his memoir *It Was All a Lie*, Stevens confessed, "I think we played too much on the social conservative side, particularly with the same-sex marriage referendum. I think that was regrettable."[39] Stevens's admission that the campaign was involved with the same-sex marriage ban referendums to increase turnout is beyond "regrettable." He and Rove were playing with LGBTQ Americans for their political sport.[40] The passage of time has exposed that cruelty.

During Pride celebrations in 2022, the year of his death, Michael Gerson (President Bush's brilliant speechwriter) finally found the words to repudiate all he had written decades before about defending straight marriage, "one of the most fundamental, enduring institutions of our civilization."[41] "The evidence appears non-existent," Gerson wrote in a personal reassessment, "that gay marriage would somehow weaken the institution." He concluded by celebrating our success as "the most dramatically successful social movement of the past few decades."[42]

"Senile Old Fag Lover"

When Al came out in support of same-sex marriage in Massachusetts (2003), the vile Westboro Baptist Church ("God Hates Fags") formally protested with a letter from their minister Fred W. Phelps urging the construction of a monument in Cheyenne (Mathew Shephard's killing state) featuring the biblical condemnation of homosexuality. Phelps called Al, "a senile old fag lover."

I will never forget how Al responded with grace and hilarity to Phelps in the style of Al's political role model, cowboy humorist Will Rogers: "Dear Rev. Phelps, I just want to alert you to the fact that some dizzy son of a bitch is sending out mailings and emails from the Westboro Baptist Church and using your name! . . . I know you are a god fearing, Christian person filled to the brim with forbearance, tolerance and love . . . and this other goofy homophobe nut must be something opposite. . . . Alan Simpson."[43]

Al did not pull back from his support of same-sex marriage. Indeed he joined with the RUC to oppose President Bush on his Federal Marriage Amendment. Al wrote, "Several Senate members want to create more anguish by pushing a proposal to amend the Constitution . . . but a federal marriage amendment would do nothing to strengthen families, just the opposite. And it would unnecessarily undermine one of the core principles I have always believed the GOP stood for: federalism." But Al knew how to make it personal, as we had presented ourselves as flesh and blood in Austin, not just about wonky support of federalism: "We all know someone who is gay, and like all of us, gay men and women need to have their relationships recognized in some way."[44]

***

In 2004 the Republican National Committee (RNC) sent out mailers in Arkansas and West Virginia saying that if people vote for liberals, the Bible will be banned and gay people will be allowed to marry. We tried everything to get a White House meeting with President

Bush, but to no avail. It was a hard thing for me to process, being locked out precisely because we had done our work so well. What they wanted was the old bargain: remain 100 percent silent on gay issues in exchange for access and roles in the administration. We settled for a meeting with Ken Mehlman, who had served as national field director for the Bush/Cheney campaign in 2000. We did not fully understand his role in the state referenda to ban same-sex marriage. We waited patiently to be ushered into Mehlman's office by our friend, the deputy chair of the RNC at the time, Maria Cino. We wanted to protest and asked him for action to stop this, but all was lost in a fog of inexplicable distraction. We were forced to make our points in the midst of messages coming in and out, interruptions, and preparations for a trip somewhere; there was no way Ken Mehlman was going to have an honest discussion with us. He gave Don Capoccia and me some dumb advice about joining with other groups on unrelated issues like Social Security privatization.

A decade later I was invited to Ken Mehlman's forty-second-floor sky-palace office at the investment firm Kohlberg, Kravis & Roberts, where Mehlman had become a private equity executive. Soaring above Central Park, the setup is designed to humble you. The purpose of the invite was to ask for our help with his new project. He had finally announced he was gay but explained he did not know that basic fact when we met with him at the RNC. He wanted us to join him in the fight for same-sex marriage in New York. He began his presentation with a heartfelt, smooth plea: "It is rare in life for one to have an opportunity for a do-over." After the erasure and exile we had been through when he headed the Bush reelection and chaired the RNC, we could forgive him when asked. But how to forget? To forget is to erase. It did happen. But since then Ken Mehlman has embodied Oscar Wilde's line, "Every saint has a past, every sinner a future."[45] His leadership to help persuade Republican members of the Senate to vote in 2022 for the Respect for Marriage Act, legislation to mandate federal recognition of same-sex marriage, was outstanding.

The Act

"If the Supreme Court says you have the right to consensual sex within your home, then you have the right to bigamy, you have the right to incest, and you have the right to adultery," Rick Santorum famously pontificated to the Associated Press.[46] This comparison was an insult we had to face. Both President Bush and Senate Majority Leader Bill Frist ran to defend Santorum. Frist, a surgeon, said ridiculously (to his permanent disgrace), "Rick is a consistent voice for inclusion and compassion . . . and to suggest otherwise is just politics." President Bush called Santorum "an inclusive man."[47] I checked with our RUC team, and we agreed to stand up to this. How could we not and maintain a shred of self-respect or dignity for millions of gay and lesbian Americans? I laid it down: "These are false and harmful comparisons. Senator Santorum owes an apology to gay men and women who support, build and have loving families all across America."[48] Dana Milbank at the *Washington Post* quoted me, "I can't imagine they [the White House] would ever want to have a national debate on incest, bigamy and homosexuality—culture war issues that Senator Santorum has so carelessly thrown out there."[49] As it turned out, the Bush team was fine with that in their run-up to pass the Federal Marriage Amendment.

Mary Cheney, smoldering, called me at my office. "You are being used by the Democrats. We should not ask Rick Santorum to apologize for anything. He owes no one an apology," Mary said to me. I could not believe my ears. Mary Cheney resigned from the RUC without public explanation and was swept back into the cocoon of the Bush reelection campaign.

I knew we were finished two weeks later on a Sunday morning while folding my socks and watching *Meet the Press*. Suddenly, the show's celebrity host Tim Russert—who likely never covered a gay story in his life—started talking about the RUC. My jaw dropped as Russert described us as headed by President Gerald Ford (wrong) and quoted our statement demanding an apology from Santorum. He put the question to his guest, Mary Matalin, who was doing her weekly gig with husband James Carville. Obviously prepared for the question, Matalin ripped into us: "They are parroting what the Democratic interpretation of what Senator Santorum, who's a wonderful, caring, loving man who spent much of his career helping the poor and homeless"—I was agog at hearing this tribute to Rick Santorum—"a devout Catholic . . . that church teaches that you must love and accept the individual but you cannot accept the act. The act is a sin."[50]

The *act*? Matalin's early era performative politics with James Carville makes for hilarious reading so many years later. She tries to close; Carville calls her ideas "cockamamy." She hurtfully concluded, "They [the RUC] have raised the tolerance bar here. . . . You now have to reject your religious doctrine—if you want to call anybody a bigot, then you should call . . ." she loses it, " . . .the pope a bigot."[51] A crazy word-salad followed about the pope. This media savvy White House surrogate, who I once liked a lot and respected, had not a word for us. It became a crazy upside-down world where words mean nothing. This was my first real experience of how Republican politics were morphing, like a digital breakup, into a place I no longer recognized.

I took a long, lonely walk that Sunday morning. Incest, bigamy, the pope, "the act." Is this what I had come to? I thought about David Mixner, the gay friend of President Clinton who felt so angry and betrayed by Clinton's support of Don't Ask, Don't Tell that he had himself arrested in front of the White House. Mixner wrote in his memoir *Stranger Among Friends*, "I could see some of my colleagues and political allies looking at us from the windows to watch the arrests. . . . I felt an overwhelming sense of loss."[52] I felt the same loss. I did take comfort looking at this misadventure with some irony, not total self-pity. Ever an English major, I thought of Mark Twain's hero Huckleberry Finn. Huck, at the moment when he decides there can be no going back if he helps his dear friend, the enslaved Jim, escape slavery and get out of the South on a raft, says, "I was a trembling, because I'd got to decide, forever, betwixt two things, and I knowed it.

I studied a minute, sort of holding my breath, and then says to myself: 'All right, then, I'll go to Hell.'"[53]

I wrote Al to tell him it was time to end the Republican Unity Coalition and that he would always be a hero of mine for standing with us. Al understood that things had turned out badly. I later became a trustee of his beloved Buffalo Bill Center of the West, a spectacular museum of Western history and art in Cody, Wyoming.

It was time for me to begin my own reckoning outside a world turned topsy-turvy. Goodbye to my illusions and the belief I could will things to get better as I saw fit . "Hey, Huck and Jim," I thought. "Got room on that raft for me?"[54]

Chapter 7

Kameny's Attic

Setting: An institutional hallway leading to service elevator doors.

Fade In: Two male, white-gloved attendants resembling nurses or guards push a gurney, transporting what looks like a body covered in a sheet, out of the elevator and down a long corridor. Following the gurney is gay civil rights pioneer DR. FRANKLIN E. KAMENY, then 81; my friend and historical novelist, THOMAS MALLON; and CHARLES FRANCIS. The attendants are fussily minding the long lump on the gurney.

FRANK (*instructing the attendants*): Decay. Exercise care, please.

The gurney rolls to a rest at a huge vault door. We are met by HARRY RUBENSTEIN, the chairman of the Division of Politics and Reform at the Smithsonian National Museum of American History. RUBENSTEIN, looking like a doctor wearing a white lab coat, turns the lock tumblers on the Smithsonian vault doors. The doors open to reveal a room that resembles a morgue.

POV: The gurney rolls into the vault, which has large drawers and cabinets from floor to ceiling surrounding a central raised platform. The gurney slides alongside it. HARRY gathers the group and gives the white-gloved attendants a nod. The attendants roll back the white shroud revealing, where there should be a pair of legs, wooden sticks, heavily nicked and numbered. As the cover is rolled back farther, we see the gurney is not carrying a body. It is carrying a jumble of old picket signs.

Close-ups: Wooden sticks and old picket signs. Hand-lettered, yellowing words. "Discrimination against Homosexuals Is as Immoral as Discrimination against Negroes and Jews." Pan to reveal, "First-Class Citizenship for Homosexuals." FRANK literally stands at attention. TOM MALLON takes notes for an article. CHARLES'S eyes tear up.

***

When I first met Frank Kameny, we were both on a bit of a downtick and open to each other. Normally he would have loathed this ex-Bush Republican from Texas. I would have pulled back from this self-described gay militant whom I had read about in high school. I was in something of a recovery from my naive delusion that I could help the old Republican Party move forward, or that I could simply will things to happen. I had failed. Frank was at a stage in his life where he was considered something of a dinosaur in gay circles. In Spanish he would be almost *uno olvidado*, a forgotten one. He detested the alphabet soup of gay identity LGBTQIA+ politics, was living largely in his anecdotage, almost destitute. We were a weird, good fit.

In 2004, at a small gathering in Washington, Frank reminded me of Rosa Parks in her situation years after the Montgomery Bus Boycott. She had become a forgotten one, an NAACP (National Association for the Advancement of Colored People) icon out of the news, and almost destitute. In a 1960 *Jet* magazine profile, Parks was described as "a tattered rag of her former self—penniless, debt-ridden—compressed in two rooms with her husband and mother," working as a seamstress in Detroit.[1] Not until she volunteered for the winning 1964 campaign of John Conyers, and Conyers hired her to run his Detroit office, was she able to restore her financial stability and get a life. Parks tapped into what James Baldwin called "the great force of history within us."[2] She invited Martin Luther King to Detroit to endorse Conyers. Conyers won and her life changed.

It is not an overstatement to compare Frank to Rosa Parks, given his historic role in creating the modern LGBTQ civil rights movement. Yale Law School Professor William Eskridge said at Kameny's memorial service that Frank was the "Rosa Parks and the Martin Luther King and the Thurgood Marshall of the gay rights movement."[3] When I met Frank, he was where Parks had once been, not knowing how to tap the "great force of history" within himself. Together we figured out how to do that.

***

My then partner Stephen Bottum and I were hosting a book party in 2007 at my apartment in Washington for Thomas Mallon, to help him launch his historical novel *Fellow Travelers*,[4] a devastating gay love story set during the McCarthy-era Lavender Scare. This was the time of the Communist and homosexual witch hunts in the State Department that destroyed careers and Mallon's doomed lovers, Hawk and Tim. I invited Frank as a guest of honor to speak about the bad old days, and he did not disappoint. We were thrilled for him to stand alongside Tom on the staircase, a merger of historical fiction and a lived life.

Frank had been dismissed from the US Army Map Service in 1957, the year of Joe McCarthy's funeral mass at St. Matthew's Cathedral, dramatized in the penultimate chapter of *Fellow Travelers*. Mallon's characters Hawk and Tim came to my mind with the specters from his novel of Richard Nixon and Alice Roosevelt Longworth. There on the staircase stood Thomas Mallon and Frank Kameny together, weaving this fiction and history that Frank lived and survived. It was a special moment.

Stephen, following a career in publishing in Boston and New York City, well described the event on his site *Band of Thebes*: "The crowd of 100 people—ages ranging literally from 18 to 82—was so intelligent and fun it was hard to remember it was DC."[5] *Band of Thebes* has been described by its many readers as an "amazing, deeply researched, smart, funny, gay book blog"; "defined my reading list."[6] For me the *Band of Thebes* was a lot more than a "gay book blog." It was my introduction to thinking *historically*—as far back as classical Greece and the Sacred Band of Theban lovers—about the LGBTQ movement for dignity and equality.

I know how much this all meant to Tom Mallon. "Words fail me—honest. You are this book's guardian angel, and I am forever grateful," he inscribed his book to me. We all were lifted.

That evening, Frank, age 82, was surrounded by bright thirtysome-things, young men and women with Washington careers and celebrities like PBS Newshour host Jim Lehrer. Frank carried a clunky briefcase and reminded me of the silent screen star Norma Desmond in *Sunset Boulevard*, surviving in contrast to the kids back at the studio. Book parties were not his thing, especially if not about him. His life had been dedicated to the fight for gay and lesbian equality in another Washington. Frank's DC was about arrests, investigations, termina-tions, and discharges. He inhabited another world, one he confronted with new militance, he emphasized for all of the fellow travelers in the room.

Shifting gears he asked, "Er, can you help me get a ride home?" Of course I went into action on behalf of this gay senior, out of his time, in a well-wrinkled suit, eyeglasses held together with tape. That was Frank, and it felt good to help him starting in 2003. I did not realize it at the time, but I had become a marked man—marked by Frank.

The phone would ring at all hours, continuously and insistently. It was Frank. "Please, please help me. I would never approach you for anything, but this once, I am in a unique bind that will soon be resolved, I can absolutely assure you . . . but until then can you spare $500?" It was heartbreaking to hear him have to beg so.

A couple of evenings later, Frank called again; this time his electricity has been turned off. A week later it was his real estate taxes. I begged off. The phone started ringing not ten times, but twenty times or more. And then again. He was shrieking. I unplugged it (we still had phones to unplug). In the coming days, I learned this had become Frank's way of living, but it always required new donors who were smitten by his past achievements, all of whom would eventually move on, frustrated by his stubborn refusal to listen to good ideas and his inability to secure his financial situation. It had gone on like this for years.

It was all so sad and troubling. I knew Frank Kameny had helped invent the modern gay civil rights movement as we know it, beginning in 1960 when he brought the first gay-related case to the United States Supreme Court—his demand to be reinstated in his job after being fired in 1957 for the sole reason of his homosexuality. I had no clue about the full dimension of Kameny's achievements or intellect. My friend Dudley Clendinen, an editorial writer for *The New York Times* who was working on a new gay history, helped explain Frank to me, if such a thing were possible. Dudley wrote, "Almost single-handedly, he formed and popularized the ideological foundations of the gay rights movement in the 1960's . . . with the confidence of an intellectual autocrat, the manner of a snapping turtle, a voice like a foghorn, and the habit of expressing himself in thunderous bursts of precise and formal language. . . . He was George Patton as gay activist."[7]

***

"Patton" answered the door of his modest 1950s red brick colonial, the headquarters of the original Mattachine Society of Washington, DC. The original Mattachine Society was named after the medieval court jesters who would wear a mask in order to speak truth to the king. This was adopted by early gay rights activists like the original founder, Harry Hay. Frank found the name useful in the sixties because it was widely recognized in the day, not because of its association with the "mask." He snapped to, on his best behavior, and welcomed me. There to drop off a donation to cover some problem or another, I had no idea what to expect. The whole scene came as something of a shock.

"Please, please sit down." He waved me to an old sofa, half covered in papers. "I so appreciate your support, thank you." It took me a moment to reset my bearings in this wonderland of paper—not newspapers and magazines, but stacks of documents, copies of documents, carbon copies, documents on his staircase in a mysterious long box tied so neatly with string, mimeographed copies, extinct gay mags like *ONE* and *Drum*, and opened mail all around. In the corner I noticed an overflowing bookcase with old astronomy textbooks with titles like *The Pulsation Theory of Variable Stars*. The dining area and kitchen were completely blocked with more stacks and documents.

"I am just back from a lengthy interview for a documentary on the so-called 'Lavender Scare,'" he said to divert me from looking around.

I responded, I think in an overly forward way, a bit overcome with the whole scene, "I hope they are paying you something."

"Oh, no, never. I never request payment. My views are not for sale. Of course, I will accept travel expenses, but that is it."

I thought of his late-night, pleading calls, at the same time trying to take in what I was seeing and feeling. The odor of old paper was the one overwhelming impression. It was an earthy smell, like a tunnel of loam. If I were less excited about this visit, I would have thought, "MOLD!" and run for it. Indeed, there were wisps of mold on the edges of many documents, and you could see its brown traces. It was all part of the scene. Writing this, I can still feel the dizziness I would experience for hours after exposure to this colony of spores, the old Mattachine headquarters, the epicenter of gay activism in Washington for many years. Frank Kameny's house was a remnant of the world of LGBTQ activism when it was a netherworld by today's standards.

An honest observer would say Frank and his house could be located somewhere on the clinical spectrum of pathological hoarding. A self-described pack rat, he had allowed the rooms to become blocked with stacks and piles upon piles of papers and boxes and to become totally unusable. This hoarding did not occur to me then. Driving home, still spore-dizzy, I thought of Frank's house and papers as a thrilling discovery. I did not know, or fully appreciate, that it was far more than that. Indeed, it was historic community archive right there on New Mexico Ave., NW, in the District of Columbia. I could not wait to study this stuff. "Start me with that copy of *Drum*," I would say. Or, "May I look inside the long black box tied with string?" I sensed there would be answers there. I knew so little.

I kept getting the calls and could not turn away. So I returned with another check, this time I think it was for a new cell phone. On this visit I was no longer startled and so was able to think clearly. "So Frank, you seem to have saved everything," I prodded.

"Oh, yes, yes. Ha-ha! I have been accused of being a pack rat."

I begin brainstorming aloud with him, as though he were one of my clients in the public affairs consulting business. "This must be an incredible collection. What do you have here? Look at this copy of *Drum*."

"Oh, yes indeed. An attractive young man on the cover, don't you think?" he laughed.

"And, Frank, what is in the black box on the staircase? And what's upstairs?" I pressed on.

"Oh yes, it is a bit messy. This is my filing system. It has gotten a bit out of hand."

I ask, "Please, may I look?"

"Yes, feel free. As I say, it is a bit untidy," he laughed.

At the top of the stairs, I walked past stacks and piles with names on top of them: "Clifford Norton," "Charles Baker," "Lilli Vincenz," "Civil Service Commission," "American Psychiatric Association," "Mattachine." A second bedroom was engorged with papers and blocked. I was a couple of paces ahead of Kameny and peered into his office—a hoarder's man cave, both thrilling and appalling. Floor-to-ceiling papers were stacked in all corners. His desk was not a desk. It was an invisible platform bearing a mountainous stack of paper, carbon, and publications, an old manual typewriter.

But here's the difference: This was not just any hoarder or pack rat; he was the grandfather of the largest civil rights movement in the country after the Civil Rights Movement of the sixties. In reality, the entire LGBTQ emergence from invisibility in Washington began here. As if I were in a dream, Frank's desk reminded me of the undiluted madness of visionary art, like the aluminum foil *Throne of the Third Heaven*, an art installation by James Hampton at the Smithsonian Art Museum. Beside this throne were two filing cabinets cascading paper, alongside many years of Yellow Pages phone directories. The scene reminded me of descriptions of Andy Warhol's house, another compulsive hoarder, after his death. Besides being gay, I knew Kameny and Warhol would have zero in common but this.

"Frank, my God, you saved it all," I said in awe and kneeled before the filing cabinets as if they were an altar.

He was not amused.

"Get out," he yelled. I jumped up. "Get OUT," he screamed in a high pitch of panic. It was the first honest and true thing I heard from him. It was the anxiety reaction of a hoarder when someone threatens to throw away their stuff. I later learned hoarders may have emotional connections, a substitute intimacy, with the stuff.[8] Realizing what a mistake I had made, getting too close to his precious papers, I ran down the stairs, skipping steps at a time.

"I'm so sorry, Frank. It's just that you have the whole history. You have it all."

He settled himself. We hit a pause. He chuckled to lighten the mood, "Yes, yes, I have told myself for years now to write a memoir or biography. It is all so distressing. People always tell me to do that, and I will get to it one day. I will. I must get to it."

It was clear he would never get to it; he was way too far down the road for that. "Frank," I responded, "these materials are valuable. Let me help you think about ways you can help yourself with this stuff; there has to be a way to use them for yourself, historians, authors, filmmakers." I was sputtering, but he got the idea. He had heard it all a hundred times before from libraries and gay collectors and writers. I sincerely wanted to help him.

Frank Kameny's files (2005)—an overflowing trove. Photo by Charles Francis.

"Frank, let me think about some ideas," I said. Charles Francis and Dr. Franklin E. Kameny shook on it.

"Okay, then," he snapped to again. "I will look forward to your earliest response."

I returned to the headquarters soon, not with money this time but with an idea.

"Frank, let me take a rough inventory of what you have. Then we'll figure out the best way to market it. I do believe," I said like a recovering ex-Republican, "it is possible for money to be 'the root of all good,'" quoting an early proponent of the prosperity gospel, the late Reverend Ike. I was trying anything to hang on to his attention and break through his prerecorded anecdotes. "If one has the right intentions and ideas, of course."

Money, the "root of all good," got it.

I suggested a new direction—creating an archive, including all of the old picket signs, and branding it. I told him we could name it the Kameny Papers. Seeing a potential solution to being perpetually broke, he opened his mind and his attic door.

The Valachi Papers. The Pentagon Papers. The Kameny Papers.

"Follow me," he said, pulling an old rope affixed to his ceiling attic door. Down dropped the most rickety ladder I have ever trusted. Normally, I would have passed. "Come on up," he yelled.

I held my breath and, doing so, traveled backward in time to my grandmother's attic in Dallas, full of old trunks for train and ship travel and iron toys and dolls from the 1930s. How I loved the smell of the moth balls up there and in all attics. Then, bang, I was back in Frank's.

It would take me weeks to comprehend and list what I saw up there. It was a life in amber. There were scores of unopened boxes. Hundreds of old *Blade* newspapers and boxes of *The Homosexual Citizen*, the magazine published by the original Mattachine Society of Washington, DC. Gay "Homophile" conference posters protesting LBJ's Great Society were in piles, as were fliers and handouts that said "Gay is Good."

At the far end of the attic, dimly lit, was a pile of picket signs—the original, nicked, hand-lettered pickets carried in front of the White House by Frank, the Mattachine Society members, and brave women from the Daughters of Bilitis, the first lesbian civil rights organization in the country. The pickets almost seemed to vibrate. They proclaimed, "End Official Persecution of Homosexuals"; "Homosexual Americans Demand Their Civil Rights"; and "First-Class Citizenship for Homosexuals." I knew these old pickets carried in front of LBJ's White House were the Big Bang of the political movement for LGBTQ civil equality. These old signs paved the way for a new political language, words for us all to find each other, to make lives for ourselves, even to survive a plague and to build families. I did not expect how they would move me. Standing before this pile of pickets, I became all in for helping Frank the hoarder find his way, and hoped that by helping him I might find my own.

We were not the only ones concerned about the preservation of the Kameny archive. "More than a few movers and shakers in Washington's gay community have recently feared that Kameny's trove could accidentally become rubbish once he's gone, if someone doesn't step in and preserve it. Lately something of a scramble has emerged," said a 2005 profile of Frank that ran in the *Washington Post*.[9]

The idea of Kameny Papers was further developed by my friend, Washington corporate public affairs strategist Bob Witeck, who had known Frank for years; our pro-bono attorney Rande Joiner, and others who created a strategy and sound legal structure to be named the Kameny Papers Project. Simply, we would have the papers and pickets appraised, raise the money to purchase the archive from Frank, and then donate all of it to the Smithsonian National Museum of American History and the Library of Congress. We would offer the pickets to the Smithsonian for display to the public and the papers to the Library of Congress for research by historians, authors, academics, and lawmakers.

We began with an appraisal from one of Washington's best-known appraisers of archives and books, Allan Stypeck, president of

Dupont Circle's Second Story bookstore. I told Frank that Stypeck had provided fair market value appraisal services to the Library of Congress, the FBI, and the US State Department, so we could trust him to be accurate and fair. No more need to panic.

At my apartment circa 2006, now filled to the ceiling with Kameny's boxes, Stypeck delivered the hard news. "Charles, few seriously collect gay papers. There's just not a market for this stuff." He was candid with us, and it stung a bit. "I mean, if these papers were signed by Eisenhower or Thatcher, or Rock Hudson, maybe there is a gay paper market. But who is Frank Kameny in this league?" He continued, "I mean I know who he is, but every member of Congress thinks they have something valuable."

I thought, "Oh, lord, do not compare us to members." I pushed back: this was a vast civil rights movement that began here in DC, and Frank played a seminal role in driving that history. "Please give us your best, fully supportable, valuation that would be acceptable to the IRS. We want to give our donors a tax deduction for their pro rata donations. And our purpose is to give Frank something he can live on. How high can you legitimately go? There are tens of thousands of pages here." I shared with him our greatest hits flip-book we had assembled—eye-popping documents like the original copy of his petition to the Supreme Court; or his 1973 "We are cured!" memo, announcing to activists and donors the delisting of homosexuality as a mental illness by the American Psychiatric Association.

"Hmm. Well there is this one. The one about 'revulsion,' the one in that long black box," Stypeck said.

I knew it. He had singled out the box that I first saw on Frank's stairs. It contained what we later named the Revulsion Letter, written in 1966 to Frank and the Mattachine Society by John W. Macy, chairman of the US Civil Service Commission. in the black box was a mimeographed copy of the letter, which is both an utterly vile description of "the deviate" and a superbly twisted legal rationale for why homosexuals must continue to be barred from working for the federal government—be they postal clerks or White House aides. No one

I knew of, no publisher, had ever seen this. It was forgotten and fading in Frank's attic.

Stypeck explained, "It is obviously a heavily lawyered document that has resonance even today." It is a single-spaced, three-page letter that laid down a viciously discriminatory federal policy that lasted for decades. The Revulsion Letter reverberates still each time a judge scrutinizes a law that targets LGBTQ Americans.

Macy, President Lyndon Johnson's leading defender of anti–gay and lesbian prejudice in public service, wrote to Frank: "Pertinent considerations here [for maintaining the ban on homosexuals in government] are the revulsion of other employees by homosexual conduct and the consequent disruption of service efficiency, the apprehension caused other employees by homosexual advances, solicitations or assaults, the unavoidable subjection of the sexual deviate to erotic stimulation through on-the-job use of common toilet, shower and living facilities, the offense to members of the public who are required to deal with a known criminal or sexual deviate" (see appendix 2).

Thanks to Allan Stypeck, I knew then we had a collection that may have some value, and we would succeed for Frank, our community, and the country itself. Thanks to the generosity of our donors, like former congressman Mike Huffington (a fellow alumni of Camp Longhorn), we were able to purchase the archive from Frank at a fair price, enough for him to live on in the coming years. At that time the Manuscript Division of the Library of Congress had no other openly gay or lesbian collections. (Okay, they had the papers of Margaret Mead, but please, she was closeted.) They were thrilled to hear from us.

To open the vault doors of the Smithsonian National Museum of American History, I made contact with Harry Rubenstein, who at the time was the curator of the Division of Political History. Harry was excited to hear about the pickets and came to my apartment to see them neatly stacked for his review and the museum's consideration. A political historian and an intellectual with a plainspoken manner,

Harry was thrilled with what we had. I thought it was a stack of pickets, a collection. But it was no mere collection to Harry; it was the American democracy story itself lying there before us, in powerful objects attesting to our democracy's steady expansion through war, sacrifice, activism, and protest. Harry Rubenstein understood what the pickets were saying.

In 2017 he was cocurator of the museum's exhibition, *American Democracy: A Great Leap of Faith*. Teaching me about the power of objects, he took me to see the show while it was under construction. He had included one of the most powerful Kameny pickets in a section of the exhibition titled "Beyond the Ballot," about the ways individuals exercise the right to peaceably assemble to bring "their interests and concerns before the nation."[10] It was thrilling to see one of the old pickets front and center: "Discrimination against Homosexuals Is as Immoral as Discrimination against Negroes and Jews"—now in the Smithsonian Hall of Democracy.

It was emotionally difficult for Frank to let go. At one point he stopped releasing the papers that we called the "good stuff," the substantive documents charting the progress of the gay and lesbian activists. One day he handed me a small stack he had reviewed, a pile of old gay newspapers and handouts, such as one for a Mr. Groovy Guy contest. I had to tell him it was junk and we would not stand for that. I brought a tape to measure the piles by the foot to emphasize our determination. No more word salads from a master. If the stacks were not tall enough and substantive, we were not going to continue with this charade. Of course Frank tried our patience. That's what he did for a living, challenging a nation that needed pushing.

On October 6, 2006, the Kameny Papers Project organized and paid for a reception to announce our gift at the Thomas Jefferson Building of the Library of Congress with suggested business attire. I could not stand the idea of the library simply blowing by yet another donation without making an occasion out of such a moment. The whole point was to fight invisibility and erasure of history. How we got Frank into business attire I will never know, but he was amazing that day.

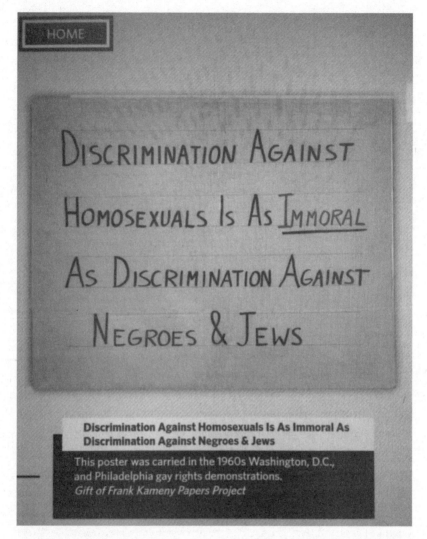

DISCRIMINATION AGAINST HOMOSEXUALS IS AS IMMORAL AS DISCRIMINATION AGAINST NEGROES & JEWS

Discrimination Against Homosexuals Is As Immoral As Discrimination Against Negroes & Jews

This poster was carried in the 1960s Washington, D.C., and Philadelphia gay rights demonstrations.
Gift of Frank Kameny Papers Project

From Kameny's attic to the Smithsonian National Museum of American History, "Hall of Democracy" permanent exhibit: "Discrimination against Homosexuals Is as Immoral as Discrimination against Negroes and Jews." Photo by Charles Francis.

Acknowledging a standing ovation, Frank said, "I have become something of a walking history book."

Thanks to the generosity of former congressman, and fellow Texan, Michael Huffington, we were able to make the purchase,

Frank Kameny's note to me: "Beyond words." The feeling was mutual.
Photo by Charles Francis.

giving Frank the income to survive with dignity for the rest of his life. The *Library of Congress Bulletin* announced the scale of the Kameny Paper Project's donation: "The nation's library accepted more than 70,000 letters, documents and memorabilia . . . from a pioneering crusader for gay rights."[11] The Smithsonian National Museum of American History received such picket signs as "End Official Persecution of Homosexuals" and "Homosexual Americans Demand Their Civil Rights." I received a handwritten note from Kay Tobin Lahusen and Barbara Gittings, pioneer lesbian activists, thanking me for helping Frank and our cause. Coming from Barbara and Kay, that meant a lot to me .

At that moment, in the Jefferson Building of the Library of Congress, I believe Frank turned his corner from yesterday's gay pioneer to a historical visionary.

***

With that recognition, Frank went on a roll, blasting the whole notion of erasure whenever he was presented with a worthy target. My favorite was the ultimate mainstream celebrity historian, Tom Brokaw, author of *Boom! Voices of the Sixties* (2007). *Boom!*, now thankfully forgotten, was a survey of all of the issues of the sixties from Vietnam to race, from sex and gender to ethnicity and the environment—without a word about LGBTQ America's emergence from invisibility and the fight for equality. Frank and I wondered how that was possible.

Frank went to the barricades. It was 1965 again. Working with him on a first draft of an open letter to Brokaw was an honor made thrilling when the old war horse returned a final draft.

"Mr. Brokaw," he wrote, "you have degayed the entire decade! As a gay combat veteran of World War II, and therefore a member of the Greatest Generation, I find myself and my fellow gays as absent from your narration as if we did not and do not exist." He closed with a riff on his famous exclamation, "Gay is good. You are not."[12] We received a mealy-mouthed response from Brokaw's editor at Random House, who added a begrudging note about Stonewall in the paperback edition.

We discussed how our history is constantly deleted by mainstream biographers—not only Brokaw—and their publishers. Three contemporary Eisenhower biographies[13] fail to mention the Eisenhower executive order that identified "sexual perversion" as a reason for a ban on federal employment. This order, omitted in these major biographies, destroyed the lives and careers of thousands of gay men and women for generations. The Eisenhower security order defined the "pervert" as a security threat to be investigated, terminated, and discharged.

Three years later, in 2009, Frank met President Obama in the Oval Office; later, he received a formal apology from the US government delivered by Office of Personnel Management (OPM) Director John Berry at the old Civil Service Commission building.

Like Rosa Parks, Frank had reclaimed his personal "force of history." This was the Kameny Papers Project's greatest achievement, made all the sweeter by its cofounding with Bob Witeck, my friend from our days at Gray & Company decades prior. Bob and Frank had been friends for years. Our handover ceremony at the library is marked in my memory and heart by the note I received from my husband, Stephen's, parents, John and Cherie, who one day would become my in-laws. "Charles & Stephen," they wrote, "the perfect setting [the Thomas Jefferson Building] for one of the proudest days of our lives, thanks to you." It was a wonderful family moment, in the broadest sense of the word *family*, for everyone.

> *Setting: Interior: Smithsonian National Museum of American History; Vault, Political History. Curator* HARRY RUBENSTEIN stands at a platform table. FRANK KAMENY, CHARLES FRANCIS, and THOMAS MALLON gather around. *The attendants lift each of the old picket signs off the gurney and meticulously place them in rows on the platform. Like a priest, curator* HARRY RUBENSTEIN *officiates at the raised platform.*

A series of close-ups:

HARRY (*turns toward a cabinet and carefully removes a small wooden tabletop writing desk*): Frank, we call this the Declaration of Independence Desk. It was Jefferson's desk where he wrote the declaration in 1776. (*He places the desk beside the pickets.*) And here is a brass inkwell of similar importance. (*He holds up the inkwell as if it were a chalice and places it on the table alongside* FRANK'*s pickets.*) This is the inkwell President Lincoln used when he wrote the first draft of the Emancipation Proclamation. These old pickets are part of the same story: the expansion of liberty to ever-widening circles of Americans.

> *Continuing his thought,* RUBENSTEIN *opens a small box that could easily display a precious stone. It contains a pin that reads, "Jail for Freedom."*

RUBENSTEIN: This belonged to the suffragette Alice Paul. Frank, Alice Paul went to jail for the right to picket the White House—and vote.

HARRY (*like a benediction*): Your pickets, gay history? It's *American* history now.

> HARRY *holds up one of the old pickets, which reads:* End Official Persecution of Homosexuals.

FRANK KAMENY: I never could have imagined. It would have been inconceivable that we are here today in this room, with these objects. We were so utterly despised . . .

> *He never trails off, but he does now. For once* FRANK KAMENY *is at a loss for words. So is* CHARLES. *They stand there in a moment of pure and reverent silence—rare in Washington.*

> *The Smithsonian staff directs the small group for a photograph.* FRANK *holds his picket high.*

FADE OUT

***

Frank passed away in 2011. In 2012 the Smithsonian National Museum of American History displayed the picket signs, along with a photograph of Frank, in the great entrance hall adjacent to the original, restored Star-Spangled Banner. The pickets had been locked away in the Smithsonian vault in 2006 when we donated them. At last they were on display.

When Frank died he became the subject of innumerable tributes. My personal favorite was the *Washington Post* editorial by Jonathan Capehart, "Frank Kameny: American Hero."[14] "Few people who set out to change the world actually succeed," it said. The editorial mentioned the Kameny Papers and cited Kameny's petition to the Supreme Court, denied in 1961—the petition we discovered in his attic that "started a revolution."[15]

After his passing in 2012, it was a thrill to hear from NASA astrophysicist Jane Rigby, who invited me to speak about Frank to the American Astronomical Society's (AAS) annual meeting in Austin.

After six years in a Smithsonian vault, the original Mattachine pickets were
displayed in 2012—next to the Star-Spangled Banner exhibition.
Photo by Charles Francis.

I was invited as a cofounder of the Kameny Papers to speak about
Frank—the astronomer—before they posthumously presented him
a certificate of appreciation. At the event I said, "Frank had the
education—a Masters and PhD in astronomy from Harvard—he had
the training, and he had the experience. Before him lay our golden age
of space exploration. Then, in 1957, at age 32, he was 'found out' gay
in the fifties, which left his career in astronomy in ruins." It was an
emotionally charged moment for the AAS, and for all of the LGBTQ

employees at NASA and in their profession. Rigby, herself openly lesbian and an advocate for nondiscrimination within NASA, went on to become the operations project scientist for the James Webb Space Telescope, NASA's $10 billion telescope that is the most powerful ever launched. Frank paved the way for so many.

Six months after being honored by the AAS, the International Astronomical Union in 2012 formally named an asteroid after Frank: Asteroid 40463 Frankkameny, which orbits the sun between Mars and Jupiter.[16]

A Pulitzer Prize finalist biography of Kameny, *The Deviant's War: The Homosexual vs. the United States of America* (2020), was written by Eric Cervini and became a *New York Times* bestseller and is now set to become a television series produced by Amazon Studios and Brad Pitt's Plan B Entertainment. We were thrilled to meet Eric when he was a student at Harvard digging into the Kameny Papers Archive at the Library of Congress. Today, we consider him part of the Mattachine family. Cervini writes in his acknowledgments, "The history of this book begins in Frank Kameny's attic," acknowledging the Kameny Papers' origin story. "Unable to pay his bills, Kameny sometimes called a friend, Charles Francis, for financial assistance. After one of these calls, Francis had an idea . . ." Eric continued telling the story, writing that the Kameny Papers "collection is so large that if you stacked its contents one of top of another, the pile would rise taller than a six-story building."[17]

Before this experience I had no idea of the meaning of "historiography," how first drafts of history are written, how history itself is invented from such "six-story" stacks. I had never thought of history as something one has to rescue, not passively receive or memorize like school kids. Reflecting on Frank's life, I thought, what if history is like one of those barbaric ultimate fights produced for cable television, but not one of fists? Our ultimate fight is against some of LGBTQ peoples' worst enemies: the fireplace, the garbage bag, the shredder and the bonfire—the morgues of our history.

Frank Kameny at his desk where he kept everything—thank goodness.
Photo by Charles Francis.

There could be no greater reward for my work as an Archive Activist than Cervini's inscription in *The Deviant's War*: "To Charles, Thank you for making this book possible." This is what Archive Activists do.

The largest LGBTQ book collection of its time was thrown into a Nazi bonfire. I will never forget when husband Stephen and I visited the site of the bonfire that was staged in 1933 in front of Humboldt University in Berlin. Thousands of books written by, and about, so-called degenerates were looted, then burned, from Magnus Hirschfeld's Institute for Sexual Science. At the time the institute held the largest collection of books about homosexuality and was deemed un-German and perverted. The minister of Nazi propaganda, Joseph Goebbels, wrote, "No to decadence and moral corruption! Yes to decency and morality in family and state! . . . You do well to commit to the flames the evil spirit of the past."[18]

Two years later a new historical, ancestral department of the Nazi SS was created in order to control the past by researching the superiority of the Aryan race. According to the distinguished British historian Simon Schama, a Nazi expedition to Tibet was conducted in 1938–39 "on the assumption that it was the racial cradle of Aryans," but as things turned out in Tibet, "Ancient bodies preserved in bogs were said to be homosexuals subjected to Aryan extermination. A round-up of 15,000 gay men duly followed. Most died in the camps."[19]

What if history depends not upon great historians but upon that one special person like Hirschfeld or Kameny with the courage, the observational capacity of a scientist and the agency to save what matters? Someone alienated enough yet fully engaged who will isolate a document or artifact and protect it. Additionally, this person has to have a safe and secure place in an accepting political environment, with a good roof where the scrapbook, cache of letters, or pickets may be protected, not burned. And this condition must last for decades—long enough to escape the clutches of a hostile society or a cleaning team with garbage bags to empty an old hoarder's house.

The story of the Kameny Papers is a miracle.

Chapter 8

Archive Activism: Recovering LGBTQ History

"Yep, that's him," I said to the man at the old, redbrick DC General Hospital. On October 12, 2011, we were asked to verify the identity—complete the positive ID—of the body revealed to us by Polaroid in a small black box.

"Be seated and brace yourself for any feelings you may have in the identification process." This is how they help people manage the shock and grief when the little box is opened. I was joined by Marvin Carter, a gay former Marine who could handle anything. Marvin headed a small LGBTQ charity, Helping Our Brothers and Sisters (HOBS), that had generously volunteered to help Frank throughout the final years of his life. In the absence of family or next of kin, we were asked to initiate the process at DC General for our friend. We did so, and it all happened with dignity and profound respect. It was the fiftieth anniversary of the founding of the Mattachine Society of Washington, DC.

Marvin and I, and all associated with HOBS and the Kameny Papers Project, were determined that Frank's legacy of activism be carried forward, his papers now safely inside the Library of Congress. We knew he loved that. He was gone now, and the unmistakable reality of his passing hit us hard. How do you like your astronomer, Mr. Death?[1] We knew the legacy would and must live on.

The District of Columbia had revoked the legal incorporation status of the Mattachine Society of Washington, DC, in 2006 due to the failure of Mattachine to file reports and pay its fees. But perhaps we could invent a new kind of LGBTQ organization in the form of a history society? I was thinking a history society not for academics and professional historians but for activists and those who want to recover erased history. It could be a new style of history society with an edge and a mission: full LGBTQ civil equality using the power of history to make our case. We might call this Archive Activism for a repurposed Mattachine.

I walked away from DC General with the beginnings a new idea.

***

We decided Archive Activism would be the new Mattachine motto. It reflected our passion to unearth erased and forgotten LGBTQ history. Inspired by community historians like Allan Bérubé (1948–2007)[2] and Jonathan Ned Katz (b. 1938),[3] we understood LGBTQ historical research was still a frontier. We discovered in the Kameny Papers a personal letter written in 1978 from a graduate history student at Columbia University. That student is today's distinguished author and historian John D'Emilio.[4] "As you know, the academic community has only rarely deemed the lives of gay men and women to be worthy of serious scholarly study. To my knowledge," D'Emilio the student wrote Kameny, "no American history faculty at a major university has yet sponsored a dissertation that deals with gays historically." In 1978 John D'Emilio's dissertation on "the gay movement in the United States" faced a real challenge, and his purpose in writing Kameny was a lack of manuscript sources. "I must be able to uncover 'manuscript' sources, that is unpublished and unique historical materials," D'Emilio wrote Kameny, the self-described "pack rat."[5]

We met gay historian Gerard Koskovich and read his eye-opening historiography "The History of Queer History: One Hundred Years of the Search for Shared Heritage."[6] It was the "silence—and silencing"[7] of LGBTQ Americans, Koskovich observed, that stimulated a new wave of community historians dedicated to uncovering LGBTQ history. That'd be us. The silence and silencing continues, with legislation passed or proposed in many states to ban the teaching of "inherently divisive history" and "Don't Say Gay" laws at all grade levels spreading across the country.[8]

Pate Felts and I—enjoying a decades-long friendship going back to our days at the Power House, where he served as chief financial officer—cofounded the new Mattachine Society of Washington, DC. We were joined by Frank's dear friend, activist and journalist Rick Rosendall, who had served as secretary of the original Mattachine Society, and by my friend, journalist and author Glenn Simpson. Our mission: to excavate deleted LGBTQ history and use it in the ongoing fight for full civil equality. We first introduced our motto and ideas about Archive Activism in 2009 to the LGBTQ Caucus of the Special Libraries Association at their meeting in Washington, DC. "Looking back on the Frank Kameny Papers Project—our effort to save and secure one of the great collections of LGBT history—I now realize saving and conserving an LGBT archive is a kind of activism," I said.[9]

We explained how our brand of citizen archivery represents those wrongly investigated and fired, their careers and lives thwarted or destroyed. Archive Activism is a rescue mission to recover the deleted, often sealed, documentation of the pure government animus that runs through LGBTQ political and policy history, and it focuses on the full range of historical erasure of government animus. Restoring "the historical memory of the repression of homosexuality in the United States," writes Professor Omar Encarnación about our work, "requires locating the empirical evidence that proves the role of animus in justifying anti-gay discrimination in federal policy toward gay people."[10]

Our innovation is in the coupling of original archival research with the professional legal counsel of an international law firm, McDermott Will & Emery, our pro bono partner for ten years. This was the one single best thing that ever happened to us. The McDermott team, led by partners Lisa Linsky in New York and Paul Thompson in Washington, DC, taught us how to convert newly discovered materials into evidentiary history and legal products that we deployed with the media, the legal community, legislators, and the courts. Our arguments were made with the documents we discovered, and we gave them a voice. Professor Dale Carpenter writes, "It is unconstitutional animus for the government to target homosexuals simply because it morally disapproves of homosexuality."[11] We targeted that animus with our discoveries and let the documents speak for themselves: "vox docs," the voice of the documentary evidence.

Archive Activism is about harnessing the power of our history. It is about finding the sealed or erased documentary evidence—from libraries to attics—and using it as a powerful tool to advocate for social change. Never again will we accept a "this didn't happen" erasure for ourselves or our community.

Uniquely Nasty

As Archive Activists we rely upon reservoirs of humor and patience to shepherd our projects through the labyrinth of stonewalling government officials and the National Archives in Washington. Beginning in 2011, we were determined to look behind the curtain of government secrecy to learn exactly what the government's lawyers were saying about Frank and all of us "homos" knocking at the government gate, under investigation, and in federal courtrooms.

For two full years we submitted our FOIA requests to the OPM and the National Archives asking for all files dealing with homosexuals, homosexuality, "perverts," "perversion," anything sexual. We called and we wrote OPM. But to no avail. We were a weekly presence in the records division of the National Archives at College Park, Maryland, working with the professional researchers there, and still nothing. We decided to become more aggressive, establishing a public profile, talking to the media and calling out the whole system of silence this many decades later. Maybe we were starting to generate some second thoughts in the stacks.

One day, unexpectedly, a research assistant at the National Archives stepped forward with a call slip seemingly out of nowhere with one word that broke the code: "Suitability." He had written down, "Suitability, Office of General Counsel, US Civil Service Commission." He told us these boxes had never been processed or formally declassified. After all of these years, they were still officially closed. Working with our legal team at McDermott, we got them opened, and damn, it was "suitability" all along. Homosexuals were unsuitable for government service.

Research = Activism (R = A)

The boxes labeled "Homosexuality and Suitability Legal Advisory Files" were brought up from the bowels of the archives to a cart for our review. Here was a trove, four hundred pages of memos, correspondence, reports, and meeting minutes covering twenty-five years of massive resistance to reform. Pate and I had expected the worst, but these files revealed the whole horrible story of government bigotry, ignorance, and pure animus baked into decades of regulation and law. We almost ran to the photocopying machine at the archives when we discovered the John Steele memo regarding "Homosexuality and Government Employment" (October 14, 1964). "Our tendency," Steele wrote, "'to lean over backwards' to rule against a homosexual is simply a manifestation of the revulsion which homosexuality inspires in the normal person. What it boils down to," Steele concludes, "is that most men look upon homosexuality as something uniquely nasty, not just as a form of immorality."[12]

At last we had discovered the smoking gun of pure government animus that had nothing whatever to do with policy or any overriding state interest. The files showed how a permanent caste of embedded, government attorneys, of both parties, maintained the investigations and firings. All of us were "uniquely nasty," not a security threat or a potential blackmail target or bad for military morale, just "nasty."

"Uncovered Papers Show Past Government Efforts to Drive Gays from Jobs," the *New York Times* announced our find in a page-one feature by Matt Apuzzo. "It was in the government's suitability files that Mr. Francis found the memo from Mr. Steele." The article continued, "While the government clearly labeled files concerning Communism and counterespionage, documents related to gays were not so neatly identified, Francis said."[13] Anodyne, gray filing names were for one purpose: to conceal. Or maybe there were no words, only pejoratives, for us.

The *Times* headline about driving "gays from jobs" was an understatement. For a high-level government attorney inside the Civil Service Commission to characterize homosexuals as "uniquely nasty" in a formal memorandum is an example of verbal assault. This goes beyond saying gays are "unsuitable" or a "security threat." "Uniquely nasty" transformed lesbian and gay Americans into something almost subhuman, unworthy of any honor or status protected by the Constitution. Seeking to understand the concept of *verbal assault*, I turned to author Daniel Goldhagen, who analyzed the incessant antisemitism of Nazi propaganda in the 1930s. Of course they are not the same, but there are similarities. He wrote "The verbal assault contributed, as much as any other policy, to transforming Jews into socially dead beings, beings who were seen to be owed few if any moral obligations by Germans and who were conceived of as being thoroughly dishonorable, indeed incapable of bearing honor."[14] Verbal assault is the only way one can describe "uniquely nasty." Can a citizen bear honor if he or she is "uniquely nasty"?

Littera Scripta Manet

Littera scripta manet, translated "the written word remains,"[15] is the motto of the National Archives and Records Administration (NARA). It was here where we discovered "uniquely nasty," two words that indeed endured and branded LGBTQ Americans for decades. What better place to receive the bad news? It inspired us to absorb the textual record at the archives facility in College Park—the largest archival building in the world, with access to some thirteen billion pages of textual records and forty-four million photographs. We citizen Archive Activists are welcomed by the archives that take pride in providing greater access to the nation's documentary LGBTQ heritage. If you have never before researched a topic at the National Archives, it is difficult to understand the grandeur of the place and its team of archivists and librarians. It reminded me of my first steps down into the Grand Canyon, a humbling realization of staggering scale. I thought, "O God, thy sea is so great, my boat so small."[16] Littera scripta manet.

The Archive's roots as a national archival institution are in ancient Greek civilization, where valuable documents were kept in the temple of the mother of the gods in the public square of Athens. Here were the treaties, laws, and minutes of the popular assembly. It is in this temple (the Metroon) where the statement of Socrates in his own defense was saved. We Archive Activists thrill at his words: "I tell you that wealth does not make you good within . . . I will never stop questioning . . . this is my teaching and if it corrupts youth, then I suppose I am the corrupter."

The archivists and librarians at the archives gave their all to help in our searches of the LGBTQ past. This had not always been the case. Mattachine's advisory board member David K. Johnson, author of *The Lavender Scare* (2004), spoke at an event we held in 2014 at McDermott Will & Emery's office in Washington, DC. He said he would meet with the government archivists requesting records of the homosexuals accused of disloyalty and would receive resistance and pushback in the name of privacy issues. The records keepers would wince at the word *homosexual* if it was raised in a political or historic context. Homosexuality? That's a *personnel* matter, and personnel information was not for release, even if the individuals involved were long deceased. Mattachine has hit the same wall. "We are not erasing or locking up your history," the argument goes. "We are merely protecting privacy rights," even when targeted as Communists or deviates by Director Hoover.

There has been a cultural shift at NARA. Today, the National Archives has an LGBTQ web page listing a host of documents, beginning with the 1778 documentation of the expulsion of a gay officer from the US Army during the Revolutionary War, and thousands of other pages of documents related to US policy toward homosexuality in the military. We were thrilled when the former NARA Archivist David Ferriero spoke to us at the same Mattachine Society event and emphasized that the archives had undertaken an institutional review of its records that were buried or organized without reference to homosexuality, "suitability," "perversion," or other tags that could be useful to researchers in the future.

***

The formulation of gays as "uniquely nasty" is of a piece with John Macy's Revulsion Letter we discovered in Frank Kameny's attic. Neither of these classic, disparaging insults have been included in a Supreme Court opinion, and they should be. The day is coming when the justices will be asked to revisit the court's opinions on LGBTQ-related cases. They will deny any bigotry is involved. Chief Justice John Roberts minimized our history in his dissent in *US v. Windsor* as "snippets of history to tar the political branches with the brush of bigotry."[17] Our evidentiary history of animus proves the lie to that. Macy's Revulsion Letter to the Mattachine Society went far beyond retching at our existence; it denies homosexuals any identity or legal status. Macy, chairman of the Civil Service Commission, wrote Kameny and the Mattachine Society, "We do not subscribe to the view, which indeed is the rock upon which the Mattachine Society is founded, that 'homosexual' is a proper metonym for an individual. Rather, we consider the term 'homosexual' to be properly used as an adjective to describe the nature of overt sexual relations or conduct."[18] We do not exist. There is only "the act."

Has this been resolved? Of course not. Ideologue attorneys continue to question the existence of LGBTQ identity in a morass of lies about pedophilia, grooming, and woke indoctrination. This goes back to the beginning.

Nasty / Unsuitable

The "suitability" files we discovered at the National Archives revealed decades-long massive legal resistance to federal court decisions and plaintiff's efforts to be reinstated in their jobs and to end federal discrimination against gays. Among them we could not find a single document that revealed an iota of empathy for their gay and lesbian targets, people whose careers were being destroyed and lives shattered with the official imprimatur of "immoral," "disgraceful," and "unsuitable."

We bundled up our "suitability" trove and headed over to the office of our partners in Archive Activism—who became our friends—at McDermott Will & Emery. They were blown away by the memos dripping in animus. Normally, Lisa Linsky and Paul Thompson met with us on Friday conference calls to review the week's discoveries and challenges. This time we met in person. Paul is a former federal prosecutor, with one of his many areas of expertise being congressional investigations; Lisa is a partner who specializes in complex litigation while being the firm's first partner in charge of LGBTQ diversity and inclusion practices. With this kind of background, it was quite something for them to validate our guess that the Steele memo was a historic find with multiple meanings for future legal and legislative action. We asked them to simply read it aloud. And they did so as if it were a terrible vow from a government bureaucrat, "something uniquely nasty, not just a form of immorality." This cemented our partnership with McDermott. Soon the McDermott team would include some twenty attorneys—partners and young associates, LGBTQ and straight, practicing and retired. We became a true Archive Activist fighting force. The McDermott team well understood the implications for future arguments to be made at the Supreme Court. They explained to us how our archival research might be used in an equal protection challenge, demonstrating how animus as a basis for specific state action could render a law unconstitutional.

At last we saw what the government lawyers were saying behind their impenetrable wall about Frank Kameny and the case he had brought to the Supreme Court. One government lawyer wrote his boss, the director of the US Civil Service Commission, "Kameny's whole brief was a constitutional argument *that he and his kind* [italics added] constituted a 'minority group' and titled to Constitutional protection under the same conditions as race and religion . . . I think we can dispose of the Constitutional question quite quickly."[19]

We discovered one astounding letter written in 1973—four years after Stonewall—by Civil Service Commission General Counsel Burton McDonald to the Justice Department. "This individual," writes McDonald, who wanted to terminate the employee, "is an open, exclusive homosexual, who has obtained, indeed sought, publicity in his advocacy of freedom of homosexual activity . . . his allegations of protection under the First Amendment cannot stand."[20]

Soon we and the McDermott team were both thrilled and galvanized to become the subject of a documentary about our Archive Activism, produced and directed by investigative reporter Mike Isikoff. I wondered what the title would be . . . and was initially a bit thrown when Mike revealed to me "Uniquely Nasty."[21] Okay, I thought, I will be proud to be "uniquely nasty" in service to our Archive Activism. Mike, a seasoned investigative reporter and student of history, well knew the terrain of the government's war on gay and lesbian Americans in the day. More important, he understood the national political dimension connected to contemporary Texas politics going back to Waco Congressman John Dowdy's racist and homophobic diatribes. Isikoff's documentary told our story, beginning with the vision of the Austin Twelve. He artfully connected the episode about us titled "The Betrayal" to the McDermott Will & Emery / Mattachine amicus brief—dubbed by the *Washington Post* the "animus amicus"[22]—in the same-sex marriage case *Obergefell v. Hodges*.

Our amicus brief in that case was powerful and clear: "The historical background demonstrated by these source materials reveals a culture of animus against LGBTQ Americans, justifications for excluding them from the privileges given to all other Americans, and a revulsion to any form of intimacy between individuals of the same sex." Our discoveries provide the evidence for the brief to conclude,

"The voices of the government officials in these important documents, and the stories of the victims of these purges, show why the government actions grounded in animus cannot stand."[23]

For that true buzz of animus, we loved the find of the letter of termination to Charlie Baker from the Civil Service Commission's Bureau of Personnel Investigations. Charlie and his partner, Rod, came to Washington to brief our team over two days at the McDermott law office. He told us in a conference room what it was like to be home living with his parents in his twenties when the awful government letter arrived. It was a disgusting bureaucratic, righteous "You're fired." He was horrified. He was frightened and angered even in our conference room, where all of us were empathizing with every word coming out of Charlie's mouth, as he read, "In view of the aforementioned immoral, infamous, scandalous, and notoriously disgraceful conduct, you are invited to show cause why you should not be disqualified for federal employment and removed therefrom to promote the efficiency of the service." Charlie's story is told by Mike Isikoff in the documentary "Uniquely Nasty." Charlie's disgrace and termination are redeemed with his marriage ceremony, when he and partner Rod marry on an open expanse of a Florida beach.

"For high court, a hateful history at close hand," Philip Kennicott wrote in the *Washington Post*. His column described our research and amicus brief as "an insider's look at how the fear and hatred of gay people was codified, disseminated, defended and adapted after homosexuals were officially banned from civil service by President Eisenhower in 1953."[24]

The "Uniquely Nasty" Washington premiere was part of the first History Film Forum sponsored by the Smithsonian National Museum of American History and the National Endowment for the Humanities. We loved that it was screened at the Smithsonian's Warner Bros. Theatre. The film featured the voices of activist and Star Trek helmsman George Takei reading the part of J. Edgar Hoover; and television, film, and Broadway star Matt Bomer, from Spring, Texas, reading the part of John Steele. Bomer's reading of the words "uniquely nasty" reminded me of the young Orson Welles's radio

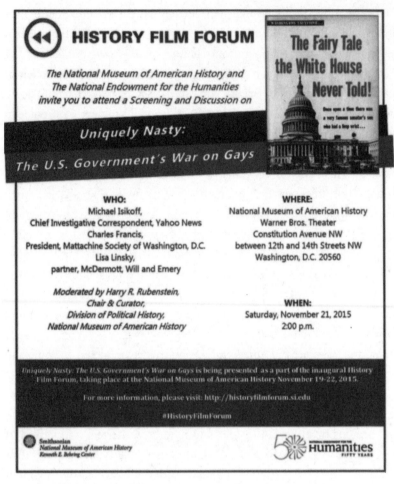

The premiere of Mike Isikoff's award-winning documentary
"Uniquely Nasty" in the Warner Bros. Theater at the Smithsonian National
Museum of American History. Courtesy of the National Museum of
American History, Smithsonian Institute.

theatre voice. Mike Isikoff was duly recognized, as were we and the
whole McDermott team. "Uniquely Nasty: The US Government's
War on Gays"[25] received in 2018 the Edward R. Murrow Award
for Best News Documentary. (Ed Murrow is the journalist who
confronted Joe McCarthy, Joe Wershba's old boss.)

Chapter 9

Lilli Vincenz, *Lebenskünstler*

"All okay up there, Lilli?" we called upward into her attic.
"Yes, yes, one moment, please," responded Dr. Lilli Vincenz in her definitive, in-charge German accent. Holding onto the pull-down ladder at her home in Arlington, Virginia, we eagerly awaited what Lilli had uncovered. I climbed up to take a look into a world of dust, Christmas decorations, and scores of boxes of her patient files.

"Charles, there, there. In the back, that crate." She directed me to begin crawling, and I obeyed—until I could not hold my breath much longer. Why wasn't I wearing a mask?

"Lilli, Pate, I can see them," I gasped, and started tugging the wooden crate, overflowing with 16 mm film reels and cans, loops of footage and files, and a vintage 16 mm movie projector. The film cans came into focus, labeled with faded masking tape: *Second Largest Minority*. And another one, *Gay & Proud*.

Born under the Third Reich in 1937 in Hamburg, Germany, Lilli Vincenz has been described as a lebenskünstler, a German word for someone who has mastered the art of living—indeed, one whose

Lilli Vincenz's 16 mm work print and trims of two LGBTQ classic
documentaries, *Second Largest Minority* (1968) and *Gay & Proud* (1970).
Photo by Charles Francis.

life itself is a work of art.[1] After being discharged from the Women's
Army Auxiliary Corp for being a lesbian, Lilli became the first
lesbian member of the original Mattachine Society of Washington, DC.
A true pioneer of the movement for gay and lesbian civil equality,
Lilli picketed the LBJ White House in 1965 with Frank Kameny

and nine other picketers from Mattachine and the lesbian Daughters of Bilitis.

Lilli was the editor of the Mattachine's newly militant monthly magazine of ideas, the *Homosexual Citizen*, with special features like "If You Are Arrested" or "Are You on File?" In later years Lilli went on to become one of the Washington area's most respected psychotherapist counselors, focusing on lesbian issues and providing counseling, along with her lifelong partner and spouse Nancy Tucker, to men struggling with HIV/AIDS-related psychological and spiritual matters. Calling themselves the Empowerment Group for People Living with AIDS, Lilli and Nancy counseled these "untouchables" when no one else would come near them in the early days of the epidemic. What an incredible life of learning and service by this courageous and compassionate lebenskünstler.

The "Zapruder Films" of a Movement

In that crate of 16 mm films we discovered Lilli's sense of history itself—capturing the early LGBTQ rights movement on film before studios, networks, or Hollywood filmmakers would touch the subject, except as a dark theme or in mockery. Lilli's attorney and friend, Rande Joiner, believed preserving Lilli's films and thousands of pages of papers was of extreme importance and so contacted us to see if we might do for Lilli what we had been able to do for Frank Kameny— organize, curate (as best we could), and help her donate her archive to a suitable library or repository. Lilli had reached that stage in her life where it was time to let go and part with many of her most treasured belongings—the ones she knew could have meaning for millions of people and history itself. Her films perfectly fit that description.[2] We presented our plan to Lilli and Rande, which included helping Lilli offer her archive to the Library of Congress. We suggested she consider donating the treasure of her films to the library's moving image collection, some 1.5 million film reels and videotapes stored in a former nuclear war mountain bunker near Culpeper, Virginia.

Lilli and me with her precious crate of films pulled down from the attic. Photo
by Pate Felts, Mattachine Society of Washington, DC.

She had the vision to take this step. The greatest reward of our Archive
Activism is the trust we build and the emotional bonds we create with
donors like Frank and Lilli, who were willing to let go with our assistance. Lilli appointed us as her agent in this effort. "Let's do it. See
that projector there?" she asked.

The projector is a 16 mm vintage Bell & Howell that weighs a ton.
It is blue and green with a reel that says "Lilli" with a smiley face.
That smiley face was her reaction to the hostility. Lilli would travel
with it to screen her films. This was how she spread the word so that

others, by the millions, would be inspired to hold Pride celebrations of their own across the country in the decades to come. She would also rent the films out for $10 and mail them by US mail to people and organizations that owned their own projectors. *ONE*, the first homosexual magazine focused on public policies and debates of the day had won the right at the Supreme Court in 1958 for gays and lesbians to ship materials using the US mail.[3] How else would anyone have seen Lilli's films? There were no ways to distribute a political LGBTQ-themed documentary film of the first Pride parade in New York. We were effectively silenced pre-internet, and no networks or studios would touch our advocacy. The television networks like CBS were utterly hostile to homosexuals and their cause.[4]

"So who is this Lilli Vincenz?"

Before we could find a home for Lilli's archive, we knew we would have to answer this question for mainstream media and libraries who were often clueless when it came to gay and lesbian history. In those days a well-known lesbian would be celebrity Ellen DeGeneres, or a closeted Eleanor Roosevelt or anthropologist Margaret Mead. To lay down a baseline, we approached the *Washington Post*, networking our way to a Style section features writer by the name of Monica Hesse. Hesse was excited to listen, learn, and work with us for many weeks of education, document identification, and endless questions about the most important lesbian activist a young reporter had never heard of. We immersed Hesse in Lilli's films and life of activism as both an activist and therapist. We introduced her to Lilli and Nancy for hours of interviews at their home in Arlington—and placed our bet that Hesse could tell the story, from Hamburg to Washington, DC. At stake was the birth of a recognized archive.

As it turned out, Hesse's piece, titled "What Lilli Saved," was brilliant. She misidentified me as this nameless "consultant" from nowhere and erased Mattachine's role. But who cared. She wrote, "Her [Lilli's] films became the ur-texts of sorts, Zapruder footage for the gay rights movement—used by groups around the country to understand what was happening or what had already happened in the early days of the crusade."[5] Hesse nailed it with this reference to Ukraine-born, Dallas dress manufacturer Abraham Zapruder's devastating 8 mm color film of the assassination of President Kennedy in Dealey Plaza. Like the Zapruder film, Lilli's films became the historical memory.

Armed with Hesse's article, I loaded the "Zapruder footage" into my car and called upon the Library of Congress's motion picture Packard Campus in the small town of Culpeper, Virginia. I understood it would take eye contact, one on one, to describe this pioneer activist to Director Mike Mashon. At the time, we Americans lived in such separate worlds, especially LGBTQ Americans and the mainstream, straight society of historians and major cultural institutions. Having now studied under two Franks, Kameny and Mankiewicz, I saw it as our job to make those connections. We knew how to translate Mattachine speak into plain English. I had Ted Kheel's "know how" and "know who." Surrounded by stacks of old Hollywood film cans, nitrate films for preservation, copyright prints of new releases, and an old Steenbeck 16 mm screening table, Mashon asked for the video cassette of *Gay & Proud* and let it roll.

Gay & Proud is a twelve-minute, black-and-white, 16 mm documentary produced and directed by Lilli in 1970, covering the first ever Christopher Street Liberation Day parade in New York on the first anniversary of the Stonewall Uprising. Lilli enrolled in a film course to learn how to use a borrowed Beaulieu 16 mm camera and hit the streets. She did this in a time when no networks would even consider a serious documentary project covering a homosexual parade. Simply put, there is nothing like Gay & Proud. The film documents the country's first Pride parade, from Greenwich Village to a Central Park queer "be-in." Think of the Broadway show or motion picture *Hair*. It is a breathtaking time machine of LGBTQ+ liberation. "Every so often a precious jewel emerges from this mountain of content that comes into the Center," Mike Mashon wrote. Lilli's films are "revelatory . . . record[ing] a seismic shift of such proportions that we're still feeling the reverberations today."[6]

After Lilli named us as her agent for the library to approve use of her films, we did so for an incredible range of progressive documentaries and film projects. Requests poured in, and we mostly gave the okay, from ABC, CBS, NBC, and PBS to a wide range of independent productions, including the PBS / Independent Lens production of *Cured* (about the delisting of homosexuality as a mental illness); a Showtime series titled *The First Lady*, featuring Viola Davis playing Michelle Obama; and a Henry Louis Gates Jr. miniseries for PBS entitled "Making Black America." We did decline a request to allow the films to be used in a True Crime Series about a serial killer in Greenwich Village. Many millions of viewers have now experienced for themselves what Lilli's borrowed Beaulieu and vintage projector heretofore made available to early lesbian and gay organizations and independent film festivals.

Lilli's films now belong to the American people. For the new Mattachine, not only were Lilli's films revelatory, but it was also riveting to see how a deleted or forgotten past can be salvaged from an attic, reassembled, and leveraged to support social change and expanded awareness of justice rooted in history. Resulting from our crawl in her attic, Lilli donated to the Library of Congress some ten thousand items, photographs, and memorabilia collected over a period of fifty years (meticulously recorded by Pate using all of his CPA organizational skills). Her patient files, of course, remained with her.

***

Working with our longtime friend, filmmaker Patrick Sammon, Mattachine produced a video documentary about Lilli titled "Gay and Proud: Lilli's Legacy."[7] We wanted the video to bring the Vincenz papers and films to audiences outside of the Library of Congress via YouTube and social media. No more 16 mm projector. It features historian and author Lillian Faderman and Senator Tammy Baldwin (D-WI) commenting on Lilli's contributions to the movement, most particularly how her films inspired them to lives of scholarship and politics. "I prize, cherish and respect not only those participants in

Lilli Vincenz honored during Pride month at the White House (2014) alongside a
picket she carried out front on the sidewalk in 1965. Photo by Charles Francis.

activism but those who recorded it so people like me decades later
could learn about them and our history," Senator Baldwin said.[8]

The last time we heard from Lilli, before an illness of memory
would take her away, she wrote us a sweet note: "Thank you for

I did not know what a "onesie" was until this.

everything you have done for Nancy and me!!!" with a heart. The last time I saw her was in 2014, a special moment of personal triumph for Lilli when she was invited during Pride month to the White House by President Obama. There she stood in the East Room alongside one of the Mattachine picket signs the Kameny Papers Project had donated years before to the Smithsonian: "End Official Persecution of Homosexuals," it proclaimed. This was the picket she had carried as a brilliant, beautiful young lesbian activist on the Pennsylvania Avenue sidewalk.

It was wonderful that I, representing Mattachine, was able to be a part of this moment at the White House. It was exactly a week before our son, Thomas, was born in Charlotte, North Carolina. At the hospital, Stephen and I knew we were there—on the edge of parenthood, two dads married and soon to become a family—thanks to pioneers like Lilli and the foundations they laid for us all. Stephen's sister Angela and her spouse, Marjorie, were cheering us on all the way. We received a onesie as a gift that declared "Two Dads Are Rad." We did not feel rad, just real. And grateful.

Chapter 10

"Negroes," "Agitators," and "Racial Perverts"

W e could not limit our Archive Activism to white Washington, DC. Fully blooded now in our searches for the deleted LGBTQ past, we were inspired to widen our chase. We wanted to look beneath the suitability investigations, revulsion firings, and "nasty" denigration down to the bedrock of racism and homophobia that underlay the discrimination against so-called Negro "homos," perverts and agitators—Black and white. We found that in Freedom Summer 1964.

When we first reported on these "Freedom Summer 'Homos,'"[1] our Archive Activism focused on the connections between LGBTQ state persecution and the Civil Rights Movement in Mississippi. In later years we saw how this bloomed to include the Mississippi legislature's ongoing threat to the rights of all the state's citizens, with profound national consequences.

Our first direction came in the opinion of US District Court judge Carlton Reeves, striking down as unconstitutional Mississippi's ban on same-sex marriage in 2014. Reeves's opinion made the connection between Mississippi's LGBTQ discrimination and the Civil Rights Movement of the sixties: "Any claim that Mississippians quietly accommodated gay and lesbian citizens could no longer be made in the sixties. . . . Segregationists called their opponents 'racial perverts,'" he wrote. "Being homosexual invited scrutiny and professional consequences . . . The Mississippi State Sovereignty Commission . . . singled out Rust College, a private historically black institution, on reports that instructors there were 'homosexuals and racial agitators.'" Reeves focused on the intersection of Jim Crow and the animus-drenched persecution of Mississippi gays: "Klan propaganda tied together 'Communists, homosexuals, and Jews'—infidels all.'"[2]

Judge Reeves inspires us today because he does not back down from the Mississippi legislature's "history of disregarding the Constitutional rights of its citizens"[3]—nor does he exclude LGBTQ Mississippi from his opinions. Reeves writes that lawmakers in Mississippi are determined to maintain "the old Mississippi." Criticizing the Mississippi legislature, Reeves "recounted the state's long history of denying its citizens constitutional rights with segregated schools, prohibitions on same-sex marriage and a 'secret intelligence arm' that enforced racial discrimination."[4] We know what that "intelligence arm" was—the racist, virulently anti-LGBTQ Mississippi State Sovereignty Commission (MSSC).

Judge Reeves's writings alerted us to an untold, erased story of Freedom Summer 1964, when openly gay African American student organizers came under attack by the state of Mississippi for being "Negro perverts." Yes, gay Black students at the historically Black Rust College in the small town of Holly Springs were organizing and fighting for their lives in 1964. For that they were targeted.

We began our Archive Activism with a police report covering a fearful town meeting in Oxford, Mississippi, in May 1964. Present were some sixty mayors, police chiefs, deputy sheriffs, county attorneys, supervisors, and other law enforcement officials for a briefing by Tom Scarbrough, a former sheriff and investigator for the MSSC, on the coming Freedom Summer. The MSSC was created by the Mississippi legislature in 1956 to fight integration, block the registration of Black voters, and thwart the civil rights organizers who were targeting the state. Scarbrough reported directly to the governor, so people that night in Oxford were intent upon his message and guidance. According to documents uncovered by the Mattachine Society at the University of Southern Mississippi in Hattiesburg, Scarbrough said he was there to help "organize the city to work in a coordinated unit to handle the racial agitators who have promised to invade Mississippi this summer." He told them that all of the major civil rights organizations, "CORE, SNCC, SCLC, NAACP and COFO have publicly boasted through the newspapers that thousands of outside agitators were planning to come to this state after the colleges close in June." Scarbrough advised the attendees that "the demonstrators will be composed of Communists, sex perverts, odd balls and do-gooders and the unfortunate thing concerning this group is that the [Kennedy] Justice Department has been and in all probability will be supporting their agitation."[5]

Of course, the "sex perverts" and "odd balls" would be among the agitator groups behind the "Negro" unrest. "The Negro has never progressed very far on his own," said Scarbrough, "his progress has come with the assistance of the white man or by the white man's mistakes, and of course, the reason Mississippi officers have done so well is that they have been organized." Scarbrough laid it down in starkest racist terms for the folks that night to get themselves organized. He told the crowd the agitators were on their way to Oxford and nearby Rust College: "Rust College at Holly Springs is very near, and it is possible that outside agitators would organize at Rust College and come down and picket . . . at the courthouse in Oxford."[6]

I was happy to wear the hat of "sex pervert outside agitator" at this stage of my life. So I went to Mississippi to uncover what had happened at Rust College.

I went to Clarksdale, Mississippi, where legend has it that bluesman Robert Johnson met the devil. There I missed the devil but caught up with my lifelong friend whom I met at the University of Virginia, former Clarksdale mayor Bill Luckett. BBQ and beer at the Ground Zero Blues Club with Bill was even better than meeting the devil.[7] Bill was a former candidate for governor, and his partner at Ground Zero,

A "Freedom Summer" special collection at the Rust College Leontyne Price
Library, with gratitude to Rust and the greatest opera diva of our time.

the actor Morgan Freeman, understood Mississippi as few others do,
especially those who oppose the anti-LGBTQ thrust of Mississippi
politics and law. Bill opened the doors for us to begin our Archive
Activism in Mississippi at the crossroads we were interested in—the
intersection of racism and homophobia.

Our first stop was in the Special Collections vault of the Leontyne
Price Library at Rust College. The library is named for the world-

famous soprano whose mother went to school there. Price performed at a benefit concert for the college in 1967, which raised money to build the library. Price herself would travel with the Rust Choir and even recorded an album of spirituals with them that includes the epic "I Wish I Knew How It Would Feel to Be Free." At the Price Library, I was able to tap into the spirit of Dr. Earnest (Earnie) Smith, who led the school as president through the trials of the Civil Rights Movement only to be branded a "homo" and a "queer" by the state and its segregationists.

Young Earnie Smith arrived on an all-night bus in Holly Springs, alone with a suitcase. Raised in the 1920s in Alabama, when people openly wore their Klan robes on the streets, he had been stricken as a child with polio. "I arrived in the early morning, still dark on a bus with exactly fifty-five cents. When I saw the first black fellow, I asked 'Where is Rust College?'"[8]

I reviewed the papers and photographs documenting how Rust, under Dr. Smith's leadership, had become a Freedom School that summer, allowing its dorms and facilities to be used by the organizers from the Student Nonviolent Coordinating Committee (SNCC), the NAACP, and others. I could see the faces of Smith and the young students in photo collages facing the challenge of their lifetime—securing their right to vote and overturning Jim Crow, which was strangling them all.

We discovered in the files of the MSSC a briefing memo written by the sheriff/investigator Tom Scarbrough. The subject of the single-spaced, five-page document was "known or suspected homosexuals" at Rust. Its purpose was to expose President Smith as "queer" and his faculty and student activists as "odd balls and homos."[9] Rust, the report stated, "had become a place for instructors who are homosexuals and racial agitators." By name it listed each of the accused "homos and perverts." Six of them were supposedly consorting with "a single man" who was "presently teaching English at Rust"; they reportedly "had been seen going in the window to his room at night." Others had been fired for "homosexual activity" in their previous teaching jobs. They fought

A Freedom Summer '64 collage of Rust College students and faculty. Courtesy
Leontyne Price Library; photo of the collage by Charles Francis.

over homosexual rivals, and one had been "beaten up by his boyfriend"
and had subsequently attempted suicide. An anonymous informant
charged that youth had been "molested" in the library. Students, "both
boys and girls," were said to be having "unnatural relations." As for
Smith himself, "Informant No. 3 stated that Smith is a known liar and
ladies' man and it has been rumored that Smith might have other queer
impulses."[10]

   "These individuals were all our friends," roared Leslie Burl
McLemore, a retired professor of political science at Jackson State
University and one of the founders of the Fannie Lou Hamer National

Institute on Citizenship and Democracy, at his home in Walls, Mississippi. In 1964 McLemore was both the president of the Rust Student Council and the founding president of the NAACP chapter there—sworn in by Medgar Evers himself a year before his assassination. Les had never seen this memo before and reacted with a progression of disbelief, laughter, and then outrage. "The rightwing rednecks would figure out any way to get at Rust, and this is how low they went." McLemore continued, "Of course many of these folks were gay, and we all knew that back then. It was not an issue for us . . . we all came from small towns in Mississippi, and we all knew gay folks."[11]

Gloria Clark, one of three female SNCC organizers at Rust that summer, was given the approval to live in the women's dorm by Dr. Smith. "I knew he got a lot of heat for doing that. I thought we were accused of being flaming hetero," she laughed, noting "the sexual hang-ups of the white Mississippi males."[12]

McLemore continued, "Dr. Smith was there, in the moment, aware of the pressure brought to bear on him. . . . If you picked up your cues from Earnie, he stood his ground, protecting us from the politics of it all while taking the heat. He is a forgotten hero of that summer."[13] Indeed, what happened to Dr. Smith has been deleted or forgotten. I learned later that he likely wanted it that way. It was too humiliating an experience.

"We heard about the resignation of Dr. Smith one day in chapel," said Frank Moorer, an openly gay student at Rust at the time who was outed and smeared during the investigation. "We were all sad and disconcerted about his departure." When I met with him at his home in Montgomery, Moorer was a retired professor of the humanities at Alabama State University. Then in his eighties, Moorer was raised on a farm in rural Pink Bottom, Alabama. "I did not sit at a desk until the sixth grade, an awful school without electricity, so I was fighting that summer for our freedom, for our rights."[14]

When I shared with him the Scarbrough memo we had uncovered, he said, "To be honest, I am taken aback by this. I did not know this document was out there, and have absolutely no idea what they are talking about except to besmirch me." According to the report handed over to the Rust College Board of Trustees, Moorer had been "caught" with two boys in the library. "This is comical were it not for such an evil purpose," he said. "The state would do anything to stifle dissent," he thundered, "rendering us beyond the pale, as sissies and faggots for registering voters and fighting for our rights . . . rights we won back in 1865." He added, "At the time, people at Rust knew who the gay faculty members and students were; it just did not pop-up as an issue for us."[15]

Back in Washington I asked Frank Smith Jr., a former DC city councilman and a founding member of SNCC, about Moorer. Frank Smith is the founder and director of the African American Civil War Museum, whose mission is "to correct a great wrong in history that largely ignored the enormous contributions of the 209,145 members of the United States Colored Troops" to end slavery.[16] Smith and Moorer were roommates that Freedom Summer on the Rust campus. "I always knew Frank Moorer was gay . . . we were risking our lives and knew that white Mississippi was not going to give up power without a fight. I loved Frank Moorer. Being gay in that context was of no concern to us. We were literally guerilla organizers, together."[17] Frank Smith speaks with the conviction and gravity of someone who lived through the Civil Rights violence in Mississippi. Alongside his office at the African American Civil War Museum in Washington is a glass case containing various mementos. One is his original copy of *JET* magazine, the 1955 issue with the shocking cover photograph of the mutilated, lynched Emmet Till in his casket, the issue that helped launch the Civil Rights Movement.

"Frank," I asked, "why is this *JET* here in a Civil War museum?"

He replied, "Seeing this cover when I was a student at Morehouse University outraged and inspired me to go to Mississippi and begin organizing in Holly Springs. This *JET* was my beginning."

Frank Smith organized voter registration and outreach programs with his gay roommate Frank Moorer and another SNCC organizer, Larry Rubin, who, being a white outsider, stood out and was arrested repeatedly.

The breakthrough in our Archive Activism to discover how Dr. Earnest Smith could have been removed as president so quietly

Remembering the sixties Mississippi police state. *Left to right*: me with SNCC organizer Larry Rubin; Frank Smith Jr., founding member of SNCC and chairman, African American Civil War Museum, Washington, DC; and former mayor of Clarksdale, Mississippi, Bill Luckett. Photo copyright Deborah Barfield Berry, USA Today Network.

and effectively came in the Paul B. Johnson Family Papers at the University of Southern Mississippi in Hattiesburg. In 1964 Johnson was elected governor with the winning campaign slogan, "Stand Tall with Paul." This was a rhyming reference to his having physically blocked federal authorities who were attempting to get African American student James Meredith through the cordon of men resisting his entrance to the University of Mississippi in 1963.

A real man of the people.

The Paul B. Johnson Family Papers are a perfect example of the archive as "the dwelling place that marks the institutional passage from the private to the public, which does not always mean from the secret to the nonsecret."[18] We suspect the secrets of Johnson were

not supposed to be found in this family passage, but we found them
thanks to the help of Assistant Curator Carla Carlson. It took three days
to discover the file. It had been buried, perhaps misfiled, among total
junk like "Latin America Trip: Governors," "Institutions of Higher
Learning," and "Junior College Commission." But suddenly the USM
archivist librarian and I came across a folder marked "Investigations"
with no other reference to civil rights, Rust, or homosexuality. Here
we found the raw investigative report by none other than Tom
Scarbrough, reporting to the governor.

"Subject: Information on Dr. Earnest A. Smith, Negro Male,
President of Rust College, Holly Springs, Mississippi." It took
my breath away to read Dr. Smith described as a "Negro Male,"
as if he were in an old Jim Crow lineup. An anonymous informant
advised that "Dr. Smith was a homosexual and had unnatural relations with both sexes; and at the present time, and for some time
past, had been attempting to get rid of a number of the profes-
sors in the College and replace them with teachers of his type."[19]
The report we found that day in Hattiesburg was signed by an investigator for the Mississippi Highway Patrol, which makes sense.
The Mississippi Highway Patrol was a partner with the MSSC,
part of the police-state tactics of the time. From this raw intelligence sprang the plan to attack Dr. Smith and the gay students
and faculty. The operation and its result were reported to Governor
Johnson. The toxic handoff was made to the Rust College Methodist board of trustees. Dr. Smith quietly retired, even though he
had been married for decades and was in all likelihood straight and
what we today call gay friendly.

It was hard to be thrilled by what I had found that day in the USM
library—the sickening intelligence, sewage really, used to demean,
denigrate, and get a good man fired in order to crush the student civil
rights organizers. Dr. Smith was allowed to resign with dignity in a
silence that would last decades. How would it help to defend himself
against the charge of being queer or a homo? It would only amplify the
lie. It was our job to uncover it all in order to show how government

can harness homophobia in service to state racism. The two work so well together.

Fortunately, for the America beyond Dr. Smith, beyond Rust College, beyond that Freedom Summer, President Lyndon Johnson signed the Civil Rights Act of 1964 and, for the time being, put an end to the madness and discrimination. The "Negroes," the "agitators," and the "perverts" soldiered on together, as we must.

The story of our discovery was published as a scholarly article in the *American Historical Review*.[20] The AHR described Mattachine's work in Mississippi as "an exemplary description of how archival work carried out beyond the precincts of the university and the seminar room can illuminate matters of great public import."[21] We took our R = A work further by discovering how the outing of the "perverts" at Rust College was so entwined with the very specific suppression of voting rights by the ex-sheriff Tom Scarbrough. What to do during registration drives? Ask Tom Scarbrough: "They should be lined up in a group . . . or be arrested . . . until given the voter registration test."[22]

Following Judge Reeves's opinion on Rust College and same-sex marriage, in 2018 he overturned Mississippi's near abortion ban. Here he connected the MSSC's attack on gay citizens organizing for their civil rights to the larger story of the Mississippi legislature's "history of disregarding the Constitutional rights of its citizens."[23] This Reeves decision was subsequently overruled by the US Supreme Court in its 2022 landmark decision *Dobbs v. Jackson Women's Health Organization*, eliminating the Constitutional right to abortion.[24] The through-line of Judge Reeves's opinion from Jim Crow racism to the sexual "perverts" to the abortion ban is voting rights and democracy itself.

Leave it to the German language's ridiculously long compounds to provide a single word for this head-spinning history that almost sounds like conspiracy theory: *vergangenheitsbewältigung*. These eight syllables mean "the struggle to come to terms with the past."[25] My heritage runs the American gauntlet from pre–Civil War colonial Virginia to Alabama secession, and then to post–World War II clueless gay youth born in privilege while being branded guilty for being queer in Texas. This is history with the wind in our face, and I lean into it. We all must. History is no recitation of the past; it is a struggle to wrestle the past down to the ground and reckon with it. In this we stand on the shoulders of community historians and Archive Activists everywhere to recover history and lead the way out of erasure to a better future.

Chapter 11

Counsel for the "Preverts" versus Waco's John Dowdy

"The acts of these people are banned under the laws of God, the laws of nature, and are in violation of the laws of man," Texas Congressman John Dowdy spewed in 1963 at a congressional hearing, launching an attack on the homosexuals who dared to raise funds for the original Mattachine Society of Washington, DC. "I think a situation which requires them to be permitted a license to solicit charitable funds for the promotion of their sexual deviation is a bad law and should be changed forthwith," Dowdy said.[1]

Born in Waco, John Dowdy (1912–1995) is a pioneer of Texas gay-bashing. It would be fair to dub him the Father of Texas Homophobia. Dowdy richly deserves this distinction. He had well learned his lessons in demagoguery as one of the only four Texas congressmen who signed the so-called Southern Manifesto of protest against the Supreme Court's landmark school desegregation decision in *Brown v. Board of Education*. Considered the "single worst episode of racial demagoguery in the era of postwar America," the manifesto accused the court of a "clear abuse of judicial power" when it ruled "separate is not equal."[2] Neither Lyndon Johnson nor Democratic

Speaker of the House of Representatives Sam Rayburn of Texas signed it. And by 1963, Dowdy had moved on—to the deviates.

"Mr. Speaker, it came to my attention last fall that the District of Columbia government had granted a society of homosexuals a license to solicit charitable contributions in the District of Columbia," Dowdy declared.[3]

Who would stand up to Dowdy on behalf of the deviates?

Too often the LGBTQ beginnings of things live in the memories of allies and elders who never sign book deals and are forgotten by the young. In the archive there is only a hole. Historians like LBJ's biographer Robert Caro or Eisenhower's biographers Jim Newton or Jean Edward Smith never tell our stories from the fifties and sixties. We are the great untold. This is why we are thrilled by the opportunity to interview those who stood up for us in the past, heroes like Zona Hostetler. Oral histories can fill in that hole.

We were so excited to have a chance to sit down with Zona (b. 1936), a public interest attorney who, over a lifetime in Washington, DC, has represented groups ranging from the SNCC, in its efforts to achieve civil rights in Southern states, to our own legacy organization, the original Mattachine Society of Washington, DC. After graduating from Harvard University Law School in 1960, Zona was among the wave of young idealists who came to Washington in the 1960s to make a difference. She chose Covington & Burling because the firm offered her the freedom to take on pro bono activities. At the time Covington was the leader in such representations. Zona was one of the founding members of the National Capital Area Civil Liberties Union (NCACLU) about the time the organization stepped up and took on the fight for homosexuals who were being fired from their federal government jobs for no other reason than their sexual orientation.

In 1963 Zona had the courage—it took that in those days—at age 27 to step forward and represent Frank Kameny and the Mattachine against Dowdy. No other law firms represented gays fighting for their basic First Amendment rights. There were no LGBTQ public interest law firms. This mattered not to Zona. She saw that Dowdy was on a

crusade to crush the homosexuals and their organization with legislation specifically targeting the "deviates" in order to strip them of their
license to raise funds in the District of Columbia. With this clearly
unconstitutional bill of attainder, a law that singles out and punishes
without trial an identifiable individual or group, Dowdy wanted to
muzzle Mattachine.

"I didn't have to think about it for a second because, you know,
it was obvious that someone should do this, and it was an important
issue," Zona told us in our interview conducted by queer historian
and author Eric Cervini, who serves on Mattachine Board of Advisors. "When the NCACLU asked me to do this, Dowdy referred to
the gays as 'preverts,' mispronouncing pervert. I was happy to be
'counsel for the Preverts,'" Zona told us. The other lawyers at the
NCACLU were less comfortable with being associated with homosexuals. "Maybe there was a suggestion that they, too, were gay, and
they were uncomfortable having that thought about them in the legal
community. I don't know," she laughed.[4] But she was serious. There
was a stigma attached, and Zona, a heterosexual woman, was utterly
secure in who she was and what she believed. It had not been easy for
a woman in the day to even think about attending law school or joining
a major law firm where there were no women partners. Raised in rural
Virginia, she was a pioneer in every aspect of her being.

"I was something of a country bumpkin even after I got to law
school in 1957," she said. "I had never been to a major symphony
or major museum, you know. I was from rural Virginia. And
Williamsburg [where she attended the College of William & Mary]
was a little Southern village. The college was completely segregated
racially. I suppose though, there obviously would have been gays . . .
but even in law school I didn't know people who were gay. Everyone
was deeply closeted."[5]

She was so secure, she took it a step further. "The NCACLU thought,
and I remember thinking that maybe, maybe if I went to the hearings
being visibly pregnant, things might go better for us. I was pregnant . . .
and this became part of our family lore. I remember telling my husband

this story and my children, too. . . . The lawyers said they thought the 'atmospherics' would be better if you did it [pregnant] than we."[6] Zona served as a pregnant counsel for the "preverts."

For Zona and the Mattachine, things went from nasty to worse when it came out during the hearing that Mattachine members had used pseudonyms in their charitable license applications and for their donors. Dowdy pressed Mattachine president Frank Kameny on this, knowing the leverage it gave him: Fake names. Fraud.

"So that isn't their names. You have got dummies registered with the District as officers of your society?" Dowdy pressed. "And that is not their true names? . . . with full knowledge that they are fictious names," Dowdy closed in.[7]

It was true. The use of pseudonyms was standard practice for gay organizations like Mattachine in the day. Donors and officers felt they had to be protected in some way from the many repercussions of openly gay and lesbian activism. Lilli Vincenz herself was "Lilli Hansen" in her role as editor of the *Homosexual Citizen*, Mattachine's magazine of ideas. The pseudonym issue triggered proceedings to revoke the Mattachine license, and Zona appeared before the District of Columbia Commissioners to help resolve the matter. In those days Washington, DC, did not have a city council. "DC was basically a plantation ruled to the nth degree by the District of Columbia Committee in Congress," Zona told us. The amendments were proposed for no other apparent reason than to "finger the Mattachine Society," she said.[8]

Ultimately, Zona and the NCACLU team got the matter settled. The Mattachine voluntarily gave up their license since they did not meet the minimum amount of $1500 an organization had to raise in order to comply. They stayed in business. The House overwhelmingly passed Dowdy's bill, but it went nowhere in the Senate; it was clearly unconstitutional. The massive publicity surrounding the whole affair, including a pro-Mattachine editorial in the *Washington Post*, invented Frank Kameny and his organization as national players. Zona and her colleagues' work influenced the NCACLU board to unanimously pass a resolution declaring that the US government's policy toward homosexuals was discriminatory—and wrong. This was huge in the day and a first for the ACLU.

And Dowdy? He later retired from Congress under indictment for bribery. In 1971 the Associated Press ran a picture of Dowdy and Mrs. Dowdy, identifying him as a Democrat from Athens, Texas, after being "found guilty of accepting a $25,000 bribe to influence a Justice Department fraud investigation of a Washington, DC, home improvement firm."[9] Convicted on eight counts, he served a sentence in prison for perjury.

Dowdy's papers were eventually donated to Baylor University's Poage Legislative Library in Waco. Ever alert to erasure, we noted the library's "Scope and Contents" description of the collection does not mention *Brown v. Board of Education*, segregation, the Southern Manifesto, or homosexuals being "banned under the laws of God, nature and man." However, it does manage to point out that Dowdy may have been the victim of a "set up" on that perjury conviction.[10]

Chapter 12

Presidential Libraries: Theirs or Ours?

F or years we Mattachine records requesters banged our heads against the walls of the presidential libraries overseen by NARA. We believed these fifteen libraries should be gold mines of White House material for community historians and activists to explore. But are they actually an expensive charade, at taxpayer's expense, for presidential museums of spin? How many of their LGBTQ-related collections are declassified, unrestricted, and open for review in a meaningful way? We know in their vaults lie the answers to many of the largest questions in LGBTQ American history. Exactly what happened to us when we were isolated and powerless? How were we disguised? Were we told "this didn't happen"?

We Archive Activists seek the memoranda, notes, drafts, and correspondence—the evidentiary history of six decades of animus— maintained at these libraries by the NARA and funded by taxpayers at the cost of $66 million per year. Doing so, we have made some great discoveries and had some mind-numbing disappointments.

Sex Deviates and the Presidential Records Act of 1978

One of the greatest days of our lives as Archive Activists was discovering key evidence of FBI director J. Edgar Hoover's Sex Deviates program, which he kept in one part of a private filing system used to undermine, denigrate, and blackmail suspected homosexuals. Upon his death in 1972, Hoover's personal secretary, Helen Gandy, was instructed by Hoover to destroy his private files. Gandy did. The many thousands of files obsessively kept on homosexuals were destroyed by the FBI shortly thereafter. We sought the remnants.

Around the same time of Hoover's death, President Nixon turned the White House itself into a crime scene with an evidence-destruction scandal called Watergate. Both of these events forced Congress to take action by enacting the Presidential Records Act of 1978. This act ended the notion, they thought, of the presidency as a personal possession—an idea being tested today. This legislation did not tweak the system: it overturned it. Legal ownership of a president's papers was transferred from the president to the American people. The act states, "Any records created or received by the President as part of his constitutional, statutory or ceremonial duties are the property of the US Government and will be managed by NARA at the end of the Administration."[1] Former presidents may not claim, "It's not theirs, it's mine" when the National Archives demands the return of White House papers. They are ours.

Former presidential library directors and classified papers experts have spirited arguments about the arcane issues of classification and declassification that require years of FOIA requests. Who can have the staying power to run these gauntlets? Archive Activists wonder why we cannot see the papers that are already opened for review. We would receive responses to our FOIA requests that a particular series was now declassified, processed, and open for review only to find out the folders had been emptied and filled with Pink Sheet Withdrawal Markers. The many exemptions for complying with the

Presidential Records Act and releasing the papers are maddening for Archive Activists, especially the kudzu-like claim of something called the P5 exemption. This is the so-called deliberative process exemption from releasing declassified documents described as "confidential communications requesting or submitting advice between a president and his advisors or between such advisors."[2] Its purpose is to protect open and frank discussions on matters of policy between subordinates and superiors. In practice its misuse deletes history itself for records requestors decades after a presidency. The insights and views of all the key players become locked away with the insertion of a P5 slip into any folder of significance.

At the George W. Bush Presidential Library at Southern Methodist University, if your research is substantively related to LGBTQ policy—domestic partner benefits (remember those?); what they called "gay marriage"; the Federal Marriage Amendment; gays and AIDS; hate crimes, sodomy law in Texas; Don't Ask, Don't Tell—it has likely been withdrawn with something called a Pink Sheet Withdrawal Marker, a P5 justification to hand you an empty file this many years after the end of a presidency. How long does this last? The Presidential Records Act restrictions on George W. Bush's papers originally expired on January 20, 2021. However, the president may invoke restrictions for up to twelve more years, with even more restrictions after those twelve years pass. The FOIA coordinator wrote Mattachine that "restrictions on President George W. Bush's records expired on January 20, 2021. However eight FOIA exemptions continue to apply to PRA [Presidential Records Act] records after the 12-year period."[3] Supposedly NARA is "proactively proposing these records for release on a rolling basis." Imagine a silent reading room because it is totally empty, with no researchers because there is nothing to see. That is where this leads, all funded by the National Archives. Dubbed the "withhold it because you want to" exemption, the P5 is the most abused exemption, "'a get out of jail free card' to avoid disclosing embarrassing or politically problematic records."[4] Just insert a P5 slip.

For Archive Activists it can be humorous to play with these P5s. For instance, we thought it would be interesting to read a two-page letter written in 2002 from the political and evangelical leader Dr. James Dobson to Karl Rove. Knowing that Dr. Dobson was, and is, a committed foe of all things LGBTQ, we thought it would be revealing to take a look. Dr. Dobson was not a part of the administration or a Rove "subordinate" providing official "advice to the president." We opened the file—BONK, a P5.[5]

Nancy Reagan to Rock Hudson: "No"

We learned the best approach to these libraries may be more roundabout. One of our greatest finds, for example, was at the Reagan Presidential Library where we were doing AIDS policy research. While going about our work, through multiple visits, an archivist tipped off Pate that we might find something about the Reagans' deceased friend Rock Hudson not filed under "AIDS" or "Rock Hudson" but, weirdly, in a file labeled "Hospitals." Who knew?

We discovered a particularly sad and angering exchange that hurled us back to the seven years of raging AIDS when the Reagans would not even mention the word. In the "Hospitals" folder there was an exchange of gut-wrenching telegrams and anguished pleas for help to Nancy Reagan from dying Rock Hudson to be admitted to a French government hospital for AIDS treatment.

"Only one hospital in the world can offer the necessary medical treatment to save life of Rock Hudson or at least alleviate his illness," wrote Hudson's publicist Dale Olson in a telegram to the White House.[6] A simple call from the White House would have made the difference, Olson said. Our discovery showed how First Lady Nancy Reagan turned her back.

"I spoke with Mrs. Reagan about the attached telegram," responded her White House aide, Mark Weinberg. "She did not feel this was something the White House should get into and agreed to my suggestion we refer the writer to the US embassy in Paris."

This revelation of Nancy Reagan's callousness and indifference to Rock Hudson echoed the administration's entire response to the horrors of the epidemic. Chris Geidner, then senior political reporter at *BuzzFeed News*, understood the power of the archive and painstakingly confirmed the facts in each of the documents we discovered and wrote the story "Nancy Reagan Turned Down Rock Hudson's Plea for Help Nine Weeks Before He Died."[7] Geidner used the archive to challenge the established narrative that it was Nancy Reagan who wanted to nudge the president all those seven years to say *anything* about the AIDS epidemic. In that established narrative, there were just "no good options" for Nancy Reagan in a "proper role for a First Lady."[8] One day later, "Nancy Reagan Refused to Help Dying Rock Hudson Get AIDS Treatment" was the headline worldwide.[9] We were pleased the HBO documentary *Rock Hudson: All That Heaven Allowed* highlighted some of the documents we discovered at the Reagan Library. Nancy Reagan's "no" "encapsulates the Reagan Administration's entire response to the epidemic," the film's narrative concluded.[10]

In film there is the concept of a "plastic particular," a single tangible image that makes an emotional connection with an audience and speaks volumes about a character and historical moment. This telegram to Nancy Reagan, a plea from their dying friend Rock Hudson—coupled with Nancy's "no"— is an eloquent particular image. It was buried in a file with a bland label. We can guess that if the file had been labeled "Rock Hudson," the contents would have gone missing or been restricted with a P5.

Gay History with the Bark Off at the LBJ Library

"I thought you would be interested in knowing that we are processing the folders in the Mildred Stegall Office Files that deal with the investigation of Walter Jenkins in October 1964," said the exciting email to us from the retired LBJ Presidential Library Supervisory Archivist Claudia Anderson. "As you probably know, Mildred Stegall's responsibilities included liaison between the White House and the FBI."

Pate Felts (*seated*) and me in the LBJ Presidential Library
recovering sealed White House history with the "bark off." Courtesy of
Mattachine Society of Washington, DC.

What fantastic news. We could be the first to see what Mildred
Stegall had been holding all these years. Austin bound, we discussed how
"processing the folders" meant they would soon be opened and available
after having been sealed until Mildred Stegall's death. Stegall had been
instructed by Johnson to hold all documents pertaining to the massive
Walter Jenkins scandal after his 1964 arrest for "disorderly conduct" in
the restroom of a YMCA. Who knew that Stegall—from Stranger, Texas
(near Waco), who went to work for Senator Lyndon Johnson in 1946 and
was his most trusted private secretary—would live to be 105?

As Archive Activists we had been highly vocal in our advocacy for
the LBJ Library to release its papers documenting the Johnson administration's discrimination and outright hostility toward lesbian and gay
Americans. We were particularly interested in Johnson appointees, like

his rabidly antigay personnel director, John Macy, and his closest aide, Walter Jenkins. They knew a lot, but Mildred knew more.

We contacted one of the library's trustees, Lloyd Hand, a long-time aide to Johnson, for assistance. Hand had known my Uncle Charlie from Houston—a Johnson insider back to LBJ's Senate days. We told anyone who would listen that LBJ always said he wanted his library to show "history with the bark off,"[11] and this was truly some "bark-off" material, involving a trio of unusual relationships inside the White House—LBJ, a young lady from Texas, and her gay "walker" (long-used slang for a gay escort). "I assure you that we are interested in seeing that researchers are able to tell the full story of the sixties," the LBJ librarian wrote us.[12]

Mildred Stegall adored LBJ beyond any normal standard of professional loyalty. She wrote that he was "one of the greatest men I have ever known. I just wish the whole world could have known the Lyndon Johnson I knew."[13] Her cache of documents reveals history with so much bark off it is painful to read. Busted, hospitalized for a "breakdown," fired, and sent back to Texas, Jenkins was in ruins. Mildred never let go of Jenkins's prepared statement that he did not know what happened that night at the Y. The statement reads, "The FBI states in its report that Mr. Jenkins admitted having engaged in indecent acts. I am certain this was a complete misunderstanding on the part of the agents who interviewed me or the result of the sedation which had been given me . . . I do not know whether I did or not."[14]

What Mildred protected until her 105th year was a series of heavily lawyered, professionally prepared affidavit-type statements to be signed by Walter Jenkins to cover for Lyndon Johnson in case yet another homosexual was revealed to be in the White House. That homosexual, with family-like closeness to LBJ, was Bob Waldron from the East Texas town of Arp. That discovery would have been catastrophic for LBJ. Yet another deviate inside the White House. The Jenkins letters lay down the story: no one here knew any deviates, ever.

Mildred Stegall classified, keeper of the Walter Jenkins documents at
the LBJ Presidential Library. Photo by Charles Francis.

"I object strenuously to the FBI statement, Mr. Jenkins has
had limited association with some individuals who are alleged
to be, or who admittedly are, sex deviates," says he letter to be
signed by Jenkins. "Never in my years of government service did
I consciously or knowingly recommend or approve the appointment
to any position of any person whom I had reason to suspect was
a homosexual." There was "one exception, Mr. Bob Waldron . . .
who was loaned to the staff on which I was working because of his
exceptional skill as a stenographer and typist."[15]

Thanks to the Johnson Library's release to us for the first
time, we now know that Bob Waldron had become an aide, travel
companion, "personal confidante, and almost family-like relation"
to LBJ.[16] Waldron served as the regular escort of Mary Margaret

Wiley, later to become Mrs. Jack Valenti, providing her the ability to travel worldwide accompanying LBJ. Waldron and Mary Margaret even joined the Johnsons onstage at the 1964 Democratic Party National Convention. Rising from receptionist for Johnson in his Senate years, Mary Margaret had come a long way from Waco and her Austin days working in the law office of Judge Homer Thornberry (1909–1995).

What happened to Bob Waldron after the Jenkins disaster? He was immediately fired. It crushed him, but over the years he became a top interior designer in Washington for Lady Bird Johnson and Linda Johnson Robb, his true friends to the end before he succumbed to AIDS.

We are indebted to James Kirchick, author of the groundbreaking history *Secret City: The Hidden History of Gay Washington*, for his generous acknowledgment of our "yeoman's work unearthing the documentary record of the federal government's animus against gay people. It was Charles who alerted me to the existence of Robert Waldron, and who therefore deserves much of the credit for my ability to share his poignant story for the first time."[17] This is the essence of our Archive Activism: discovery and outreach to a respected journalist such as Kirchick, expanding the archival base for new histories that will not erase us again.

We ask ourselves, did any of this Johnson / Waldron / Mary Margaret / Jenkins behavior have policy implications? Certainly not for gay Americans like Frank Kameny and Lilli Vincenz, who were outside on the sidewalk picketing, nor the thousands of LGBTQ Americans under investigation in the Johnson years, fired from their civilian jobs or discharged from the military. LBJ and the Great Society never considered homosexuals as having a civil rights claim.

"Dear Mr. Kameny," wrote Vice President Hubert Humphrey in a letter we discovered in Kameny's attic. "Neither the federal Executive Orders on Fair Employment nor the Civil Rights Act . . . are relevant to the problems of homosexuals."[18] And it was John Macy who wrote the Revulsion Letter to the Mattachine Society of Washington.[19] For Lyndon Johnson, the Jenkins disaster and the personal relationship with Bob Waldron were a terrible political entanglement. He had become so close to both of these men. Walter Jenkins and Bob Waldron were willing to be closeted, to have no life and no family time, to meet the 24/7 demands of Lyndon Johnson, who craved their full attention—until they had to go, broken.

Macy Gone Missing

Pertinent considerations here [for maintaining the ban on homosexuals in government] are the revulsion of other employees by homosexual conduct and the consequent disruption of service efficiency, the apprehension caused other employees by homosexual advances, solicitations or assaults, the unavoidable subjection of the sexual deviate to erotic stimulation through on-the-job use of common toilet, shower and living facilities, the offense to members of the public who are required to deal with a known or admitted sexual deviate.

John W. Macy letter to Franklin Kameny and the Mattachine Society of Washington, DC, 1966 (see appendix 2)

Who was the architect of all of this misery?

Walter Jenkins and Bob Waldron were the human wreckage of the government playing the endgame of exposure. But it began with President Eisenhower, encouraged by J. Edgar Hoover, issuing in 1954 Executive Order 10450, declaring "perversion" a national security threat. Over the years the national security rationale morphed from security and the possibility of blackmail to "revulsion" felt by coworkers. It then moved to harming "morale" of the civil service. The final excuse was a lack of general "suitability" for government service. "Suitability" was broad enough to mean anything the government wanted it to mean.

Behind this evolution was a master bureaucrat. He was the signer of the infamous 1966 Revulsion Letter to the Mattachine Society, chairman of the US Civil Service Commission, and LBJ's personnel man, John W. Macy Jr. Described as Lyndon Johnson's "dogged defender of anti-gay prejudice,"[20] Macy was the driver of the administrative evil that cost untold thousands of gays and lesbians their careers—and some their lives.

Macy was an administrative colossus in Washington. Originally appointed by President Eisenhower as Executive Director of the US Civil Service Commission at age 35, Macy had served under President Kennedy as Chairman of the Commission on Equal Opportunity in Hiring. Johnson dubbed him as "my talent scout."[21] He identified or cleared every political appointee and significant promotion in the Johnson administration: assistant secretaries, undersecretaries, ambassadors, agency heads, and commission appointees. Macy discussed them all for hours on end with Johnson.

We believed the LBJ Presidential Library must be keeping his secrets, so we refused to remain silent or passive about this. We asked archivists and everyone we knew, "Why haven't the papers of John Macy been opened?" With the help of legal counsel and the empathy and interest of the LBJ library staff, we got our first answer: Macy had them sealed. He held on to his papers for eleven years after the Johnson administration ended in 1969 and then negotiated a deed of gift (a common practice) in 1980.[22] This agreement permitted him to seal the papers to prevent "an unwarranted invasion of personal privacy"[23] of people who may be mentioned by name.

We argued that this privacy restriction should be interpreted liberally and removed after more than thirty years, with many of the named individuals deceased and many of his victims—who fought him and the Johnson administration in federal court—openly gay now anyway. The privacy of so many thousands of gay and lesbian federal employees had been shattered by Macy's professional interrogators and investigators. We cited examples like William (Billy) Lyman Dew, an African American who fought the Civil Service Commission in federal court for six years to be reinstated in his job as an air traffic controller after he was accused of being an "unreformed" homosexual. Dew, married with children, had made the mistake of admitting (while hooked up to a lie detector) to homosexual relations when he was an undergraduate. Macy had no concern for Dew's privacy rights.

With Macy's deed of gift, we were confronted by the fact that the Presidential Records Act of 1978 did not apply to President Johnson since his administration preceded its passage. Thus, a guy like Macy could take his papers home if he wished and bargain for conditions like sealing them. Our arguments were rooted in historical justice and President Johnson's statement about his library providing "history with the bark off." To this day Johnson defenders, like his press secretary Bill Moyers—a Texan, raised in Marshall, educated in Denton at North Texas State College (now the University of North Texas) and in Austin at the University of Texas—decline to criticize Macy. Moyers told the *Washington Post* in 2015, when asked about Macy's war on homosexuals, "I am bewildered" by Macy's words and those of us who refuse to forget about it all. Moyers claimed that Macy never evinced any signs of homophobia or animus. "It was a time of vast denial," Moyers deflected when asked about the Johnson/Macy policies of brutal investigations and firings.[24]

At last we were informed that the personal papers of John W. Macy would be processed—slowly. We were told that the Macy papers were dense, with hundreds of pages of copies that would require review for privacy issues. The archivist reassured us, "We want to tell the full story of the sixties." We were grateful to the archivists who opened the collection's 126 boxes of memos, letters, and reports from 1963 to 1969.

And were the contents ever boring.

We were treated to hundreds of personnel matters and appointments; boatloads of warm regards and long-winded think pieces on improving the Civil Service Commission. Goodness gracious, one would think John Macy was a dutiful public servant. The archivists and librarians could find no files or series of papers with names like "suitability" or "morale of the service" or anything to do with the "infamous and scandalous." Nothing is there on "homosexuality," "homosexuals," "Kameny" (with whom he fought in near hand-to-hand combat for years);[25] nothing on any of the high-profile court cases, like NASA employee Cliff Norton's lawsuit to be reinstated,[26] or victorious Billy Dew, who was reinstated with back wages. We asked ourselves, Is this kind of gap the result of what eleven years of private possession can do to a collection of papers? Is it possible for archival collections to deflect? Reviewing the personal papers of John Macy, we learned the answer to that can be "yes."

However, even the most thorough culling of one's papers can miss telling scraps that provide irrefutable evidentiary history. In Macy's papers there were two buck slips, one of which was most revealing—a short note of transmittal from JWM to Macy's Civil Service Commission counsel Lou Pellerzi. We were thrilled by this discovery.

Memorandum for Mr. L. M. Pellerzi
Subject: Proposed response to the Mattachine Society
February 14, 1966

I have reviewed with thoughtful care the proposed response to the Mattachine Society. I believe it is most effectively done and sets forth a humane, public interest position. I would appreciate it if you would review this with the other Commissioners and the Executive Director and return it to me for signature.

JWM[27]

The other note we discovered regarding the Mattachine Society was revelatory: "I believe our position is increasingly untenable in refusing to receive representatives of this organization [the Mattachine]. There is no need for us to negotiate or explain. But to continually refuse to listen cannot be defended."[28] Macy did not attend the meeting but responded to Frank Kameny with the Revulsion Letter.

This is the evidentiary history we sought, proof that Macy not only called for meeting with the homosexuals but also supervised the writing of the infamous Revulsion Letter, the one we discovered years before in Kameny's attic. The Macy papers correct any notion that Macy was not the man behind the whole revulsion argument. We recalled how our appraiser Allan Stypeck believed the letter was heavily lawyered and was, in fact, a comprehensive statement of federal policy. Macy believed his homophobic, vile comments about revulsion of fellow federal employees and the ban on homosexuals in federal employment was "humane." Any legal analysis by the Supreme Court of historic, imbedded animus toward LGBTQ Americans in federal law must now address this letter to Frank Kameny and the Mattachine Society.

Macy went on to become the first president of the Corporation for Public Broadcasting and wrote a high-minded book titled *Public Service: The Human Side of Government*, in which he portrays himself as a progressive. "Assailed by accusations that Uncle Sam is a bigot and that he is practicing discrimination in reverse, the government employer has been at stage center in the drama of equal employment opportunity," he wrote, sounding very progressive.[29] The decade-long brawl with Mattachine and gay and lesbian federal employees (including postal workers to the White House), the investigations and ruined lives, the major court cases—all is erased. The last of the discriminatory policies Macy supported remained intact until 1995, when President Bill Clinton ended, by executive order, the denial of security clearances on the basis of sexual orientation.

I love the expression *gone missing*. When someone loses something, it often is described in the passive voice as having gone missing. No one threw anything into the fire. Nothing was shredded. No individual tossed a garbage bag. It all has just gone missing. An entire history erased.

Can one reasonably believe nothing was documented or received by memo or correspondence by the chairman of the US Civil Service Commission when thousands lost their jobs and legions of the self-avowed were terminated? It is not "bewildering,"[30] to use Bill Moyers's word, for anyone who suffered through this or had family or friends destroyed. Generations of LGBTQ Americans have not gone missing for Archive Activists. We got the buck slips.

Chapter 13

Ex-Ex in Paris

On the road to Paris (Texas, not France), headed north toward Oklahoma, we are driving through old cotton prairie under a sky that is dizzying in scale. As a boy, I knew this was tornado country, peppered with shelters in earthen berms where bees built hives and real men rolled their own. Pate and I knew we were getting close to the home of the Rev. John Smid and Larry, his husband, when we saw the sixty-five-foot Paris, Texas, Eiffel Tower with the red cowboy hat perched on top. A gay friend back in Washington had quipped, "If anything could turn an ex-gay gay again, it would be that little Eiffel Tower with a cowboy hat." Gay to ex-gay and back to gay. (I will call them Double-Exes, like a ranch brand.) Maybe that's why John Smid, a famous Double-Ex, is a Parisian now—where anything goes, we laugh to lighten the mood. Oh, how we wanted an original copy of the Rev. Smid's *Love in Action Handbook*. He invited us to Paris to examine his archive and take what we wanted. He was done with it.

Here is the drill, according to Garrard Conley, author of the powerful memoir *Boy Erased*. Once you were checked in to the secure residential conversion therapy facility in Memphis by your parents, you were allowed to keep two items: a Bible and Rev. Smid's handbook with your name on it. The 274-page ex-gay handbook becomes your life.

"Welcome (your name goes here)!" it says. "You are a product of the world (and the Devil)."[1] The handbook sets the tone for your massive conversion to come, far away from the "World-Flesh-Satan" wreck of your teenage life. These words were written by Smid, the founder and president of Love in Action (LIA), once the largest residential gay conversion therapy operation in the country. The *Love in Action Handbook* was your personal roadmap to heterosexuality. Many believed, or hoped, it would do something even more than that: provide the key to returning home somewhere in the South. Like many, you had been kicked out of the house until you could get "straight." You could be pure again. You were not allowed to journal, photograph, or record in the facility, so the handbook became one's memory.[2]

We wanted that handbook, and we wanted everything that went along with it in the collection—the moral inventory sheets, the gay addiction workbooks, the 12-step program to become straight, the slick brochures, the singing and swaying rally videos in San Rafael, California, where it all began in 1973, and the *Larry King Live* interview with Smid himself. He was the great example who had once been a doomed homosexual. "Putting sin, shame and Satan behind us," the handbook proclaimed to parents paying $1500 (for a claimed 87 percent success rate) to check in their kids. For one of those kids, Garrard Conley from Mountain Home, Arkansas, the handbook became the only evidence that the conversion therapy nightmare really happened to him. Garrard writes in his memoir, an account that will always make me tremble in anger along with him, "I will open the LIA Handbook, read a few sentences, and feel the old shame wash over me until I can no longer focus."[3]

***

We Archive Activists longed for the LIA ex-gay handbook with all the trimmings. Pate and I explained to Garrard Conley over coffee in New York City, where he was thriving at the time, teaching and writing, that the purpose of our Archive Activism was to deliver the texture of queer history—what things felt like, what the particulars were, what was coded, what documents revealed the wrenching fear. We showed him in his beautiful memoir our highlight of each document that would deliver that texture for researchers and historians. "It is our mission to rescue it all," I said. I think he was moved by the word *texture* and began thinking how we might work together. He said he would think about giving Mattachine his one precious copy of the handbook. This would be a profound letting go. He strategized with us about contacting Smid, something that was unthinkable for him to do himself. We heard there may be files and boxes and old ex-gay handbooks in Paris.

"To Paris," we raised our coffee on Broadway.

***

The Rev. John J. Smid, in a sweeping American reinvention of self, declared conversion therapy a failure and decamped from Memphis to Paris, Texas, got a divorce from his wife, and married his new husband, Larry—a total repudiation of his teen conversion therapy mill and a renunciation of sexual orientation change therapy (SOCE) itself. In this Smid fell in line with the American Psychological Association and American Psychiatric Association in making claims that sexual attraction cannot be changed through SOCE.[4] Smid kindly agreed to meet with Pate and me. Our rental car loaded with empty boxes and tape, we hit the road to Paris. If only we could get those materials back to Washington, we thought, we could defang them with a conversion of our own—into an archive.

Smid's house is in the middle of a horse farm. This is definitely not Kentucky bluegrass or Ocala, Florida, horsey country. This is a world of cattle pens, galvanized watering troughs, and screeching windmills crying out for oil. We had read Garrard's account of Smid's LIA Lie Chair. This was the chair where gay youth would be psychologically interrogated by Smid: "You must tell all that must be told. Anything you resist is the very thing you need to share!" says the handbook. "Pretend to see a father

Ex-conversion therapy minister (Love In Action) John Smid with his vintage
Pontiac in Paris, Texas. Photo by Charles Francis.

you don't . . . and confess everything negative you have ever felt about
him before the full room." Smid—neither a psychiatrist nor a licensed
therapist—would instruct them to tell the truth . . . in the Lie Chair.[5]

A fire-engine-red, vintage Pontiac convertible parked in Rev.
Smid's driveway came as something of a surprise to us, either a greeting or a warning of things to come. Kind of Satanic Sixties, I thought.
John Smid had been expecting us and laid it on, putting us at our
ease. His husband, Larry, warmly received us, welcoming us into their
home. I am not sure what we were expecting—maybe a Lie Chair
on a concrete slab? Hardly. It was all oak-country antiques and cozy,
not the "tell me everything" John Smid. It was country grandpa Smid
standing beside two long tables, both neatly displaying exactly what
we had come for: his LIA archive. We were delighted and boggled by
the warm reception in contrast with what we knew to be his past.

It was thrilling to review the boxes and files. "Please, take whatever you want," he generously offered, explaining how he had been working through a long night to pull all of these materials together. Having researched LIA at the James Hormel LGBTQIA Center at the San Francisco Public Library, we knew this was the texture of a conversion therapy enterprise that had grown from a small church in Marin County, California, to the disaster that unfolded in Memphis.[6] His generosity was so emotionally open; we will always appreciate that. He must have been so thrown by the news that one of his alumni had written a memoir that was about to become a major motion picture starring Nicole Kidman, Russell Crowe, and Lucas Hedges.[7] He had earnestly recanted and decided to let go of it all.

"All I can do is acknowledge and release the rest," he said. He was standing on a national stage now, not as a fundamentalist spiritual leader but as a villain. He could not accept that. Otherwise, he might have shredded everything—an Archive Activist's worst fear.

The materials so neatly displayed for us ranged from 1986, when he began his life as a conversion therapy counselor and house leader in San Rafael, to his time as executive director of LIA, the largest ex-gay ministry in America. Included are the papers and lawsuits and press releases documenting the controversy of youths treated for their sex addiction at LIA. It was all there—the gay demonstrations and a year-long lawsuit filed by LIA against the state of Tennessee Department of Mental Health, claiming religious discrimination. Tennessee acted on its genuine interest in protecting minors treated inside Smid's cult-like walls. All of this is supported by hundreds of pages of manuals, handbooks, lessons, fundraising appeals, audio cassette sermons sold worldwide, and news clippings with headlines like "Born Agains on Polk Street, Ex-gays Hit the Bible Trail."[8]

It was difficult for us to read in Smid's living room about the prohibition on journaling at LIA, so we maintained our focus and moved on to an Archive Activist mindset. We knew we had something here. We outlined how we would conduct a complete inventory, organize the materials, and offer them to an appropriate repository. Our first choice was the Smithsonian National Museum of American History. John Smid liked that approach—expressly wanting history to be his judge. Indeed, that will happen as historians, survivors, and, we hope, Supreme Court clerks study these documents to understand where we have been and where the whole issue of banning conversion therapy may go in the future. Smid donated his collection to the Mattachine Society of Washington, DC, and the folks at the National Museum of American History were excited to accept it all from us.[9] There will be new LIA-type organizations and arguments for conversion therapy wrapped in the language of parental rights and religious liberty. But the archive is now loaded with the truth.

Garrard Conley, the "Boy Erased"

"I wish none of this had ever happened. Sometimes I thank God it did," Garrard Conley wrote in his memoir about his conversion therapy experience in Memphis.[10] But it did happen, we Archive Activists always insist, especially so in the LGBTQ world, where so much is erased.

In working with Garrard, we thought about ways to educate others with the Smid archive and all that we now knew. First, we introduced Garrard to the McDermott team, led by partner Lisa Linsky. Lisa and Garrard initially fell "in like" as working partners, then "in love" as friends joined in trust that allowed our team to interview him extensively and begin writing a comprehensive history of LIA. This history was completed and released as a white paper at Washington's National Press Club in 2018, titled "The Pernicious Myth of Conversion Therapy: How Love In Action Perpetrated a Fraud on America."[11] Thanks to John Smid's full cooperation, and hours of interviews with Lisa, this history goes far beyond anything Garrard could have known as a kid. Without such a legal history, judges and their clerks or lawmakers in Washington could not fathom the whole story of LIA's devolution from a small church to a failed enterprise.

The white paper traces the rise of LIA and the events leading to its eventual demise. Smid explained to our team how LIA developed into

The Team. McDermott Will & Emery attorneys celebrating *Boy Erased* author Garrard Conley (*front center*). *Front row, left to right*: Lisa Linsky, Conley, Paul Thompson. *Standing, left to right*: Britt Haxton, Jim Camden, Mike Stanek, Charles Francis, Ryan Leske, Irene Firippis, and Lisa Gerson. Photo by Pate Felts, Mattachine Society of Washington, DC.

the new paradigm for conversion therapy and the ugly truth about its false claims perpetrated on young people and their families—namely, its impotence to change sexual orientation. "What we were doing to people is wrong," Smid told our team. "We were playing with peoples' minds. . . . We were working in a genre that we were not educated or equipped to work in," he confessed.[12]

As a public policy matter, the white paper addresses the reemergence of conversion therapy today. It outlines "the threats posed by those working to roll-back the advances made by the broader LGBTQ community over the last decade and the role that conversion therapy is playing in the larger debate over equality."[13]

As Archive Activists, we were excited to share all of our research with WNYC's Radiolab, produced by Jad Abumrad. Using our materials and much other investigative material, Abumrad, working with Garrard, produced an electrifying four-part podcast titled *UnErased*, with its last segment titled "Smid." "It is a story of identity, making

Garrard Conley with his personal copy of the Love in Action conversion
therapy handbook and Archivist Frank Robinson at the Smithsonian National
Museum of American History. Photo by Charles Francis.

amends and Smid's reckoning with this life," says the Radio Lab
program in an understatement.[14] We were credited and acknowledged
for all that our Mattachine/McDermott team had contributed to this
radio reckoning.

In Paris we deeply appreciated John Smid's gift of the handbook, which is now safely inside the archives of the National Museum of American History. It belongs there. "If it weren't for the handbook . . . I might still be second-guessing my sanity about what really happened during those few weeks," writes Garrard.[15] "What I had been involved in was a cult," Garrard says in a video produced by Mattachine, "Mattachine and Me."[16] We are satisfied that the ex-gay handbook will not hurt anybody anymore. It can only teach and remind. This was Mattachine's gift to Garrard Conley: a gift of history.

One Zeke at a Time

The key to Archive Activism is not only finding the stuff but also using it. The Archive Activist must use discoveries to make the world a better place. Since Garrard was an Arkansas native and Pate had long-standing ties to the state as a former chief-of-staff to Arkansas senator David Pryor (ret.), we headed for Fayetteville, Arkansas— a wonderful college town, home to a great state university and the David and Barbara Pryor Center for Arkansas Oral and Visual History. Formed in 1999, the center's mission is to "document the cultural heritage of Arkansas" by creating audio and video histories to share with scholars, students, and the public.[17] The Pryor Center was excited to produce an oral history video of Garrard and his mother, Martha Conley, from their family history in Mountain Home all the way to the release of the motion picture based on their searing experience not so far from Fayetteville.

We shared what we had with the Pryor Center and helped support their efforts. We arranged for Garrard and Martha to partic- ipate in many hours of video interviews about themselves, their family, and their lives, including the Memphis experience. With the permission of the Pryor Center, we were able to use some amazing material drawn from these interviews for a video of our own titled "Welcome, Garrard" (hat tip to his ex-gay handbook).[18] To mark the occasion, the Pryor Center hosted a panel discussion. It was thrilling to see the turnout. Students, faculty, and news reporters were there to hear from Garrard and Martha about their lives in Arkansas and beyond. Martha revealed so much: "I just wish that everyone would not have to go through the fourteen years that I went through to get to where I am."[19]

This became an important event for all who attended. Arkansas remains embroiled in controversy, hopelessly ensnared in politics over all things LGBTQ. This has a terrible impact on LGBTQ youth in the state. One young student, I will call him Zeke, approached me with sincere thanks and appreciation for what we were doing.

"When my dad found out, he kicked me out," Zeke said. "The only place I had to go was my truck." Zeke took his truck, a country kid's safe place, to Fayetteville, a college town oasis. He found a life there. He told me that he saw himself in Garrard's story of pain and honesty. This is what makes our Archive Activism thrilling—reaching one Zeke at a time, along with his friends, straight and gay, and an entire community in the American South.

With Garrard we delivered our finds from Paris to a mental health collections vault at the Smithsonian Museum of American History in Washington. The curator, Katherine Ott, was pleased to receive them and to help us put our discoveries into the context of the American medicalization of homosexuality.

"When I donated my ex-gay handbook to the Smithsonian," Garrard says in the video "Mattachine and Me," "they took me into a vault to see the tools that were used against gay people in the past . . . the living reality, what the lobotomy tool looks like," the straitjacket, the electroshock boxes. "It is so important to not have blinders on, to think we are on a straight line of progress that will lead us out of this terrible history," he continues. "Hey, here's a document," he waves an imaginary paper like a torch: "You cannot do this now."[20]

Chapter 14

Asylum Seekers

" **A**sylum Seekers, Insulin shock therapy. Lobotomies. Seclusion and restraints. The history of LGBTQ pain at St. Elizabeths Hospital and how two 'archive activists' are bringing it to light," said the cover story about our work published by the *Washington City Paper*.[1] We had moved well beyond ex-gay handbooks into the deeper waters of lobotomies and exotic therapies (insulin shock, for one) that were funded by the federal government at Washington's infamous St. Elizabeths Hospital. At St. Elizabeths one might be "cured" or learn to conform—or not be released.

St. Elizabeths Hospital played an independent role alongside the FBI and the US Civil Service Commission in the federal assault on LGBTQ America through six presidencies. The documents we uncovered told a story so devastating and far-reaching, we wondered whether it might be better to simply put a face on the nameless patients who endured so much. Where were the faces of the LGBTQ patients who had become a voiceless, subaltern population?

Among the ruins of St. Elizabeths Hospital, Washington, DC. Charles Francis
(*left*) and Pate Felts (*right*). With permission from the *Washington City Paper*.

Looking for answers, we were excited to visit an exhibition about
St. Elizabeths at the National Building Museum. Titled "Architecture
of an Asylum: St. Elizabeths, 1852–2017,"[2] the exhibition told the
story of the hospital in powerful photographs, documents, and etiological diagrams. It was a stunning exhibition about the sprawling
mental hospital that housed almost eight thousand patients committed behind locked doors until 1961. The exhibition told the story of
how specific identity groups were treated and how they coped with
being committed for their various psychiatric treatments. We learned
how African American patients were segregated in a "Colored Wing"
and how Native Americans were brought to St. Elizabeths from the
Hiawatha Insane Asylum in South Dakota. There were stark etiological diagrams of the various mental conditions. To our initial dismay,
we realized the entire exhibition had been degayed.

To degay is to deliberately strip LGBTQ-related content or context
from art, literature, culture, and the historical record itself. Degayed
history is the deletion of our existence. The erasure of LGBTQ patients

at St. Elizabeths was so complete that we asked the curator about it. She referred us to a slice of an etiological diagram, an early twentieth-century drawing of circles depicting the cause of an alcoholic woman's mental illness. She was identified as "Alcoholic Woman #2," and there were two slight mentions of her problem: "Repressed Homosexuality" and "Homosexual Tendencies and Phantasies." That was it: "Alcoholic Woman # 2." The curator later responded to a reporter who asked why there was so little information on homosexuals committed to St. Elizabeths. "We tried to do a lot, but if museums can do anything, they should encourage people to explore more on their own."[3] That sounded to us like a perfect invitation for Archive Activism.

We may never know the backstory or reason for the erasure, even though we made several FOIA requests that turned up nothing. But the fact is, there was not a single story in this entire exhibition about the gay, lesbian, and gender nonconforming experience of individuals committed to St. Elizabeths. We know they were committed under the DC Sexual Psychopath Act of 1948, passed after a panic in Washington over sensational sex crime reporting. Homosexuals, voyeurs, rapists, and murderers were bundled together as some kind of sexual-terrorist organization that was abusing children. The Sexual Psychopath Act of 1948 stated that "if a patient is adjudged a sexual psychopath, he must be committed to St. Elizabeths Hospital and confined until released in accordance with the Act. He or she is released when the Superintendent of the Hospital finds that he has sufficiently recovered so as not to be dangerous."[4] The act decimated the District gay community. In conjunction with the Sexual Perversion Elimination Program, hundreds of men were arrested for sodomy and "cruising" between 1947 and 1950. The law legitimized and codified gay conversion therapy and "cures" such as ice-pick lobotomies and insulin shock therapy.

The Subaltern

"Every historian of the multitudes, the dispossessed, the subaltern and the enslaved is forced to grapple with the power and authority of the archive and the limits it sets on what can be known . . . and who is endowed with the gravity and authority of historical actor," writes Saidiya Hartman in a history of early twentieth-century "wayward" Black girls living in Harlem.[5] In a "wayward" class of their own, individuals committed to St. Elizabeths by their families or the courts as queer psychopaths had zero standing to write about, report, or freely journal their experience. As homosexual subalterns behind bars in an asylum, they were displaced entirely, without human agency. In this case the authority of the archive was controlled by the doctors, psychiatrists, and keepers of the asylum. They were the historical actors. This was our archival challenge: to find the pieces of a silenced, subaltern puzzle apart from what was recorded by the doctors.

Our first breakthrough was at the Jean-Nickolaus Tretter Collection in Gay, Lesbian, Bisexual, and Transgender Studies at the University of Minnesota. We learned through gay friends that the Tretter Collection held the papers of Dr. Benjamin Karpman, who served as senior psychiatrist at St. Elizabeths from the 1920s to the 1960s. The Tretter Collection had not opened the papers for researchers until they could process and fully protect the privacy interests of Dr. Karpman's many patients. Our interest in St. Elizabeths track record helped us gain permission to visit the archive and its highly restricted Karpman Papers. This collection includes approximately seventy-seven thousand pages of records, compiled under the direction of Dr. Karpman, that "relate to his studies of criminality and behaviors that were regarded as sexually dysfunctional or deviant at the time the records were prepared," according to the Karpman Archive description at the University of Minnesota.[6] At the Tretter Collection, we went through twenty-one boxes of Dr. Karpman's materials, taking notes with only one pencil, no writing down any names or other identifiers such as hometowns, no photos and no photocopies allowed. Even so, we were able to understand the unique sorrow and horrors of being a confined LGBTQ patient undergoing treatment for a cure of your homosexuality—under the DC Sexual Psychopath Act of 1948—at this federal mental institution.

Reviewing thousands of pages of patient records, psychiatrist commentary, and even dream analyses—and photographs of the asylum and some patients—we were confronted with the evidence that St. Elizabeths not only was a center for confinement and experimental treatments for homosexuals, but it had also evolved into a kind of shadow think tank for federal policy formation over decades of dealing with homosexuals. Dr. Karpman wrote, "Chasing all of the homosexuals out of one city (even assuming such a thing were possible) would not solve the problem of homosexuality, any more than chasing all of the thieves out of one city would solve the problem of dishonesty." As a more enlightened alternative, Dr. Karpman proposed, "Psychiatry should take time out from discussing homosexuality as an individual 'disease' and offer a constructive plan for dealing with it as a social problem."[7] We could see where this social problem was going—straight to Capitol Hill policymakers to devise solutions.

St. Elizabeths superintendent from 1937 to 1962, Dr. Winfred Overholser, helped create military guidelines for the psychiatric examination of draftees during World War II, advising officials on how best to prevent gays and lesbians from entering the service and how to deal with those who did. Dr. Overholser chillingly said in 1947, "Some of these perverts are potentially dangerous . . . they should be dealt with and not allowed to remain at large."[8]

Since we could not identify the "perverts" from the Karpman Papers—their identities, crimes, and backgrounds redacted, their lives redacted—we took this as our challenge. We wanted to connect with their humanity in the archive. Then we discovered the St. Elizabeths magic lantern slides.

Vintage Slides or Super-Reality Photographs?

The vintage glass slides were heavy. Each is nearly four inches square, designed for projection in an old magic lantern device. The seventy slides we discovered were identified as teaching slides to instruct the

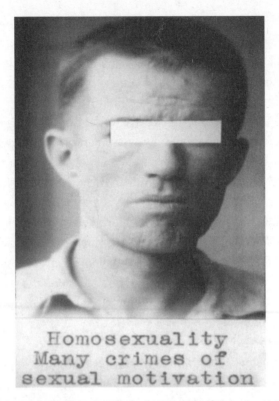

Homosexuality
Many crimes of
sexual motivation

Magic lantern teaching slide, St. Elizabeths Hospital (for the Insane), Washington, DC. Glass plate slide SEH 5-029; St. Elizabeths Collection; Otis Historical Archives; National Museum of Health and Medicine, Silver Spring, MD.

nurses, medical students, and psychiatrists about psychopathic, criminal homosexuals and gender nonconforming patients.[9] They portray human specimens in a queer gallery of crime and mental illness—or just plain oddities. There is a haunting photograph of a kind of queer zombie I cannot forget, a handsome gay man with eyes redacted, captioned "Homosexuality, many crimes of sexual motivation."

We learned the magic lantern slides were kept in the St. Elizabeths lobby museum until it closed in the 1980s, when they were subsequently transferred to an archival vault at the National Museum of Science and Health on the base of the US Army's Forest Glen facility in Silver Spring, Maryland. It took us weeks navigating a pre-COVID security clearance process to gain access to the base and museum. If one is not fully prepared to experience this museum, it can be quite disturbing to see the nineteenth-century exhibits of battlefield surgeries and primitive prosthetic devices. Here we saw the actual bullet dislodged from Abraham Lincoln's brain during his autopsy—an example of the atmosphere in this place. It's not for kids. We were there for a serious reason: to answer the question, Who were the invisible and erased gay, lesbian, and transgender patients committed to St. Elizabeths?

We shared the slides and diagrams with historians familiar with the bad science and psychosexual theories of the time. The historians pointed to the disturbing interweaving of homosexuality and criminal or pathological behavior. Of course, by definition, homosexuality in the day was a criminal condition. And you were therefore deemed insane. The suturing of homosexuality, mental illness, and criminality was finalized at St. Elizabeths. Indeed, if one were indicted and institutionalized under the DC Sexual Psychopath Act of 1948, you could not leave St. Elizabeths until certified by the hospital superintendent as "cured." We discovered the queer etiological diagrams inside these magic lantern slides. "Guilt/Guilt/Guilt" was at the bullseye of a key diagram; we also came across something called "Mixed Hysterical Psychoneurosis," a condition we learned is the relieving of stress through screaming.

On our way home, we rolled down the windows; we swerved; we did feel like screaming.

We also vowed as Archive Activists to get beyond anger and tell the story of this find in ways that people could accept and understand. How might we humanize these nameless people from the nineteenth and early twentieth century with the haunting, redacted eyes? We wondered if somehow new artificial intelligence (AI) programs might be applied to these historic photographs. And how might we as Archive Activists explore the new AI frontier in powerful and constructive ways? Might we think about something called "super-reality photographs," we wondered, to attract interest and convey the gravity of what we had experienced in that vault?

These photos may be called deepfake or deep nostalgia super-reality photographs, and they have generated a good deal of controversy for their political or propagandistic misuse. There is now an explosion of "text to image generators faster than AI companies can shape norms around its use and prevent dangerous outcomes."[10] But our idea was to use AI to generate a powerful sense of empathy with queer patients committed to St. Elizabeths. Without infringing on anyone's privacy protections, these one-hundred-year-old, anonymous (eyes redacted), educational slides could be a perfect application of the new AI tool, we believed. We struggled with the idea of using them in this way until we saw, and were moved by, an AI-treated photograph of Frederick Douglass released in 2021. The most photographed celebrity of his time, Douglass, as treated by the AI, is animated and powerful beyond words or text and went viral, generating some 2.5 million views.[11] "Brace yourself and press 'play,'" the Tweet said.[12] So we did. Douglass's head turns slightly, his eyes blink, his face becomes slightly expressive. It is a lot to absorb. This is no Disney animatronic president. So we went forward, working with our director and his editor and tech expert to figure how best to use which of the available programs.

Respectfully and with much forethought, we applied an AI program to three St. Elizabeths magic lantern slides to achieve an empathetic point of connection to the queer patients. We included them, brought to subtle, powerful life behind the bars of their redacted eyes, in a video we produced titled "The Acknowledgment." This video makes the case that it is time for Congress to formally acknowledge and apologize for what happened at St. Elizabeths and beyond. These people had been objectified and presented as mentally ill or criminal or both, or maybe simply as oddities for the psychiatrists, medical students, and nurses to study. Through AI we aimed to resurrect their humanity. Until now, their stories had been erased. How could they not have been included in the St. Elizabeths Hospital exhibition at the Building Museum? We saw how this technology can help free these individuals from the silence and ignorance that enshrouded them a century ago.[13]

Wes Holloway, an artist from Katy, Texas, contacted us when he read the "Asylum Seekers" article. We were thrilled to see how he interpreted our research and the magic lantern slides with an artist "zine" and short film titled *Queering the Medical Model: St. Elizabeths Hospital, Washington, DC.*[14] Using painting, computer collage design, and research, his presentation of the magic lantern slides lifts our research to a whole new plane of understanding and empathy.

Neither deep nostalgia nor deepfake, the use of super-reality photographic AI can be deeply human. When usage of such photographs becomes "look at this cool thing we did," historians rightly express concern, especially today when we see geopolitical deepfake videos. What are the key issues these projects raise or how might they serve as a model for Archive Activists in coming years? What are the ethics, beyond full disclosure requirements, of manipulating the historical record? Our AI-enhanced photographs of the queer "insane" more than a century ago is not a "cool thing" novelty. Instead, we see how the queer faces of St. Elizabeths can lead students and historians into a deeper understanding of erased history and our shared humanity. No more degayed St. Elizabeths.

From St. Elizabeths to Dallas's Memorial Auditorium

There is a straight line from St. Elizabeths to the modern era. It leads to Dallas's Memorial Auditorium. The line runs to the second most important LGBTQ moment after Stonewall: the Annual Meeting of the American Psychiatric Association in 1972 at Dallas Memorial Auditorium.[15] It was at Memorial Auditorium in May 1972 (and afterward, at the Adolphus Hotel) where gay and lesbian activists took their stand, led by Frank Kameny and Barbara Gittings, to demand the psychiatrists drop homosexuality from the *Diagnostic and Statistical Manual,*[16] their list of mental illnesses. Like Stonewall, it was one of those historic breaking points from the past when the disguised gay psychiatrist Dr. H. Anonymous appeared on the Dallas platform that spring day. Wearing a fright wig and a distorting rubber mask, his voice was disguised with a buzzer. "I am a homosexual. I am a psychiatrist. I am in disguise tonight in order that I might speak freely," he said. One might say the psychiatrists went nuts. In a controlled fury, Dr. Anonymous demanded an end to psychiatry's search for a cure and its war on homosexuals. It was not revealed until twenty-two years later that Dr. Anonymous was Dr. John Fryer, who today is considered a hero.[17]

To help close the deal, Frank and Barbara and her partner, Kay Lahusen, distributed in Dallas a now-historic handout, "Gay, Proud and Healthy." It said, "This is why we, as homosexuals, are here at the Dallas conference. . . . We have traditionally been the people least consulted. . . . We are bringing that to an end."[18]

In his trademark, media-savvy hyperbole, Kameny wrote to one psychiatrist experimenting with hypnosis to cure homosexuals, "We consider efforts to persuade, pressure, or compel unwilling patients into conversion to heterosexuality to be tantamount to genocide, and to be a matter of our collective concern."[19] A year later, the APA delisted homosexuality as a mental illness. "VICTORY!!!! We have been 'cured,'" wrote Frank Kameny in a memo to his supporters, a memo we discovered in Frank's attic. "The psychiatrists passed the Civil Rights Resolution at approximately 8:30 AM, on Saturday, December 15, 1973, 'curing' us all, instantaneously, en masse, in one fell swoop by semantics and by vote, instead of therapy," he wrote. Kameny coined the sixties slogan—taken from Stokely Carmichael's "Black Is Beautiful"—"Gay Is Good." At Dallas's Memorial Auditorium in May 1972, Gay was furious.

Dramatized in the highly acclaimed PBS / Independent Lens documentary *Cured*, coproduced and directed by Patrick Sammon and Bennett Singer, which aired nationwide in 2021, the effect of the disguised psychiatrist at the Dallas convention was electrifying. It was our Archive Activism, focused on the centrality of Dr. Anonymous, that inspired Patrick to create this film. "I had come across this story and read about it in some queer history books. My friend Charles Francis had written a treatment about the life of Frank Kameny. In the treatment was the story of Dr. Anonymous. So I owe it to Charles for sparking the idea," he said.[20] It would have been more accurate to say, "I owe it to Archive Activism."

Having discovered the Kameny documents, we were pleased to become the fiscal sponsor of *Cured* to ensure that this powerful documentary could find an audience, light years beyond Memorial Auditorium in 1972. Our film treatment dramatized the cinematic moment of havoc when Dr. Anonymous took the mic. And we loved the Hollywood-style punch of the *Cured* poster: "Doctors called them sick. The remedy was rebellion"—in Dallas, of all places.

Chapter 15

A Queer American Spy Story

S he wanted to know what had happened to her deceased gay father. She told us this had been a painful family mystery running through her and her husband's and sister's lives for decades—since the McCarthy loyalty investigations had cost her father his career as a Foreign Service Officer. She thought, after reading about our Archive Activism in the *Washington Post*, that perhaps, through us, she might be able to find some answers. Would we like to take this on?

We are not private investigators or an old-time detective agency, but we are always intrigued by the vicious intersection of McCarthy-era loyalty and homosexuality investigations. We listen, especially if there is a large box of papers already involved. The daughter explained how her father, Army Lieutenant Thomas Stauffer, had used the Freedom of Information Act before his passing to find some answers. She had inherited the box of papers in a jumbled mess. Was it all about loyalty and his association with Communist sympathizers? Did homosexuality have anything to do with his problem? And what had happened in Berlin? He had been assigned to the Office of Denazification in 1946, the year after Hitler's suicide. When he arrived in Berlin he was 30, fluent in German, French, and Greek after a classical education at the University of Chicago, which he entered at age 16. He was obviously a brainiac of some kind. What secrets did he carry unto his death?

Berlin 1945. We were on it.

"I have never read an adequate description of Berlin in the early days of the Occupation; I think it would best be a subject for fiction," wrote one observer.[1] Indeed, it would take a Hollywood director, Billy Wilder, in his film *A Foreign Affair*, filmed in Berlin in 1947, to capture the haunting, surreal moonscape of the city in the immediate aftermath of the war. Estimates are over three hundred thousand Berliners and eighty thousand Red Army soldiers lay dead after the two week battle.[2] Dramatic exteriors were filmed driving through ruins radiating around the soot-covered Brandenburg Gate. Marlene Dietrich sings a tribute to "The Ruins of Berlin." We thought Stauffer, and these materials, might be a queer point of historical connection to this world of rubble and the emerging Cold War. We agreed to go to work, if the family would donate to us all of the materials in their possession. They kindly did so, and we began an excellent working partnership built on mutual affection and respect.

When the jumbled mess of paper arrived, our first thought was "jigsaw puzzle." Where are the corner pieces? Find the straight edges, the clusters that reveal a glimpse of queer Berlin. Roll it all out on a long table. Piece together a chronology. Most important for us at the Mattachine Society, we began with a broad homosexual or queer view. As Larry Kramer once wrote, "God save us from the heterosexual historian!"[3] We wanted to look at the boxes of papers using queer imagination. We believe there is such a thing. With it we could make imaginative leaps to understand how events affected Stauffer, not only the army. There are solid facts, but there are also the pictures with young men on the beach, the letters, his poetry. By the time that he was posted in Germany, we could see that he had already lived an open (for the day) gay life, even having had an intense affair with the celebrity composer (and diarist) Ned Rorem (1923–). Rorem wrote in 2013, "I meanwhile was having an affair with Thomas Stauffer, a university graduate in philosophy, proud of having hosted Bertrand Russell. . . . Athletic, Stauffer was tall, with a brush cut, superciliously sadistic with me, physically exciting, but a boor and musically reactionary."[4]

Our research commenced at the National Archives, where we were directed to the OMGUS (Office of Military Government for Germany US) papers of World War II. OMGUS was established in 1945 to administer the US zone in Germany, with de-Nazification as one of its primary tasks, presided over by the US Army. Here we learned that Stauffer's job was to vet nominations to assess suitability of Germans for "high policymaking and precedent making appointments, for instance, candidates for top slots often involve (former) IG Farben officials who worked for the Third Reich."[5] IG Farben was the German chemical conglomerate that supplied the poison gas for the gas chambers that killed over a million German Jewish victims of the Holocaust. To "vet nominations" is bureaucratese for de-Nazification.

Lt. Thomas Stauffer, Office of de-Nazification, Berlin, 1945.
Courtesy of Mattachine Society of Washington, DC.

They nicknamed their operation the "skunk works" because of the foul smell of some of their subjects, like the so-called innocent banker referred to General Eisenhower for a position. According to Stauffer, General Lucius Clay, then deputy to General Dwight Eisenhower in Allied-occupied Germany, asked Stauffer for a twenty-four hour turn-around on this guy. Stauffer did his work and discovered the truth. That banker had been involved in whitewashing the property stolen by the Nazis from thousands of Austrian Jews—otherwise known as the Aryanization of Jewish property.

In addition to vetting, their larger idea was to teach Germans about American democracy and culture, from politics to baseball, in order to purge all Nazi elements and ideology from occupied Germany. Looking at young Lt. Stauffer, we discovered our first big answer about his problem in Germany inside fifty-two boxes at the archives.[6] It took days, but we found what we were looking for: a morals charge related to fraternizing with a German youth.

Stauffer was teaching the virtues of American democracy to German youth while researching Germans suspected of being former Nazis.

When we told his daughter about our discovery of the morals charge at the "skunk works" with the German youth, she replied, "We are not surprised. All my life, indeed until he died in 1986, Dad and Mom (when they were together) had young people around." It was not all black and white. "Yes, some of these young men were likely sexually involved with my dad, but probably the minority. Our family had taken in all kinds of young adults." Stauffer had lived a double life in the closet in the years after the war.

Tom Stauffer, this "supercilious" man,[7] was already in trouble by 1946, a year after he arrived in Berlin. Here soldiers would be sorely tempted to take advantage of the lawless situation. In Stauffer's case as a gay soldier, he might have yielded to the anything-goes tempta-tions amid the desperation and sexual license of the time. He never told his family about that morals charge.

Another memo we discovered in OMGUS boxes provided more context: "The alleged derelictions arise from his association with

German youths. . . . I can only express my utter astonishment," one friend back in Washington wrote to Ambassador Robert D. Murphy, a career diplomat who was the American military governor of occupied Germany. During the war Murphy had worked for William "Wild Bill" Donovan and his newly formed Office of Strategic Services (OSS, the precursor to the Central Intelligence Agency, or CIA) in North Africa.[8] The Stauffer friend and ally emphasized to Murphy, "For even a suspicion that he is, or ever has been, addicted to immoral practices . . . I can only believe that a charge of this nature has been made by someone with a cowardly turn of mind."[9]

"1946: SPECIAL ORDERS FOR AMERICAN-GERMAN RELATIONS." GIs were forbidden contact with the conquered population: forbidden to shake hands with Germans, visit their homes, play games or sports with them, exchange gifts, take part in social events with them, or walk with them on the streets or elsewhere. This was the strict nonfraternization, familiarity, or intimacy policy in Occupied Germany.[10]

We learned, with continued digging, that Lt. Stauffer admitted that the youth had gained entry to his apartment; the place was robbed, with cash and lots of cigarettes stolen, and his superiors found out about it. We kept building our file. We knew this could not be the end of the story. It was only a pause. Somehow, some way, Stauffer survived the morals charge and was allowed to continue his service to his country, no longer in the army but as a Foreign Service Officer at the Department of State. Stauffer then began a series of postings across the Middle East that boggle the mind. Of course, it could make perfect sense to send him where French was the colonial language, to cities like Beirut or Casablanca. In 1948 he was assigned to the embassy in Cairo, "reporting on all developments affecting the organized labor movement" there with no special background or interest in the Middle East. "He is doing an extraordinarily good job," a declassified State Department review from the Cairo embassy declared.[11]

Following Cairo, Stauffer undertook missions to Beirut and Damascus, then was on to Jerusalem. For the next two months, he was assigned to the Iranian Economic Mission in Tehran. At this point, it became obvious from the archive (letters, memoranda, reports, pleas for support) that this American army lieutenant had become an asset, being moved around the Middle East beyond anything conceivable in his past. It seemed Stauffer was no longer his own man or the American high achiever who spoke fluent German to the benefit of OMGUS. He had undergone a transformation of identity unknown to anyone but himself and his Washington handlers—whoever they were.

We were reminded of an unusually gay poem written by Stauffer in 1940—using the closet language of "unknowing," "misleading," and "masque"—that we found in the jumble donated to us by his daughter. His poem, titled "Night Masque," is eerily prescient, blending the imagery of furtive, old-time homosexual encounters with the style and language of espionage.

Come walk with me the street,
Talk of one another's days,
Watch other unknowing lovers meet,
Walk unknowing separated ways.

Leave them unknowing we who walk
Among the other lovers at mischance
Walk not to watch them nor to talk,
But to mislead each other in the dance.[12]

The documents we examined indicate Stauffer was finally summoned to Washington, DC, from yet another city—Alexandria, Egypt. This time it was not about his homosexuality; it was about his loyalty. Stauffer's associations in Berlin with economists and intellectuals sympathetic to the Soviet Union and Communist ideology had emerged. "It is URGENT that Mr. Stauffer be brought to Washington for interview by the Loyalty Review Board," the State Department memorandum said.[13] His problems were rooted in guilt by association with a pro-Soviet economist in occupied Berlin by the name of

Juergin Kuczinski and a colorful, queer poet—a surrealist—Edouard Roditi (1910–1992). Roditi, born in Paris of American parents, had served as an interpreter at the Nuremberg war trials and at the United Nations Charter Conference in San Francisco. Roditi's problem was not garden-variety American "disloyalty" but being a Parisian homosexual who had studied at Oxford, and now, as a State Department interpreter, he had become ensnared in the uniquely American Communist witch hunt and the Lavender Scare. (Many years later, Roditi would visit Stauffer and his family, becoming Uncle Eduard to Stauffer's children.) Stauffer was informed he was facing "charges that you are a member, or in sympathetic association with the Communist Party, with habitual or close association with persons known, or believed to be, in this category."[14]

"I am not a member of, nor affiliated with, nor in sympathetic association with, the Communist Party," he testified to a Loyalty Review Board. "I would not at any time have joined nor supported, and do not now belong . . . ," but it was too late for that.[15]

We might have stopped here, with the fairly typical revelation of yet another gay man in the State Department caught up in the Lavender Scare. But the documents revealed still more trap doors and free falls.

We saw in the legal documentation that Stauffer had returned to Washington to begin a series of meetings with his attorney to prepare for his Loyalty Review Board hearings, and likely his termination from the Foreign Service. He could be tagged for life as a Communist sympathizer, a homosexual, and a permanent, unemployable security risk. And what did he do only days before his hearings? He got himself arrested by the DC Metropolitan Police in Lafayette Park. Here at the notorious homosexual cruising ground of the day, Stauffer was arrested at 1:10 a.m. on a charge of "soliciting for lewd and immoral purposes." He admitted to a "conversation on sexual matters with a total stranger," the arresting officer stated. His State Department examiner berated him, saying, "in a hangout place for homosexuals, and you stated that you frequented a number of places in the District of Columbia which also are frequented by homosexuals. You explained your presence in Lafayette Park by 'fatigue, loneliness and need for cigarettes" . . . when you could have 'procured' cigarettes at your hotel."[16]

Stauffer's attorney appealed for mercy: "It would be grossly unfair to require him to prepare for two hearings at the same time" (homo-sexuality and loyalty). Stauffer's counsel was concerned that the arrest in Lafayette Park might be taken into consideration by the Loyalty and Security Board in connection his case. Still, he continued, "My client is solely responsible for his present plight."[17] Indeed, we see now in the archive that he was responsible in a world that was hostile to a gay Foreign Service Officer. Studying these archival materials, with incomplete context, one can only ask, Was this his final breakdown? Cruising Lafayette Park days before one's Loyalty Review Board hearings not only is reckless bad judgement but could also be compul-sive, self-destruction. We asked ourselves, Was this the final disinte-gration of various "Night Masque" identities at once? We raised all of this with his daughter and her husband in regular updates. She and the family had no clue about the arrest in Lafayette Park and the compounding of his problem, all on the eve of the loyalty hearings charging him with being a "Fellow Traveler."

It is as if Stauffer was playing to the State Department's type. "Many of the men who have studied homosexuality tell us that homosexuals are neurotic, characterized by emotional instability, that they represent a type of regression to man's primitive instincts and that they live a life of flight from their inversion and of fear of detection," says a State Department confidential memorandum written in 1950 and declassified in 1998. "We believe that most homosexuals are weak, unstable and fickle people who fear detection and who are therefore susceptible to the wanton designs of others."[18] Were those stereotypes true in Stauffer's case, when the homophobic political and social pressure exacerbated self-destructive tendencies? We think not. This man was neither "weak" nor "unstable," just, perhaps, conniving and lost.

Elbridge Durbrow, chief of the Division of Foreign Service Personnel, wrote the final wrap-up in what we think is the most important document in the collection of materials we discovered. This is not a boilerplate charge:

> By your conduct on the night of August 28–29, you displayed a lack of personal dignity and allowed your name to come into disrepute. You showed a substantial disregard of the standards of accepted behavior . . . gross lack of judgement . . . in a notorious place, at a very late hour, opening a conversation on sexual matters with a total stranger. . . . this rendered you unsuitable as a representative of the United States. . . . You are notified of your right to be present at a hearing, of your right to present orally or in writing information on your behalf, and of your right to be accompanied by a representative of your choosing.[19]

This must have been crushing for Thomas Stauffer, all coming down to Lafayette Park. It was the end.

There were three Loyalty Review Board hearings.[20] The Mattachine legal team successfully requested the hearing transcripts be declassified and released to us. Stauffer was questioned at length about the matter with the German youth and his arrest in Lafayette Park. The Loyalty Review Board chairman Howard Donovan asked, "one further point, I am afraid, Mr. Stauffer, according to information available to the Board, you were within the last few days arrested by the Metropolitan Police. Do you care to comment on that in connection to these proceedings?"[21] His attorney responded with a stock denial.

***

Stauffer wrote his father, asking for money:

> Dear Father,
> As you know Senator McCarthy and others make life unpleasant for the State Dpt. Charges have been brought against me, and I was brought back to this country for a hearing. The preliminary findings of the Loyalty Board is adverse, and I am now suspended without pay, pending a final decision.

The charges are not true, and all my associates and superiors have given me strong support in evidence, etc. The matters at issue relate entirely to <u>political matters in Germany</u> of which you and mother have no knowledge. You will not, of course discuss this with anyone but mother.

If the final decision is adverse, there is a long process of appeal, etc. during all of which I will have no income. My able lawyer is serving without fee, but even so I have no other resources, and the question arises as to whether and to what extent you will be able to help me, until the matter is determined. . . . In any event, such is the situation—you will realize from my opening that there are bigger issues than my career at stake . . .

Yours, in sorrow and anger, Tom[22]

He could have written the old rhyme, "No mon. No fun. Your son." It was half the story. Could he have revealed in 1951 to his father that his homosexuality and reckless behavior had cost him his job, in addition to the McCarthy charge of being a Communist "fellow traveler"? In the years prior to his passing in 1987, could he have told his ex-wife or children anything at all? He never did. He died with those secrets— and one other thing. We learned Thomas Stauffer had become a spy for Wild Bill Donovan's OSS. Bill Donovan (1883–1959) was chosen by President Roosevelt to direct America's "excursion into espionage, sabotage, 'black' propaganda, guerilla warfare and other 'un-American' subversive practices."[23] Donovan's OSS eventually enlisted over thirteen thousand Americans.

***

On an Archive Activist search like this, there may be no end. You hit impossible walls and false leads that can become obsessions. The archive can be maddening. Or, if the story reaches a logical ending, it is pencils down; you let go of it. We were ready to tell Stauffer's family we were at that point when an archivist called us into her small office research area adjacent to the main reading room. In her hands was a three-ring binder printout of twenty-four thousand names that had been declassified in 2008 as a result of the Nazi War

Crimes Disclosure Act.[24] She explained this included a listing of the men and women who served during the World War II as intelligence officers in Donovan's worldwide intelligence organization.

There in this ledger was the name Thomas Stauffer.

Stauffer was in the OSS. No wonder he survived his morals charge with that German youth in Berlin. Ambassador Robert Murphy, the American military governor of American-occupied Germany, had received and read the memo about Stauffer's morals charge with a German boy—and nothing had happened to Stauffer. With the OSS ledger, we can see method in the madness of Stauffer's postings from Tehran, Beirut, and Damascus to Jerusalem and Cairo with zero background in the Middle East or with labor issues. Murphy and Donovan had a longtime relationship going back to French North Africa in preparation for the Allied landings, so a hand-off of Stauffer to Donovan makes some sense.

We felt some vertigo in this cube of classified homosexuality, American intelligence services, occupied Berlin, and the emerging Cold War. There were no heroes. Stauffer was not one. He was not a foreign spy. He was one of ours. There was no clear right or wrong. There was only real life in Berlin 1946.

We were not done. On the printout the archivist pointed to a blank space. There was no serial number. She explained and we grew ashen. The blank space in her printout means the Thomas Stauffer file has gone missing. "It appears," she continued, "the file was removed or transferred to the CIA," a body blow requiring a formal request to the CIA. And good luck on that. Oh, the Stauffer file must be fabulous, we thought, and we started to plan next steps.

We can contact queer friends who once worked at the Agency. We had heard that "Wild Bill" Donovan had an enlightened atti-tude toward homosexuals working in the OSS. We well know that OSS officers "were swept up by Joseph McCarthy . . . and some forty-seven OSS employees suspected of being communists or party sympathizers" had been identified by OSS security investigators.[25] One of our advisory board members, formerly with the CIA, shared some very general thoughts with us on how best to fashion a formal request for information on Stauffer. One day we may move forward on that.

We had already arrived at our destination. The jigsaw image came into view. It was a stark picture of how a society and its victims can become disfigured in a collision of history—McCarthyism, Lavender Scare homophobia, and the Cold War. It converged on one man caught between his Loyalty Review Board hearings and terrible personal judgement in a park. OSS/CIA historian Richard Harris Smith believes rediscovering the erased "'love that dare not speak its name' helps explain puzzling wartime alliances and friendships." He writes, "There still seems to be relatively little mention of such things in conventional military, diplomatic and intelligence histories which leads me to wonder if those histories may be, to some degree, off the mark in explaining what really happened and why."[26]

There is no need to wonder. Histories written within the decades of animus may be "off the mark" because of the scorn that surrounded the queer players. Assistant Secretary of State Carlisle H. Humelsine (1915–1989) wrote a State Department policy memorandum we discovered as we looked into the Stauffer situation at the National Archives. Subject: "The Problem of Homosexuals and Sex Perverts in the Department of State": "Most homosexuals are weak, unstable and fickle people who fear detection and who are therefore susceptible to the wanton designs of others," Humelsine wrote.[27] This memorandum was submitted to Congress to support the firing of homosexuals working for the State Department, which later became known as the Lavender Scare, "the systematic firing and banning of LGBT people from the federal government."[28] It is estimated one thousand gay men and lesbians were fired in this episode, careers ended and lives wrecked.[29] Humelsine testified, "When we find homosexuals, we eliminate them from the Department."[30] Humelsine went on in 1977 to become chairman of the Colonial Williamsburg Foundation. Today, Williamsburg, Virginia, has a major parkway named for him, the Humelsine Parkway. How could there have been an alternative version of diplomatic history generated (or erased) by people so celebrated that there is a parkway in Williamsburg named for them, especially given the recent Biden White House proclamation of acknowledgment on the seventieth anniversary of the Lavender Scare?[31] The White House proclamation addressed the long queer deceased: "We acknowledge what you lost and what you wrongfully endured." There will be no reparation of any kind. There was no apology.

We tell the Thomas Stauffer kids and loved ones all about what we found, our theories, and the true story about their "Night Masque" dad, a queer spy for "Wild Bill" Donovan and the OSS. This is now a secret that will be kept by the CIA , a story suitable for one of Washington's most popular attractions, the International Spy Museum.

Chapter 16

International
Inspirations

When we were contacted by the CIA in 2015, we thought, "At last." Our dream was to find ways to declassify and access documents long held at the agency's headquarters in Langley, Virginia. This could be our first opening into an international archive of answers, we thought. Instead, we learned an awful truth about the agency's past, and our past, too.

We were contacted by Tracey Ballard, the first openly-gay and transgender officer at the CIA. Ballard came out at the agency in 1988, years before President Clinton's executive order overturning the ban on sharing classified information based solely on sexual orientation. A true pioneer, she founded the CIA's LGBTQ employee group, ANGLE (the Agency Network of Gay, Lesbian, Bisexual and Transgender Officers and Allies).[1] We agreed to meet with her and a colleague identified to us only as John C. at the neighborhood Commissary restaurant in Washington's Logan Circle. An inscription above the Commissary's bar sets the very diverse tone of the place: "I like my beer cold, my TV loud, and my homosexuals flaming! Homer Simpson." This was an appropriate place for us to speak plainly.

Before our meeting, a gay friend on the congressional staff tipped us off to the existence of an unpublished transcript of a hearing held in executive session, which means "closed." It was a 1950 hearing on the topic of "perverts" in government—and what needed to be done about this menace.

Weed them out, of course.

Historians are well aware of this hearing, chaired by Senator Clyde R. Hoey (D-NC), chairman of the Investigations Subcommittee of the US Senate Committee on Expenditures in the Executive Departments. What made the tip exciting was that this was the closed executive session with the key witness being the first director of the CIA. We began a very targeted search, both online and through archival sources, and found our copy—with the proviso that it could not be published or posted in full; the digital rights had been sold. That was more than okay with us. When we found the testimony on page two-thousand-something of the entire document, we knew we had exactly what we needed for our meeting. We had the truth.

We immediately liked Tracey Ballard, an impressive and serious individual who was direct about her mission: to strengthen the CIA's diversity, recruitment, and mission-ready talent worldwide without regard to sexual orientation—just the best. You can imagine the strength of character emanating from Ballard, a transgender CIA officer leading the way for their LGBTQ employee group. We could imagine how transgender CIA employees could bring kaleidoscopic perspectives and identities to intelligence gathering. She introduced us to her colleague, John C., who turned out to be the senior video producer at the agency. She wanted to know all about Pate and me, how we met forty years ago in Washington and what our mission was as Archive Activists. She had done her homework on us, of course, as we had done ours on her. We explained our work and prepared her for the document we had discovered, now in our possession: the "pervert" statement delivered by the first director of the CIA, Admiral Roscoe Hillenkoetter. That got a reaction. She told us she had never heard of this testimony, nor seen it. How interesting, we thought, that this was news to someone like Ballard—perhaps confirmation we had something worthwhile. This made our day.

Ballard explained that ANGLE was pulling together a first-time, historical exhibition for Pride month on LGBTQ Americans and the CIA to be unveiled in a hallway reception area at the agency's headquarters. This was Obama-era reform and progress for the deeply closeted LGBTQ employees of the CIA. The hallway exhibition would include historical background regarding gay and lesbian employment at the CIA and might include any materials we may have discovered. In addition, John C. was producing and directing a documentary video that would accompany the exhibition. Perhaps we might agree to an interview for that video? Gulp.

"Would you think about that, Charles?"

Alarms went off in my head. "So, John," I pressed, "would we be able to see a script for this video?"

"No."

"Where will the video be shown?" (At headquarters? Worldwide?)

"Can't say."

"Will Pate and I be able to see it when completed?"

"We may not show it to anyone outside of the agency," he said flatly.

Better to shift gears, I thought. It felt like a good time to share their first director's views on "moral perverts." Scoopage on Roscoe Hillenkoetter would be a nice, safe subject—a perfect Washington chat for the Commissary.

Admiral Hillenkoetter served on the front lines of World War II, in both the Pacific and Europe. He was wounded at Pearl Harbor when serving as executive officer of the battleship *West Virginia*, and organized intelligence operations reporting to the Pacific Fleet's commander in chief, Chester Nimitz. In Europe during the war he also served as naval attaché in Paris and Vichy, France, as Admiral Nimitz's intelligence officer. All of this before Hillenkoetter was named by President Truman, in 1947, as the first director of the CIA. With this extraordinary international background, one might think Hillenkoetter would have a more worldly point of view regarding homosexuality. Instead, it takes an effort in our time to conceive of a man like Hillenkoetter. Rabidly homophobic, a self-important alpha male—how is it possible to connect with this man? We soldiered on at the Commissary by connecting with his agency.

"Speaking for the agency," Hillenkoetter testified, "We do our best . . . to leave no stone unturned to make certain we do not employ any perverts of any sort, and if we do find them, we get rid of them as fast as we can."

Okay, but what do you really think? He left no insult unturned.

"Perverts are vulnerable to interrogation by a skilled questioner. They seldom refuse to talk about themselves . . . and have other exploitable weaknesses, such as psychopathic tendencies, physical cowardice, susceptibility to pressure, and general instability."

"Hey, here's a good one." I read aloud:

"Some perverts who make a great TO DO about their discretion are actually quite indiscreet. They are too stupid to realize it, or else due to inflation of their ego . . . they are usually the center of gossip, rumor, derision and so forth."

We continued walking Ballard and John C. through our find. Hillenkoetter compared these "moral perverts" to criminals, smugglers, and dope addicts. These queers (our word) show "consistent symptoms of weakness and instability which accompany homosexuality, almost always danger points of susceptibility from the standpoint of security." He concluded, "The moral pervert is a security risk of so serious a nature that he must be weeded out of government employment wherever he is found."[2]

Looking back on our lunch, we may have gone a bit too far with the Hillenkoetter discovery, but there it was—a total buzzkill. Things might have gone better if we were lower key and spoke in the standard language of LGBTQ diversity and inclusion. However, we believed history "with the bark off" mattered, especially in their secret world. We were thanked but never heard again from Ballard and John C.

"Gays Ghosted by the CIA," we laughed at our imagined tabloid headline. Nor were we invited to that Pride hallway exhibition at

Langley headquarters. It would have been nice. We learned that Admiral Hillenkoetter was also deleted in this exhibit; it's funny to have that in common with him. We "stupid," "psychopathic," "unstable" queers from another time found our peace by rediscovering his words. Hey, who needs a hallway exhibition?

MI6 Apologizes

Unlike Hillenkoetter, Richard Moore, chief of the British Secret Intelligence Service (SIS, also known as MI6) rarely makes any public statement, much less a public apology. You will not see Moore pontificate on personnel issues for SIS, which he heads as its only publicly identifiable member (aside from Ian Fleming's James Bond). SIS is analogous to the CIA, focused on foreign intelligence gathering, not on public relations. So it was an astounding and historic moment when Richard Moore lit up a Twitter account in 2021 with a lengthy statement of apology on behalf of MI6 "for the way LGBT+ colleagues and fellow citizens were treated, and I express my regret for everyone whose life was affected." He said, "It was wrong, unjust and discriminatory."[3]

We were thrilled to hear such a statement of apology, a result of years of grassroots activism and governmental support across all lines of ideology, class, and parties in Great Britain. This was our inspiration to seek such an acknowledgment and apology in the United States. We looked to the Brits.

The McDermott Will & Emery team activated their London associates to analyze and report on exactly how Britain's apology was achieved so that we could credibly brief congressional staff and allies in the United States. Our research drew upon interviews with the players, the Official Parliamentary Reports, the National Archives of the UK, and the statement of the Republic of Ireland's prime minister, the Taoiseach. Of course the movement was propelled by and anchored to the mathematician and cryptanalyst Alan Turing, the computing genius who, working out of the storied Bletchley Park, broke the Nazi's Enigma code—a spectacular computing achievement. Turing was convicted of homosexuality after the war, with a punishment imposed of chemical castration, leading to his death by suicide. It was the horrifying case of Alan Turing, the man and all he represented, that generated the popular energy to achieve the acknowledgment and formal apologies in Britain. The Turing acknowledgment and apology movement lasted nearly a decade, beginning with the first apology petition (2009) posted by software engineer John Graham-Cumming. His petition, the subject of a BBC feature, led to a formal apology delivered to Parliament by Prime Minister Gordon Brown. Queen Elizabeth, four years later, granted a royal pardon to Turing in 2013. By the time the British public had seen the moving portrayals of Turing by Ed Stoppard in the television docudrama *Codebreaker* (2011), or by Benedict Cumberbatch in the *The Imitation Game* (2014), there was no stopping the popular momentum. Bringing this to an ultimate conclusion, Parliament enacted the Turing Law (2017), proposed by Lord Sharkey, a posthumous amnesty/pardon to over forty-thousand men who had once been convicted of offenses that criminalized homosexuality.

The entire process of acknowledgment, apology, and pardons in Britain culminated with the formal apology from MI6, still drawing upon the energy unleashed by the Alan Turing reckoning. We knew this could never be replicated in America. If there were a mural of this history, it would be of a galaxy-like swirl, with Turing as the big bang connecting all Brits with the unifying legacy of their World War II experience, the mixture of endurance and brilliance that defeated the Nazis and fascist violence. After research and study of the pieces, we believe it was the emotional, blood connection to another era's sacrifice and heroism that generated the formal apology and the cascade of pardons.

But Americans have no Turing. We do have Britain's example of how divisions of ideology, party, and society may be overcome by appealing to the nation's conscience and personal ties of allies and kinship that still bind us together. In the United States, the recent bipartisan passage of the Respect for Marriage Act (2022) shows us the way.

Darker Inspirations

Under the leadership and curatorial guidance of the US Holocaust Memorial Museum, German archivists and activists had worked diligently for two years in Germany to uncover the erased stories of the homosexual men arrested, imprisoned, and murdered in camps by the Nazis. In 1933 Hitler had banned all gay and lesbian organizations because of homosexual "degeneracy," and this savagery was the violent conclusion. The Holocaust Museum's research was conducted in archives across Germany, including the Bundesarchiv in Koblenz (the Federal Archives of Germany); the Schwules Museum in Berlin; the Staatsarchiv Würzburg; the Dokumentationsarchiv des Österreichischen Widerstandes in Vienna; and elsewhere. We have visited the Schwules Museum, which contains some 1.5 million items—the largest LGBTQ collection in Germany. The researchers for the Holocaust Museum focused their efforts on preserved Nazi records and archives. They discovered hundreds of photographs, many of them the booking shots of the gay men dragged from their lives in Berlin to prisons and camps. This was part of an ambitious undertaking to tell the stories of the one hundred thousand men arrested, the fifty thousand who served prison terms, and the five to fifteen thousand sent to Nazi concentration camps, where many died from starvation, beatings, castration, and murder.[4]

Adding to its significance, the exhibition "Nazi Persecution of Homosexuals, 1933–1945" (2002) was the first time the US Holocaust Museum had focused on other groups besides Jews, beginning with homosexuals.[5] The curator of the exhibition was honestly concerned that before the opening, America's religious right, including Orthodox Jews, might criticize the exhibition for daring to bring homosexuality into the context of the Holocaust. Might Jerry Falwell or Pat Robertson, or—God forbid—Bush/Rove ally James Dobson spark a new antigay outrage by criticizing the exhibition? I was asked to help if possible, using whatever influence I might have with the White House (which was fast becoming next to none at this point). I reached out to Houston civic leader Fred Zeidman, who had been named chairman of the US Holocaust Museum by President Bush. He agreed to write something supportive. Still, I wanted to help this unique research effort that put names, faces, and real peoples' stories onto the sickening numbers. The archival research was wholly original, including historic discoveries. In desperation I contacted the vice president's office to see if Mary Cheney could at least attend a private preview and speak to the curator about the exhibit's purpose. Thankfully, Cheney did come by the exhibit before it opened for such a walk-through. The Holocaust Museum curator and his staff were so appreciative for this morsel of encouragement. If worse came to worst, at least they could say the vice president's daughter had seen and blessed the exhibition. Things were that bad. But the exhibition turned out to be a great success.

In 2016 Germany's parliament, the Bundestag, enacted legislation to compensate victims of homophobic violence under Nazism. A €30 million fund is meant to cover some five thousand surviving victims, with payment amounts determined by the length of time one spent in prison for being gay. The government of Chancellor Angela Merkel enacted a plan to expunge the records of some fifty thousand men jailed because of their crime: homosexuality.[6]

The "Disappeared of the Disappeared"

As North Americans, we are inspired by LGBTQ Archive Activists in South America and Europe who deal with issues of life and death—even being "disappeared." Their searches have continued for decades as part of national truth telling and reparations projects. In Spain there is the Association of Ex-Social Prisoners of the Franco regime, launched in 2004, headed by Antoni Ruiz. The so-called social prisoners were political prisoners who opposed the dictatorship of Francisco Franco until the Generalissimo died in 1975.[7] This association is devoted exclusively to documenting the oppression of LGBTQ people in Spain under the Franco regime. In Latin

America the Comunidad Homosexual Argentina has for years been working to include the gay victims of the so-called Dirty War into the findings of the National Commission on the Disappeared (Comision Nacional Sobre la Desaparicion de Personas). So far they have not been successful because the commission claims that it is unclear whether homosexuals during the Dirty War were disappeared because of their sexual orientation or because of their political beliefs. Professor Omar Encarnación, author of *Out in the Periphery: Latin America's Gay Rights Revolution*, questions the commission's inability to state clearly what happened to gays in Argentina. "Gays are the disappeared among the disappeared," he said.[8] This is the deadly international variant of the historical erasure Archive Activists fight worldwide.

These campaigns to recover the truth begins with Archive Activists searching for the erased and disappeared. What keeps these activists going is their belief that "injustice is routinely documented by those who perpetrate it."[9] All we have to do is find the paper.

Chapter 17

Remember

A decade into our Archive Activism, I thought, How long ago was I mentally ill, according to the American Psychiatric Association? Or just plain guilty of sodomy, according to Texas laws still on the books. Spiritually, I was damned by most all of the churches in Dallas. This was a perfect confluence of doom. But somehow I survived because I received unquestioning love from my family, partners, friends, and mentors along the way. That horrible isolation banished, I now see through the lens of Mattachine's Archive Activism that we Archive Activists are part of a worldwide movement of truth and reconciliation. Here citizens must answer the profoundly simple question about large scale government wrongdoing: "Do you want to remember, or to forget?"[1] How do I reckon with what happened these many years, from my coming up gay in Dallas through the decades-long federal assault on LGBTQ Americans? How to settle the verbal assaults as if they were accounting entries?

deviate
fag/faggot
homo, self-avowed homo

infamous
unnatural
abnormal
the "verts": pervert and invert
revulsion
the five "dis"es: disordered / "objectively disordered,"[2] dishonor-
    able, disloyal, dismissed and disowned
the interventions: "pray away the gay," conversion therapy,
    electroshock therapy, lobotomy
the double *s*: sodomite sinner
unsuitable
queer, the original meaning

If you are under 30, there will be a quiz.

The federal assault spanning decades, from the 1940s to the modern era, demands an answer: Remember or forget? Well over a hundred thousand LGBTQ Americans who served in the United States Armed Forces, the Foreign Service, and the Federal Civil Service were terminated for one cause: their sexual orientation. Many more were investigated, ruined professionally and financially, and rendered socially dead. For many their lives ended at that moment, sometimes with suicide. Others were able to claw back some portion of their dignity through FOIA research to reveal how they were abused and terminated; some who served in the military have taken their cases to court for judicial review and an honorable discharge. The living and dead, the families and children ask, Where do all of us go for honor to be restored? There is no restorative window in Washington. The honor is in official remembrance.

So we must remember.

Thankfully, many of America's allies—including Britain, Canada, Germany, Australia, Spain, the Netherlands, and Brazil—have already decided to acknowledge what happened. They have apologized for their mistreatment of LGBTQ citizens. The head of Britain's MI6 intelligence service apologized for excluding LGBTQ employees: "It was wrong, unjust and discriminatory," he said.[3]

***

For ten years the Mattachine Society of Washington, DC, researched and documented the animus. To break through the government stone-walling, we were forced to file a lawsuit. Through FOIA requests and litigation, *Mattachine Society of Washington, DC, vs. US Department of Justice*, we obtained thousands of pages of documents that had not already been destroyed.[4] The importance of our litigation was under-scored by national media coverage. The AP reported, "A gay rights group sued the Justice Department for failing to produce hundreds of pages of documents related to a 1953 order signed by President Dwight Eisenhower that empowered federal agencies to investigate and fire employees thought to be gay." Mattachine's counsel Paul Thompson spoke plainly to AP: "What the lawsuit is for us is the final step in saying, 'No, we really are serious, and we're not going to stop until we feel like we have exhausted all possible avenues to obtain these records.'"[5] US District Court judge Royce Lamberth, appointed in 1987 by Ronald Reagan, scorched the FBI when they claimed they had no more documents responsive to our lawsuit: "The Government states that there is not a single responsive document amongst the results," Judge Lamberth wrote in his opinion. "Respectfully, this strains credu-lity." He continued, "It is suspicious at best and malicious at worst for the FBI to assert in one paragraph that the review of 5,500 documents (mentioning the word "pervert") would be burdensome."[6]

Judge Lamberth is described as a "shoot from the hip Texan known for taking a hard line against what he sees as government incompe-tence" (and was valedictorian of his San Antonio high school class).[7] Judge Lamberth agreed with our outrage when the government claimed delivering the documents to us would be "overly burden-some." The court ruled in our favor, finding the FBI's search was flat out "inadequate." If words mean anything, the "pervert" word count is an appalling measure of pure bigotry. Think about it: five thousand uses of the pejorative "pervert" turned up in FBI files by computer search. This is the heavy footprint of animus as we had been empha-sizing all along.

We pressed our case and obtained hundreds more pages.

Congress led the charge with relentless purging of these accused perverts from public service, so we documented that. We could not let another generation forget this or bear it another day. We formed an Acknowledgment and Apology group to work with our project leader and board member Jeff Trammell. We enumerated the evidentiary history for the untold thousands whose careers were upended and ruined—which we believe requires a reckoning. The final product of a two-year research project by a core team of five attorneys guided by Lisa Linsky and Paul Thompson, the Mattachine/McDermott white paper is titled *America's Promise of Reconciliation and Redemption: The Need for an Official Acknowledgment and Apology for the Historic Government Assault on LGBT Federal Employees and Military Personnel.*[8]

The federal assault was not only about LGBTQ Americans. It was also about civil rights itself. Our white paper highlights how homophobia was used to undermine the Civil Rights Movement of the sixties. In an effort to derail Dr. Martin Luther King's March on Washington, the arch-racist senator from North Carolina Strom Thurmond delivered a forty-five-minute diatribe on the floor of the Senate attacking African American Bayard Rustin. "Mr. March on Washington himself," Thurmond sneered.[9] Thurmond outed Rustin for "sexual perversion," instantly transforming Bayard Rustin into *the* most famous homosexual in America.[10]

The word *intersectionality*, a scholarly term controversialized by Florida's ban on teaching it, is the connection between issues like gay rights and civil rights. "Not the same struggle, but a shared struggle," it has been well said.[11] I prefer the more prosaic term *crossroads*, where people join together on their way to a common destination. Civil Rights icon John Lewis wrote, "I have fought too hard and too long against discrimination based on race and color not to stand up against discrimination based on sexual orientation."[12]

***

Our destination must be obtaining a formal acknowledgment and apology from the United States Congress. We remain inspired by

Queen Elizabeth's royal pardon granted to Alan Turing. But how to possibly make our case for an acknowledgment in this time of roiling polarization? That was the question we posed Jeff Trammell, a six-foot-seven-inch-tall standout collegiate basketball player and former rector (chairman) of the board of visitors of the College of William & Mary who serves on the Colonial Williamsburg Foundation board of directors. Jeff combines an athlete's discipline with a historian's perspective. He served as senior advisor for LGBTQ outreach on both the Gore (2000) and Kerry (2004) presidential campaigns. We were thrilled Jeff stepped forward to head Mattachine's Acknowledgment and Apology Project. Trammell and our attorneys began by examining all such apologies ever delivered by Congress. These apologies cover a debris field of government wrongdoing, in part redeemed by the truth. Over the past thirty years, such formal apologies have gone to Native Americans, twice to African Americans, and once to Japanese Americans, Native Hawaiians, and American descendants of Chinese immigrants.

Jeff composed Mattachine's resolution and worked to shape the final draft with Senate legislative staff and the McDermott legal team. It is a historic resolution with a "Whereas" for every count of mistreatment and discrimination, culminating in a formal Article of Acknowledgment with apology.[13] Introduced in the Senate in 2021 by Senators Tim Kaine (D-VA) and Tammy Baldwin (D-WI), the four-page resolution begins: "Whereas the Federal Government discriminated against and terminated hundreds of thousands of lesbian, gay, bisexual and transgender individuals who served the United States in the Armed Forces, the Foreign Service, and the Federal Civil Service for decades, causing untold harm to those individuals professionally, socially, and medically, among other harms . . ." (see appendix 3).

Richard Baker, the Senate's first official historian, a post he held from 1975 until his retirement in 2009, wrote to us some years back, "with my appreciation and respect for your work in opening new chapters in the Senate history." From this distinguished historian of the Senate, we drew inspiration.

117TH CONGRESS
1ST SESSION **S. RES. 275**

Acknowledging and apologizing for the mistreatment of, and discrimination against, lesbian, gay, bisexual, and transgender individuals who served the United States in the Armed Forces, the Foreign Service, and the Federal civil service.

IN THE SENATE OF THE UNITED STATES

Mr. KAINE (for himself and Ms. BALDWIN) submitted the following resolution; which was referred to the Committee on _____

RESOLUTION

Acknowledging and apologizing for the mistreatment of, and discrimination against, lesbian, gay, bisexual, and transgender individuals who served the United States in the Armed Forces, the Foreign Service, and the Federal civil service.

Whereas the Federal Government discriminated against and terminated hundreds of thousands of lesbian, gay, bisexual, and transgender (referred to in this preamble as "LGBT") individuals who served the United States in the Armed Forces, the Foreign Service, and the Federal civil service (referred to in this preamble as "civilian employees") for decades, causing untold harm to those individuals professionally, financially, socially, and medically, among other harms;

Senate Resolution of Acknowledgment and Apology to LGBT Americans introduced in 2021 by Senators Tim Kaine (D-VA) and Tammy Baldwin (D-WI).

Archive Activism goes nowhere without reaching out to the public, so we went to film and video producer/director Patrick Sammon, who by now had become a member of our extended Mattachine family. We asked Patrick to think as an Archive Activist to make our most persuasive case to Congress. He did so with an R = A passion as Mattachine's producer, director, and writer of "The Acknowledgment." Archival sources for the video included the Eisenhower Presidential Library, the US National Library of Medicine, the National Museum of Health and Medicine, the US Senate Historical Office, the National Archives, and the Library of Congress. "Support is growing in Congress for a formal acknowledgment and apology to LGBT Americans for six decades of mistreatment and discrimination," the video begins. "It all began with Stonewall."[14]

The resolutions introduced in both the Senate and House lay out the case for acknowledgment and apology in fully documented statements of fact that may no longer be contested or disputed with so-called counterfactuals or plain denial. It is tough to read the twenty-nine damning statements aloud without a tear—each one of them documented by us, our attorneys, and our teams of allies and congressional staff. These statements are an indisputable montage of terminations, discharges, investigations, harassment, and purges. Appalling and all true, they are ultimately inspiring because they are both an acknowledgment and a redeeming statement of fact. Both the Senate and House resolutions acknowledge, and on behalf of the United States, apologize and reaffirm the commitment of the federal government to treat all with equal respect and dignity.

***

We were gratified with the response we received from the LGBTQ community. An *LGBTQ Nation* opinion piece said it all: "An American apology for decades of anti-LGBTQ persecution is long overdue." The commentary said, "It's not as if such an apology is unprecedented. Congress has acknowledged past injustices, apologizing to Native Americans, Japanese Americans and Native Hawaiians, among other marginalized groups they've harmed. . . . The apology would be largely symbolic—the bills do not seek reparations for those harmed by the decades of persecution. But even as a gesture, the apology would mean a lot to many."[15]

Omar Encarnación wrote in his persuasive book *The Case for Gay Reparations*, "America's gay rights revolution seems unfinished or incomplete in the absence of a national reckoning with the country's shameful systematic anti-gay discrimination."[16] In his title Professor Encarnación uses the word "reparations"; we do not. "Reparations," however defined—whether as commissions, memorials, pardons, or financial reimbursement—range over a multitude of historical reckonings. We do not argue for financial reparations. Of course, there is no comparison with the atrocities underlying the case for racial reparations. Despite our emphasis on acknowledgment and apology, Omar Encarnación continued, "I wholeheartedly endorse the efforts by the Mattachine Society of Washington, DC, the leading American advocate for gay reparations, to secure an official acknowledgment and apology from the US Congress inspired by the pardon issued by the British parliament."[17] Professor Encarnación devoted the second chapter in that book, "Digging Up a Painful Past: Archive Activism," to describe Mattachine's mission and work documenting the facts and making the case for an official acknowledgment and apology from the Congress.

The separate Senate and House resolutions are set on a foundation of history, contributed to and verified by our team of authorities and friends like Evan Wolfson, founder of Freedom to Marry; David K. Johnson, author of *The Lavender Scare: The Cold War Persecution of Gays* (2004); and Aubrey Sarvis, former executive director of the Servicemembers Legal Defense Network, who played a key role in advocating the repeal of Don't Ask, Don't Tell. This acknowledgment and apology will one day happen for the benefit and full dignity of future generations of LGBTQ Americans and our families. It will be impossible to erase. The twin Congressional Resolutions of Acknowledgment and Apology stand as a baseline of facts about our past for citizen Archive Activists to come.

"We believe the time has come to understand and acknowledge the historical animus that LGBTQ federal employees and military personnel faced for generations from their own government to ensure it can never happen again," Jeff Trammell said.[18] With a sense of history, we have bearings in today's ongoing fights over teaching history and "saying gay." Without our history we stand naked before the chaos of hatred, seen at its violent worst at the barricades during the storming of the US Capitol on January 6. Distilled in a chilling moment of video, the Capitol Police bravely fought the mob as it assaulted them in hand-to-hand combat. Above the roar, a crazed rioter hurled the worst insult he could imagine at a besieged officer: "F——ing prick! FAGGOT!"[19] The verbal assault was delivered to stun. The barricades were breached.

Chapter 18

In Buffalo Bill's Cody: Traveling While Gay

T his might be one of the best days of my life.

I was thinking such a thing in 2015, holding our son, Thomas, while giving him his bottle in front of a small hotel in Cody, Wyoming. He was wearing his Superman tee. It was one of those sparkling, Western summer mornings. We are the same as most families—but not. We are a nontraditional family, a kid with two dads.

Stephen, Thomas, and I were on our way to Yellowstone Park. I was serving as a trustee of the Western art and history museum The Buffalo Bill Center of the West, named for the great showman Buffalo Bill (with his Wild West Show starring Annie Oakley). I loved writing the Center's credo—an optimistic statement of belief in The Spirit of the American West.

While absorbed in the world of Buffalo Bill and Thomas, I was approached by a friendly police officer and his female colleague. It was all so casual, I thought nothing of it. "Howdy," he said. "You and Superman look like you're enjoying yourselves."

"Yes, for sure, always glad to be in Cody," I replied, still not understanding what was happening.

"What brings you here?" he responded.

I told him all about my service as a trustee over the years at the Buffalo Bill museum, Cody's number one tourist attraction. He continued his questions, and I gamely told him about my husband and I being from Washington and loving the Yellowstone / Big Horn region. I thought a second about using the *husband* word, but why edit myself? I was entirely comfortable in my own skin at this point in my life out West. Stephen frequently counsels me to speak honestly about being a gay dad with a husband and not using the usual self-protective terms like *my friend* or my *partner* ("*pard*" in Western parlance).

Then things got honest. The officer's partner walked forward to stand at his side above me on the bench, still dealing with a baby bottle.

"Sorry to bother you," he said, "but we got a problem."

I understood then. If they had a problem, so did I.

"We have a report of a missing child in the region and need to ask you some questions. Are you his grandpa?"

I caught my breath. "No, his dad."

"His dad." I flashed back to what a joy it first was for Stephen and me to say that about our son Thomas Francis Bottum, our Superman kid. We were blessed to welcome Thomas into our family in 2014. Our deep gratitude for this and everyone who helped us on our surrogacy journey to parenthood kept me strong even as I was questioned by the police. I understand now my brother and sister-in-law's reactions—parents themselves and fans of the Dallas Cowboys—when I told them Stephen and I were expecting. "Welcome to the NFL," my brother said, playing off the saying "Welcome to the big time"— sometimes a very rough big time.

I told the officers that Stephen and I were married, staying in the hotel. "I'm here for a board meeting of the Buffalo Bill. Our chairman is Senator Alan Simpson—a great friend of mine, he will speak for me," I scrambled. The officer asked for some identification, so I juggled baby Thomas, dug into my wallet, and handed over my driver's license. This wasn't enough.

"So do you have something with his name on it? You are his parent?" This required that we all go upstairs to the room where Stephen, without warning, was brought into the scary unfolding drama. I explained it all to him—thinking how much worse for my credibility if I had not told the whole story that I had a husband.

The officers apologized once again, but pressed on. At this point, thank God, Stephen pulled Thomas's passport from his pack. Stephen is always so organized, but how could he imagine we would suddenly be under suspicion in a missing child multistate hunt with no description of a suspect?

The police explained they were contacted by our hotel about two men registered with a child. I am sure my blood pressure skyrocketed when I heard this. Profiled by a homophobe. We had been staying at this place for years. Evidently, the new lady at the front desk became suspicious when she got word of a missing child bulletin with no description of a suspect, because there were no suspects. I wondered, had she even *seen* an LGBTQ family before? Of course she had, but to her they were invisible beings in line at the Walmart.

The officer examined Thomas's passport (thank goodness we had one) and apologized again for the awkward questioning. We told him we understood completely, and could only imagine what the parents of the actual missing child must be going through. Situation resolved, I thought, and began putting the day back on track. Roll with it. Don't be a victim, I thought. "Pull your socks up, sonny," as they say in Scotland.

But it was not resolved. The police returned within a half hour.

"We still have a problem," he said. I was so angered to hear this. My explanations did not hold up back at the station. They were now worried that our son resembled the missing kid—same blonde hair.

So back to our room we went for further questions and comparisons of our boy's face to the pics of the missing child. It was a scary, invasive, and angering moment. And it got worse. The police wanted to take our kid's picture and send it to a headquarters somewhere.

We pushed back. Would it be published? How would it circulate, and how could we protect his privacy as a child and ours as well?

I kept telling myself, "Do not lose it. They are doing their jobs. Be very cool," thinking how easy it would be for me to be hauled into custody as an out-of-control, homosexual male suspect in a missing child case. Can you imagine?

In order to cooperate, and still mindful of the parents' agony, we relented. They took the photograph, emailed it somewhere, and we waited. Minutes passed like days before we got the all clear over their radio. Our son did not have a unique, identifying birthmark on his neck. Now, at last, they were satisfied. They said they were sorry about it all. Our family was no longer under suspicion.

Of course we wanted to help. It was a heartbreaking tragedy that was occurring somewhere. Still, we felt the earth shake beneath our feet. We mistakenly thought, always thought, that we stood on solid ground. That feeling of humiliation and helplessness was new to me, mixed with the primal fear of losing our child—of anybody losing their child. When we hear about others profiled, pulled over and questioned for "Driving while Black," we have a pained empathy. The Talk that Black parents must have with their kids about dealing with the police is not abstract for me now. No matter how gay-vanilla we thought we looked, two men with an infant was a big red flag to a desk clerk in a small town. Gays and lesbians as parents, foster parents, adopted parents—especially as teachers—have had some version of "child protection" thrown at us for decades.

Oh, how we thought of going after that desk clerk with a formal letter of complaint to the hotel's corporate headquarters. But we concluded it was better to let it go than to let the anger poison us. Today, we are card-carrying members of the Family Equality Council, an organization that advocates for the legal and lived equality of LGBTQ families like ours.

While our family's experience was upsetting, and obviously novel to this Wyoming hotel clerk, I'm encouraged the times are changing. The last census reported nearly 1.2 million people are part of same-sex couple households.[1] I managed my anger to learn how hotel chains like Marriott are stepping up their game, training staff to recognize sketchy situations and differentiate them from families like ours. Beyond fantasies of revenge, we realized no matter how we might wish to fit in and be part of that optimistic Spirit of the American West, we could not pass that day. Our progress remains vulnerable unless all of us—our friends, families, and allies—experience a similar moment of their own or learn about the many kinds of nontraditional families and get involved. What is taken for granted is easily threatened.

We now travel with two of the most important papers in our family archive—a marriage certificate and birth certificate with two dads' names. For us, that is traveling while gay.

***

We became a legal family long before the cloud of suspicion in Cody, because in 2013 federal courts expanded marriage rights for all of us in two landmark rulings. Following court decisions in *Windsor v. United States* and *Hollingsworth v. Perry*, it was held that the federal government could not restrict same-sex marriages and also that same-sex marriages in California could resume. It meant a lot to us that California US District Court judge Vaughn Walker entered the John Macy Revulsion Letter to the Mattachine Society as a "Findings of Fact" in his 2013 decision.[2] This was a momentous and historic year for LGBTQ Americans. For me, it had been more than a decade since the days of the Austin Twelve.

Stephen and I knew it was our turn now. After ten years as partners (or "pards") with zero legal recognition of our relationship (remember when hospital visitation rights were in question?), we became engaged that summer of 2013 on a steep and breathtaking gulch trail overlooking Cook Inlet near our summer home in Homer, Alaska, a community of 5,700 people with its own glacier and twenty-six well-maintained trails cared for by a nonprofit alliance of "avid hikers and walkers."[3] We have renamed that trail— as though it became our private trail; sorry, Alaska—Engagement Trail. We take Thomas there for an annual Engagement Trail hike to the shoreline defined by three active snow-capped volcanos on

Family float-tripping at the Maclaren Glacier, Delta Junction, near Denali,
Alaska. *Left to right*: Charles Francis, Thomas Francis Bottum,
and Stephen Bottum. Photo Francis/Bottum family collection.

the horizon overlooking Cook Inlet. I call them the Bitter Queens.[4]
(Oh, how I could have become one.) From Engagement Trail and the
Bitter Queens to the District of Columbia, we were married at the
decidedly less romantic DC Superior Court. We loved our District
of Columbia officiant (and her name), Despina Belle-Isle. Before
she began the ceremony, she hit us with a simple question: "Do you
know how serious a commitment and moment this is?"

"Yes, ma'am, Ms. Belle-Isle, we do."

There with Stephen's mom, Cherie, and his sister, Angela,
and her partner (soon her spouse), Marjorie, and dear friends like
Bob Witeck, my Mattachine Archive Activist compadre Pate, and
Jason Raymond, who helped Mattachine uncover eye-popping
documents, we gathered beneath the most gorgeous plastic bower
of flowers we had ever seen with a superb view of the National
Mall. We understood the gravity and wonderfulness of our personal

decision, supported by lifelong friends Jacqueline LaPierre and Chris Coffin. We tapped into our entire community's newly acquired marriage equality and celebrated at our reception with Al Simpson, in from Cody, who stood with us all the way. Stephen's uncle and his dear lady friend from the small farm community of Tulare, South Dakota (population 211 in 2020), joined us. Ours was definitely not a destination wedding, but it was the destination of a lifetime. Nine months later, we were blessed with the birth of a baby boy. Today, we walk to elementary school as a family with Thomas Francis Bottum on a street renamed Frank Kameny Way.

What a long road to Frank Kameny Way.

Chapter 19

At Hoover's Grave

The J. Edgar Hoover Foundation, now defunct, was not pleased with the media coverage or snickering about the proximity of Hoover's grave at Congressional Cemetery to his spouse-like partner and FBI deputy Clyde Tolson. The problem kept arising. Tolson inherited the Hoover estate, moved into the man's house, and accepted the flag that draped his coffin. In 2007 Linda Harper, chairperson of Congressional Cemetery, received a stern letter of complaint: "While it may be understandable that your Association wishes to garner the public's interest with colorful tours of the Congressional Cemetery, the Board of Directors and I are deeply offended by the cheap shot mischaracterization of former FBI Director J. Edgar Hoover on a recent tour of the cemetery." The problem of Hoover's relationship with Tolson, "rumored to be his homosexual lover," was directly addressed: "At Hoover's family grave, with perhaps a misplaced attempt at humor, she [the tour guide] reduced Mr. Hoover's life to rumors of homosexuality, a personal and monumental distortion . . . an attempt to assassinate the character of J. Edgar Hoover."[1]

The mission of the Hoover Foundation, chaired by the FBI's retired number three man after Hoover and Tolson, Cartha "Deke" DeLoach (1920–2013), was to protect the reputation of Hoover, maybe defend him from outright ridicule, but it could never stave off tour guides, Archive Activists, and history's final judgment. Standing alongside Hoover's grave is the perfect place to ponder the rumors and the actual deeds of the man who invented the FBI's Sex Deviates program, a program to rid the government of homosexuals.

The Sex Deviates program established Hoover's "uniform policy for the handling of the increasing number of reports and allegations concerning the present and past employees of the United States Government who assertedly are sex deviates," the Hoover memo states. This memo, which the Mattachine team discovered, explains how the FBI would forward this information to the US Civil Service Commission (today's OPM) for action to investigate and terminate the untold thousands of federal employees whose careers (and often their lives) were ruined. The Hoover sex deviates memo continued, "Each supervisor will be held personally responsible to underline in green pencil," Hoover obsessed, "the name of individuals mentioned in any report, letter, memorandum, newspaper or article or other communication who are alleged to be sex deviates."[2]

We were excited to share this find with Hoover experts like Douglas Charles, author of *Hoover's War on Gays: Exposing the FBI's "Sex Deviates" Program*,[3] and Matt Apuzzo, the *New York Times* journalist who confirmed its importance. "Mr. Francis has been collecting documents on the government's anti-gay policies, filling a gap that he sees in the archives of the gay rights movement. . . . Mining government documents has typically been the purview of scholars," wrote Apuzzo.[4] We like the idea of "mining" government documents. Some activists in the seventies famously stole them.

Thanks to the breathtaking activist burglary of the Media, Pennsylvania, FBI office, America learned there were two FBIs— one public and one dark. The dark FBI ran a domestic spying program focused on one project: crushing American dissent.

"Hoover's secret FBI was a lawless and unprincipled arm of the bureau that suppressed dissent of Americans," wrote Betty Medsger in *The Burglary: The Discovery of Hoover's Secret FBI*.[5] Medsger focused on the Civil Rights and antiwar movements, but like so many histories, Medsger barely mentions Hoover's obsessive war on homosexuals, green pencils and all. It takes a lot to degay the J. Edgar Hoover story. The FBI's files on homosexuals reached some three hundred thousand pages over twenty-five years until they were destroyed, one of the triggers of the Presidential Records Act of 1978 and our own frustrations in the archive.[6] More revelations, such as the Sex Deviates program, would be for others, including us, to research in later years as Archive Activists.

My friend Dudley Clendinen, a former *New York Times* national correspondent and editorial writer, discovered shortly before his passing in 2012 how Hoover had destroyed his godfather, Arthur Vandenberg Jr. Dudley published his conclusions, drawing upon our research, in the *Times*. "Just before Christmas in 1952, J. Edgar Hoover . . . let President Eisenhower know that the man Eisenhower had appointed as Secretary to the President, his friend and chief of staff, my godfather, Arthur H. Vandenberg, Jr., was a homosexual." Vandenberg was dropped and professionally ruined. Clendinen well understood what happened. "It was part of a pattern of persecution that would destroy thousands of lives and careers," he wrote.[7]

The question is often asked, Was Hoover gay? The importance of the Sex Deviates discoveries moots that question with a, Who cares? Launching the government assault on LGBTQ Americans with President Eisenhower and turning the FBI into a central player of the so-called Lavender Scare antigay purge at the State Department, Hoover was the most determined government foe, gay or straight, we ever faced.

In front of his grave, one can reflect on this confirmed bachelor's assault on our democracy—bugging, investigating, and threatening to expose his targets, like Martin Luther King. Hoover's personal passion was to investigate homosexuals, civil rights activists, and accused

Communists, like the infamously outed Bayard Rustin—a twofer for
Hoover. The afternoon Hoover was lowered like a piano into his grave
in a 1,400-pound lead coffin, President Richard Nixon delivered his
eulogy (a month before the Watergate burglary). It was a nauseating
discourse on this *giant* among Americans who "personified integrity"
and "personified honor."[8] Our mission as Archive Activists is to shake
that lead coffin with documents, truth, and reckonings of our own.

Humor is essential in this as well. As a gay Texan, I can laugh at
the awful friendship of Hoover, Clyde Tolson, and old oilmen Clint
Murchison Sr. and Sid Richardson, another lifelong bachelor. Year
after year this loving, self-interested foursome would reunite at the
Murchison-owned Hotel del Charro in La Jolla, California. Hoover
and Tolson held court there for two weeks in summer from 1953 to
1971, paid for by Murchison.[9]

Members of the British royal family are traditionally buried in
lead-lined coffins because it supposedly helps preserve the body
far longer. Preserving Hoover's body is a Gothic thought. There is
always humor to be found. This is why I am smiling, not scowl-
ing, at the graveside with our Mattachine same-sex marriage amicus
brief that prevailed.[10] Richard Nixon should have told the story
about when LBJ and his close aide and bag man, Bobby Baker, were
driving past Hoover's common forties red-brick house, now hilariously a DC landmark. Baker, while enjoying his afternoon beer in
the waning months of his life at an assisted living facility in Florida,
told us there stood Hoover and Tolson in the front yard.

"Well, there's Mr. and Mrs. Hoover," Johnson quipped to Baker.[11]

It is perversely funny, too, that Washington's storied Mayflower
Hotel, with its gilded hallways, has a bar and restaurant named the
Edgar Bar & Kitchen. The Mayflower captions the Edgar Bar &
Kitchen on their website as "The Ultimate DC Power Player, J. Edgar
Hoover, Dined Here Daily."[12] Alongside the Edgar Bar is the Tolson,
a venue for meetings and special events. "Tolson promises to surprise
as the alter ego of Edgar," the Mayflower goes on.[13] I wonder how
the J. Edgar Hoover Foundation might react if it were still around?

Hoover and Tolson did have lunch daily for twenty years at their corner table in the Mayflower. A Washington humorist might play with the Edgar Bar & Kitchen and the Tolson as if it were all a big campy joke, but we are in the twenty-first century now. Washington has the highest LGBTQ population percentage in the United States,[14] and this scene is a few blocks away from DC's largest LGBTQ neighborhoods, Dupont and Logan Circles.

We all need to reckon with this history. At least legislation has been introduced to create a national commission to rename the J. Edgar Hoover FBI headquarters.[15] Moving on to another Washington hotel, let's meet several blocks away at the Hay-Adams by Lafayette Park, where the first organizational meeting of the Mattachine Society of Washington, DC, was held in 1961 at 8:00 p.m. in room 120.

An FBI informant reported back to Hoover that sixteen men were there to hear Frank Kameny's presentation on a new society dedicated to full equality for gays and lesbians—eight years before New York City police raided the Stonewall Inn. Author James Kirchick writes, "The most meaningful way to recognize Kameny and the positive change he effected would be for Room 120 of the Hay-Adams to earn a place in American history as illustrious as that of the Stonewall Inn."[16] Whether by plaque or national registry, we should get this done.

Like paintings in an exhibition, each of our archival discoveries and the stories we tell have their own subjects and moods, ranging from erasure to horror. And each has a tone. The cool ones are about self-invention and resilience. There are those that are smoking hot in anger and struggle for equality and civil rights. There are the dark themes of diagnosis, psychiatric "cures," and governmental verbal assault. There are movements of emergence with bursting spring colors of Pride. What ties them all together, running through my imaginary exhibition, are the hues of the American prairie, an image of LGBTQ Americans inventing for themselves a new world in which we may openly live and love as pioneer citizens under the Constitution. At Hoover's grave, I think of these American pioneers and the history they lived, preserved and bequeathed to us all.

Chapter 20

"What's Today?"

"What's today?" cried Scrooge calling downward to a boy
in Sunday clothes. . . . "What's today, my fine fellow?" said
Scrooge.

"Today?" replied the boy. "Why it's Christmas Day!'"

"It's Christmas Day," said Scrooge to himself. "I haven't
missed it. The Spirits have done it all in one night. They can do
anything they like. Of course they can."[1]

After a long night, Ebeneezer Scrooge threw back the curtains, opened
the window, and had a moment of ecstatic clarity and hope. It was
not too late. Ever since I was a boy in Dallas, reading along with
one of my 45-rpm talking storybooks narrated by Charles Laughton,
this Dickens moment has thrilled me; even now it represents a fresh
start full of hope. It can be that same moment for all of us, even in
the turmoil of our politics and historic divisions that challenge the
existence of American democracy.

It's not too late, if only we do not give up on each other.

Like Rosa Parks, Frank Kameny, and so many other LGBTQ
pioneers, we need to connect with what James Baldwin called "that

THE
MATTACHINE SOCIETY
OF WASHINGTON DC

Frank Kameny on Kameny Way. Illustration
by permission of the artist, Eric Orner.

great force of history . . . within us."[2] When Baldwin wrote these
words for *Ebony* magazine, he was writing about the fight for racial
justice. Yet as a Black man mocked and disparaged for being queer, he
would approve, I believe, of his ideas' application to LGBTQ Americans.[3]

We share a queer kinship with James Baldwin. Today, as never before, all of us must pay attention to our history, the big-sky story that unites us as we steadily expand the notion of individual liberty and democracy—yes, even from the darkness of 1619 to the Spirit of '76 to Montgomery and Stonewall. LGBTQ America has no mythical past, only an erased or minimized history, easily taken for granted by those among us who never knew the "bad old days." Archive Activists know there is nothing inevitable or permanent about our legal status or civil equality. We are traveling while LGBTQ.

***

"Make yourself useful" is a secret to happiness one hears from an older generation of Texans. I like this bracing advice because of its simplicity. How are you giving yourself to help the other person cross the river? "When you help them across, lo, thy boat has crossed the river, too," the saying goes. Here, then, are some Unclassified Principles of Archive Activism we draw from our own excavations. I hope you will consider them—and make yourself useful as an Archive Activist. Our community depends upon that spirit, and always will.

Lilli Vincenz's 16 mm projector on the set of C-SPAN's *Reel America*.
Lilli's citizen film distribution, our inspiration. Photo by Charles Francis.

Conclusion

The Unclassified Principles of Archive Activism

"There will come a time when you believe everything is finished. That will be the beginning."

Louis L'Amour[1]

1. Think historically in the archive, not only politically in the news. Place current events into the broad historical sweep of things, beyond candidates, polls, or "electeds." Looking back on our experience, we learned how to "be comfortable being uncomfortable" as open LGBTQ Americans, making ourselves more vulnerable and more convincing, educating people over decades. When the Austin Twelve met with Governor Bush, 35 percent of Americans polled by Gallup believed same-sex marriage "should be valid." Today, the approval number has soared beyond 70 percent,[2] with some seven hundred thousand people in same-sex marriages.[3] Congress affirmed this progress with a strong bipartisan vote for the Respect for Marriage Act (2022), repealing the Defense of Marriage Act. President Biden signed the bill surrounded by dozens of same-sex couples and their families who sued for marriage rights. Think historically.

2. This is for LGBTQ seniors: It is within your power to reach across generations during this revolution. "This happened." "I was investigated." "I was discharged." "I fought for my dignity." "I loved and was loved." The best way to do this is to save and donate your personal papers to a library or history society. The key tool of the archivist is a long folding table. Like Lilli Vincenz, pull out the crates, lay your papers on that table in piles, then stacks, then move the stacks around. Label them. Make it impossible for someone to toss or shred your papers after you are gone. The fireplace, in the old days, and the garbage bag or shredder, today, is our worst enemy. Do not let that happen. Washington journalist Chris Geidner, a self-avowed Archive Activist, warns a time of maximum threat to LGBTQ papers and historic photographs is when elders move out of their offices or downsize to an assisted living facility or move in with family. Make a plan to save your materials.

3. See yourself as a pioneer. Chris Geidner continues, "The indispensable role of Archive Activism is to correct the record and challenge the established narrative."[4] If you are not a professional historian, glory in that. You have fewer constraints. Despite the fact that a vast majority of Americans believe history is a set of facts and dates, understand that history belongs in the liberal art of *explaining* what happened. In Mississippi, researching our "Negroes," "Agitators," and "Racial Perverts" project, we asked questions like "why" and "how" about erased wrongdoing, not so much "when." We kept asking, "How was this secret maintained?" "And why was it buried by all of the players complicit in silence?" Correct the record with Archive Activism.

4. For youngers, talk to LGBTQ elders. Make those connections. Tear down the walls between LGBTQ generations, the distrust and ageism rampant in our community. Frank Kameny was in his 80s with a world in his attic. Pull down that ladder; climb up there. Think like historian Allan Bérubé, who researched a cache of letters discovered in a dumpster to begin his groundbreaking history of

gays who served in the military in World War II.[5] There is a vast store of materials and memories that can set you on the right path as an Archive Activist. Seniors are not invisible window panes. They can be gold mines of experience and local history. Geidner writes, "If you know someone who has lived between Stonewall and the Nineties who played a role in some aspect of the movement, interview them; get the information down. Ask them questions."[6] A good example is the Invisible Histories Project in Alabama, which is focused on saving Southern LGBTQ history by collecting to "tell the story of the Queer South." I love their tagline: "Archives for All, Y'all."[7]

5. Practice and study public history. "LGBTQ+ history is American history," declared the National Parks Foundation as it worked to preserve our histories across the country.[8] Remember R = A (research = activism), and become part of that movement. Learn how to research primary materials, transcribe and interpret sources, learn about historiography, and put Google in proper perspective as a secondary resource. Then volunteer in your community.

6. If you cannot get an advanced degree in archival studies, there are shorter certificate programs that focus on archival studies that may be completed in two or three semesters.

7. Defend your local library. Librarians are on the frontlines. In 2022 there were 1,269 demands to censor library books and materials, nearly double the 729 book censorship attempts in 2021.[9] According to the American Library Association (ALA), "The vast majority (of these books) were written by or about members of the LGBTQ community and people of color."[10] These numbers will continue to grow. Speak out. Remember the Nazi bonfire. Defend the power of books. Meet archivists and LGBTQ librarians. Their minds are tumblers that unlock vaults, and they love stories. They'll know about people like 105-year-old Mildred Stegall, who guarded LBJ's stash. Our work at the National Archives on the gay World War II–spy Thomas Stauffer would have been impossible without the coaching and imagination of librarians.

8. Attend an archives bazaar where museum curators, archivists, and librarians teach people how to properly preserve their own materials. Start a local LGBTQ archives bazaar. We need them.

9. Support the National Archives of the United States when it opens presidential papers and investigates violations of the Presidential Records Act. America's archive is the bone marrow of our democracy. Consider becoming a Citizen Archivist for the National Archives. This volunteer program had some six thousand members in 2022, transcribing documents and tagging photographs with keywords to make them more searchable.

10. Support the cause of archives worldwide that open their files to researchers and historians and human rights activists, as Ukraine did in 2015, or like the Russian human rights group that won the Nobel Peace Prize in 2022, "Memorial," that has created a memory archive of Joseph Stalin's victims as well as human rights violations in Russia.[11]

11. Get involved with public interest law firms and the major law firms in your city. Many have a strong volunteer component. Our Archive Activism could not have happened without our unique partnership with McDermott Will & Emery. "The first project I got involved with was the Supreme Court amicus brief in the Obergefell [same-sex marriage] case. I think the highlight of my career was being able to sign my name to that amicus brief," said one McDermott partner in our video *Archive Activism and Evidentiary History*.[12] Write a letter (not an email) to a partner or associate who is openly LGBTQ. Better yet, introduce yourself to one of these folks at a Pride month gathering, or come up to them at a bar association event and invite them for lunch or coffee. They will know about the public history projects and active cases in your area. You may need their help in accessing documents that are often locked away or sealed or are available only by formal public-records requests. They need Archive Activist partners.

12. If you already see yourself as a self-avowed Archive Activist, whether LGBTQ or not, run for election to a local school board. Support local schools' efforts to strengthen the teaching of history apart from politics, using critical thinking skills to understand our American heritage.

13. Finally, harness the power of history wherever you may live. The St. Louis LGBT History Project worked with Washington University to create a mapping project of key historical LGBTQ sites from 1945 to 1992 in St. Louis. The Southwest Virginia LGBTQ+ History Project in Roanoke is "an example of queer public history practice combined with the strategies and tactics of grassroots community organizing," an excellent example in the South.[13]

There is so much need in the American town square, where civic engagement is vital. Great debates and policy challenges need volunteers who understand R = A. Flip over the rocks. The media has little time and no budget. Share your research on a platter of joyous activism.

***

My "uniquely nasty" journey started with a historical family heritage that gave me a frame of reference for the years to come. Then, twenty years ago, facing my own moment of truth ("All right, then, I'll go to Hell"),[14] I learned to embrace our LGBTQ history, not run from it—or myself. With this I understood the importance of the Kameny attic, where we helped rescue both the man and his papers. The pace quickened as we uncovered documents produced by a government operating on the idea that I and millions more like me were damaged, deranged, disloyal, and unworthy of legal protection for our relationships. Like the German antisemitisms of the '30s, we were labeled a uniquely nasty people.

The story heightened when I met my husband, Stephen, who taught me about degayed history, such as what Mattachine discovered at St. Elizabeths Hospital for the Insane. Discovering thousands of pages of documents and photographs, Pate Felts and I were joined by the McDermott Will & Emery team, who helped us translate raw animus into evidentiary history. Through amicus briefs, litigation, white papers, articles, press events, and videos, we shined a bright light on the bigoted ideas and put them in proper legal, historical context. We exercised our First Amendment rights—not to cancel anybody but to put bigotry and bad theories through both rigorous analysis and a reckoning in the form of Resolutions of Acknowledgment and Apology in the Senate and House of Representatives.

We did this in the spirit of Archive Activism.

We are not historians. We are activist citizens with library cards—a tough combination to beat with uncensored, well-funded public libraries. Public libraries are where Archive Activism lives—like the Archives of Sexuality and Gender at the New York Public Library, home to the papers and photographs of pioneer activists Barbara Gittings and Kay Tobin Lahusen; or the Denver Public Library, home to the papers of Equality Colorado, which fought Amendment 2 and "the bare desire to harm a politically unpopular group."[15] In Florida, where the teaching of history is now actually regulated, the Stonewall National Museum and Archives in Fort Lauderdale, which celebrated its fiftieth anniversary in February 2023, remains an important resource.[16]

If you visit Washington, DC, do not be intimidated by the Library of Congress. The library and its dedicated staff love Archive Activists. A review of the papers of Frank Kameny or Lilli Vincenz in the Library's Manuscript Division is a thrilling way to experience the work of these pioneers. There are college and university LGBTQ archives, like the new William & Mary Archive of American LGBTQ Political and Legal History in Williamsburg, Virginia; and the collection created by the avid collector, Jean-Nickolaus Tretter in his St. Paul apartment, today the Tretter Collection in Gay, Lesbian, Bisexual and Transgender Studies at the University of Minnesota. In Texas there is the University of North Texas Libraries Special Collections, containing the Dallas Way LGBTQ historical archive. All of these are worth visiting in person or online. The largest LGBTQ archive,

ONE Archives at the University of Southern California Libraries—the leading repository of early Mattachine Society materials—works with community partners across California to offer an LGBTQ-inclusive history curriculum. In Washington, the DC History Center has developed an innovative archival processing program, partnering with Washington's Rainbow History Project and the US Naval Academy. Newly reexamined collections that "queer the archive" across the country explode possibilities. This is the archive, a sea of data for exploration and passionate use. Here is where you will find the voice of the documents, and your voice, too: the vox docs.

The archive is there for you to rekindle James Baldwin's "great force of history" that we carry within us. Feel it.

Sign in.

Appendixes

Some Archive Activist Discoveries

Appendix 1: "Uniquely Nasty" Memorandum

Discovery site: Homosexuality and Suitability Legal Advisory Files; Records of the US Civil Service Commission, Record Group 146; National Archives at College Park, MD.

Homosexuality and Government employment
By John W. Steele
Chief, Program Systems and Instructions Division
US Civil Service Commission
October 14, 1964

In considering this subject, I believe it is necessary to distinguish at the outset between homosexuality as a security factor and homosexuality as a suitability factor.

The security requirements for Government employment are set forth in Executive Order 10450. The Order provides that the occupant of a sensitive position must have a full field investigation designed to develop information as to whether the employment of that individual is clearly consistent with the interest of national security. Among the kinds of information identified by the Order as pertinent in this regard are the following:

Any criminal, infamous, dishonest, immoral, or notoriously disgraceful conduct, habitual use of intoxicants to excess, drug addiction, or sexual perversion.

Any facts which furnish reason to believe that the individual may be subjected to coercion, influence, or pressure which may cause him to act contrary to the best interests of the national security.

Although there are dissenting voices, our society generally regards homosexuality as a form of immoral conduct. Also, our social attitudes being what they are, a homosexual is extremely vulnerable to blackmail: exposure means public opprobrium and, in the case of a Government employee, the loss of his job. Thus, under the terms of the Order, evidence of past or present homosexuality renders the individual unacceptable for a sensitive position. Action in these cases, therefore, is determined not so much by policy as by the intent of the Order.

On the suitability side, the essential instructions, standards and guides . . .

From the foregoing, it is evident that we set homosexuality apart from other forms of immoral conduct and take a much more severe attitude toward it. In evaluating other morals cases we consider such factors as the seriousness of the act or acts, the age of the individual at the time the conduct occurred, the individual's general reputation, the recency of the conduct, and so on. In evaluating cases of homosexuality, we automatically find the individual not suitable for Federal employment unless there is <u>evidence of rehabilitation</u>. This is our stated policy. There is room for considerable variation in the application of this policy, however, because nothing whatever has been issued to indicate what the term "evidence of rehabilitation" contemplates.

The result is that our evaluations are quite subjective, depending on the strength of the reviewing official's personal aversion to homosexuality in general and his reaction to the circumstances of the particular case at hand. . . .

Some feel that "once a homo, always a homo" and tend to find against anyone who has ever engaged in such activity. This may have been at the root of the sustention of the FAA's action in the Dew case, although the rationale was something like this: homosexual conduct is the evidence of some emotional imbalance and indicates instability or immaturity; the work of an airport control tower operator is pressure-filled, rigorous, and demands a high degree of steadiness; since there is reason to believe that Dew may have a basic emotional flaw which may someday give under pressure, he is less than a good risk in a job where the safety of human lives is at stake. The fact remains, however, that Dew's homosexual conduct occurred in his youth; that for many years thereafter he lived a normal life with no recurrences of or apparent interest in homosexual activity, that he had a good work record; and that, to all intents and purposes, he was "rehabilitated."

In summary, it seems clear that this is an area in which there is little objectivity. Although it is Commission policy to rule in favor of the individual if there is evidence of rehabilitation, in actual practice we rarely find evidence of rehabilitation. Really, we do not apply Commission policy at all; we apply our own individual emotional reactions and moral standards. *Our tendency to "lean over backwards" to rule against a homosexual is simply a manifestation of the revulsion which homosexuality inspires in the normal person. What it boils down to is that most men look upon homosexuality as something uniquely nasty, not just as a form of immorality* [emphasis added]. It is problematical whether any study of the subject could result in overcoming an attitude this ingrained.

Appendix 2: The Revulsion Letter

(Cited by US District Court judge Vaughn Walker as a "finding of fact" in his opinion in *Perry v. Schwarzenegger*, striking down California's Proposition 8 banning of same-sex marriage in California.)

Discovery site: Dr. Franklin E. Kameny's attic, Washington, DC; correspondence now part of the Kameny Papers Archive, Manuscript Division, Library of Congress

By John W. Macy Jr.
Chairman, United States Civil Service Commission
To the Mattachine Society of Washington, DC
February 25, 1966

Gentlemen:

Pursuant to your request of August 15, 1965, Commission represent-atives met with representatives of the Society on September 8, 1965, to enable the Society to present its views regarding the Government policy on the suitability for Federal employment, of persons who are shown to have engaged in homosexual acts.

The Society was extended 30 days to submit a written memorandum in support of the positions set forth at these discussions to ensure that full consideration could be given to its contentions and supporting data by the Commissioners. On December 13, 1965 the Society filed five documents, which, along with the substance of the September discussions, have been considered by the Commissioners.

The core of the Society's position and its recommendations is that private, consensual, out-of-working hours homosexual conduct on the part of adults, cease to be a bar to Federal employment. In the alternative it is asked that the Commission activate continuing discussions with representatives of the Society to take a "progressive, idealistic, humane, forward-looking, courageous role" to elicit the holding of objective hearings leading to the adoption of the Society's recommendation.

The Commission's policy for determining suitability is stated as follows:

"Persons about whom there is evidence that they have engaged in or solicited others to engage in homosexual or sexually perverted acts with them, without evidence of rehabilitation, are not suitable for Federal employment. In acting on such cases the Commission will consider arrest records, court records, or records of conviction for some form of homosexual conduct or sexual perversion; or medical evidence, admissions, or other credible information that the individual has engaged in or solicited others to engage in such acts with him. Evidence showing that a person has homosexual tendencies, standing alone, is insufficient to support a rating of unsuitability on the ground of immoral conduct."

We have carefully weighed the contentions and recommendations of the Society, and perceive a fundamental misconception by the Society of our policy stemming from a basic cleavage in the perspective by which this subject I viewed. We do not subscribe to the view, which indeed is the rock upon which the Mattachine Society is founded, that "homosexual" is a proper metonym for an individual. Rather, we consider the term "homosexual" to be properly used as an adjective to describe the nature of overt sexual relations or conduct. Consistent with this usage pertinent considerations encompass the types of deviate sexual behavior engaged in, whether isolated, intermittent, or continuing acts, the age of the particular individual's participation, the recency of the incidents, the presence of physical, mental, emotional, or nervous causes, the influence of drugs, alcohol other contributing factors, the public or private character of the acts, the incidence of arrests, convictions, or of public offense, nuisance or breach of the peace related to the acts, the notoriety, if any, of the participants, the extent or effect of rehabilitation efforts, if any, and the admitted acceptance of, or preference for homosexual relations. Suitability determinations also comprehend the total impact of the applicant upon his job. *Pertinent considerations here are the revulsion of other employees by homosexual conduct and the consequent disruption of service efficiency, the apprehension caused other employees of homosexual advances, solicitations or assaults, the unavoidable subjection of the sexual deviate to erotic stimulation through on-the-job use of common toilet, shower and living facilities, the offense to members of the public who are required to deal with a known or admitted sexual deviate to transact Government business, the hazard that the prestige and authority of a Government position will be used to foster homosexual activity, particularly among the youth, and the use of Government funds and authority in furtherance of conduct offensive both to the mores and the law of our society.* [Emphasis added.]

In the light of these pervading requirements it is upon overt conduct that the Commission's policy operates, not upon spurious classifications of individuals. The Society apparently represents an effort by certain individuals to classify themselves as "homosexuals" and thence on the basis of asserted discrimination to seek, with the help of others, either complete social acceptance of aberrant sexual conduct or advance absolvement of any consequences for homosexual acts which come to the attention of the public authority. Homosexual conduct, including that between consenting adults in private, is a crime in every jurisdiction, except under specified conditions, in Illinois. Such conduct is also considered immoral under the prevailing mores of our society.

In the light of these pervading requirements it is upon overt conduct that the Commission's policy operates, not upon spurious classification of individuals. The Society apparently represents an effort by certain individuals to classify themselves a "homosexuals" and thence on the basis of asserted discrimination to seek, with the help of others, either complete social acceptance of aberrant sexual conduct or advance absolvement of any consequences for homosexual acts which come to the attention of public authority. Homosexual conduct, including that between consenting adults in private, is a crime in every jurisdiction, except under specified conditions, in Illinois. Such conduct is also considered immoral under the prevailing mores of our society.

We are not unaware of the numerous studies, reports and recommendations. . . .

We reject categorically the assertion that the Commission pries into the private sex life of those seeking Federal employment, or that it discriminates in ferreting out homosexual conduct. The standard against *criminal, infamous, dishonest, immoral, or notoriously disgraceful conduct* [emphasis added] is uniformly applied and suitability investigations underlying its observance are objectively pursued.

To be sure if an individual applicant were to publicly proclaim that he engages in homosexual conduct, that he prefers such relationships, that he is not sick, or emotionally disturbed, and that he simply has different sexual preferences, as some members of the Mattachine Society openly avow, the Commission would be required to find such an individual unsuitable for Federal employment. The same would be true of an avowed adulterer, or one who engages in incest, illegal fornication, prostitution, or other sexual acts which are criminal and offensive to our mores and our general sense of propriety. The self-revelation by announcement of such private, sexual behavior and preferences is itself public conduct which the Commission must consider in assaying an individual's suitability for Federal employment.

Hence it is apparent that the Commission's policy . . .

We can neither, consistent with our obligations under the law, absolve individuals of the consequences of their conduct, nor do we propose by attribution of sexual preferences based on such conduct, to create *an insidious classification of individuals. We see no third sex, no oppressed minority or secret society, but only individuals; and we judge their suitability for Federal employment in the light of their overt conduct.* [Emphasis added.] We must attribute to overt acts whether homosexual or heterosexual, the character ascribed by the laws and mores of our society. Our authority and our duty permit no other course.

By direction of the Commission:

Sincerely yours,

John W. Macy Jr.
Chairman

Appendix 3: Acknowledgment and Apology

117th Congress
First Session
S. RES. 275

(For complete text see: https://www.congress.gov/bill/117th-congress/
senate-resolution/275/text?s=1&r=26)

Acknowledging and apologizing for the mistreatment of, and discrimination against, lesbian, gay, bisexual, and transgender individuals who
served the United States in the Armed Forces, the Foreign Service, and
the Federal civil service.

*(Introduced, July 2021 in both Senate and House of Representatives
by Senators Tim Kaine (D-Va.) and Tammy Baldwin (D-WI) with
21 co-sponsor in the Senate; and H. Res 544, Reps. David Cicilline
(D-R.I.) and Mark Takano (D-Ca.)*

IN THE SENATE OF THE UNITED STATES
JUNE 17, 2021
RESOLUTION
Acknowledging and apologizing for the mistreatment of, and discrimination against, lesbian, gay, bisexual, and transgender individuals who
served the United States in the Armed Forces, the Foreign Service, and
the Federal Civil Service.

Whereas the Federal Government discriminated against and terminated hundreds of thousands of lesbian, gay, bisexual, and transgender (referred to in this preamble as "LGBT") individuals who served
the United States in the Armed Forces, the Foreign Service, and the
Federal civil service (referred to in the preamble as "civilian employees") for decades, causing untold harm to those individuals professionally, financially, socially, and medically, among other harms;

Whereas Congress enacted legislation, led oversight hearings, and issued reports and public pronouncements against LGBT military service members, Foreign Service members and civilian employees;

Whereas the policy that led to the discharge and systematic screening of gay, lesbian, and bisexual military service members was codified in a 1949 decree by the newly consolidated Department of Defense, which mandated that "homosexual personnel, irrespective of sex, should not be permitted to serve in any branch of the Armed Forces in any capacity and prompt separation of known homosexuals from the Armed Forces is mandatory"; . . .

Whereas the Federal Government maintained policies to drive hundreds of thousands of LGBT military service members, who honorably served the United State in uniform, including many who were fighting in wars around the world, from its military ranks;

Whereas in 1993, Congress enacted the National Defense Authorization Act for Fiscal Year 1994 . . . which contained the so-called "Don't Ask, Don't Tell" policy that prohibited lesbian, gay, and bisexual miliary service members from disclosing their sexual orientation while they served in the Armed Forces;

Whereas, despite the "Don't Ask, Don't Tell" policy, LGBT military service members continued to be investigated and discharged solely on the basis of sexual orientation of those military service members;

Whereas historians have estimated that at least 100,000 military service members were forced out of the Armed Forces between World War II and 2011 simply for being LGBT, while countless others were forced to hide their identities and live in fear while serving; . . .

Whereas military leaders have likewise acknowledged that, in addition to lesbian, gay, and bisexual military service members, transgender service members also serve the United States just as bravely and well as other service members;

Whereas, under the pressure of the Cold War, and at the instigation and lead of Congress, the Federal Government also pursued anti-LGBT policies, which resulted in tens of thousands of LGBT civilian employees being terminated; . . .

Whereas following Senator Joseph McCarthy's targeting of gay employees in the Department of State in 1950, the Senate held hearings on "The Employment of Homosexuals and other Sex Perverts in the Government," which (1) led to the issuance of a widely read report that falsely asserted that gay people posed a security risk because they could be easily blackmailed; and (2) found that gay people were unsuitable employees because "one homosexual can pollute a Government office"; . . .

Whereas more than 1,000 Department of State employees were dismissed due to their sexual orientation, and many more individuals were prevented from joining the Department of State due to discriminatory hiring practices; . . .

Whereas the effort to purge gay and lesbian employees from the Federal Government was codified in 1953 when President Dwight D. Eisenhower issued Executive Order 10450 (18 Fed. Reg. 2489; relating to security requirements for Government employment) which—(1) defined "perversion" as a security threat; and (2) mandated that every civilian employee and contractor pass a security clearance;

Whereas, over many decades, the Federal Government, led by security officials in the Federal Bureau of Investigation, the Civil Service Commission . . . and nearly every other agency of the Federal Government, investigated, harassed, interrogated, and terminated thousands of lesbian, gay, and bisexual civilian employees for no other reason than the sexual orientation of those employees; . . .

Now, therefore, be it
Resolved, . . .

The Senate—

1. Acknowledges and condemns the discrimination against, wrongful termination of, and exclusion from the Federal civil service, the Foreign Service, and the Armed Forces of the thousands of lesbian, gay, bisexual, and transgender individuals who were affected by the anti-LGBT policies of the Federal Government;
2. on behalf of the United States, apologizes to (A) the affected LGBT military service members, Foreign Service members, veterans, and Federal civil service employees, and (B) the families of those service members, veterans and Federal civil service employees; and
3. Reaffirms the commitment of the Federal Government to treat all military service members, Foreign Service members, veterans and Federal civil service employees and retirees including LGBT individuals, with equal respect and fairness. . . .

Endnotes

Introduction

1. Amicus curiae brief of the Mattachine Society of Washington, DC, Obergefell v. Hodges, 576 US 644 (2015), by counsel McDermott Will & Emery; and of the Respect for Marriage Act to repeal the Defense of Marriage Act and require the federal government to recognize the validity of same-sex and interracial marriages.
2. Philip Kennicott, "In America's Past, a Culture of Animus against Federal Workers," *Washington Post*, April 27, 2015.
3. Amicus brief of the Mattachine Society, *Obergefell*, 576 US 644, introduction and summary of argument, p. 4.
4. George Santayana, *The Life of Reason,* vol. 1, *Reason in Common Sense* (New York: Scribner, 1905), 284.
5. John Steele, Office of General Counsel, "Homosexuality and Government Employment," October 14, 1964; Homosexuality and Suitability Legal Advisory Files (Suitability Files); Records of the U.S. Civil Service Commission, Record Group 146 (RG 146); National Archives at College Park, MD (NACP).
6. A widespread pejorative for Dallas after JFK's assassination.
7. "Cuzzin' Linnie," DJ Linwood Henderson, broke the color barrier on Dallas "white radio," KLIF-AM; Robert Wilonsky, "Dallas Radio Has Lost a Legend, Linwood Henderson, Better Known as Cuzzin' Linnie," *Dallas Observer*, July 1, 2011.
8. Rick Santorum, in an Associated Press interview, April 7, 2003, said, "Every society in the history of man has upheld the institution of marriage as a bond between a man and a woman. Why? Because society is based on one thing: that society is based on the future of the society. And that's what? Children. Monogamous relationships. In every society, the definition of marriage has not ever to my knowledge included homosexuality. That's not to pick on homosexuality. It's not, you know, man on child, man on dog, or whatever the case may be." https://usatoday30.usatoday.com/news/washington/2003-04-23-santorum-excerpt_x.htm.

Chapter 1

1. "Young Pianist Heard," *New York Times*, August 10, 1953. "Van Cliburn, 18, pianist from Kilgore, Texas, was a soloist at a concert this afternoon with the Chautauqua Symphony Orchestra conducted by Walter Hendl."

2. Edmund Morris, *Edison* (New York: Random House, 2019).

3. Ellis Davis and Edwin H. Grobe, *The Encyclopedia of Texas*, vol 1, *Short Biographies of Prominent Texans* (Dallas: Texas Development Bureau, 1922), 246.

4. Obituary for Charles Franklin Carter: "Pioneer of Dallas Claimed by Death: Citizen Prominently Identified with Early Growth of Dallas Passes Peacefully," *Dallas Morning News*, November 18, 1912; re: Dallas cotton market see Jim Schutze, *The Accommodation: The Politics of Race in an American City* (Dallas: Deep Vellum, 1986), 45.

5. Interview with Charles Carter Sr., "Nearly a Centenarian, Mr. Charles Carter of Alabama Tells of the Past," *Dallas Morning News*, September 18, 1892.

6. Genealogical research report from Victor S. Dunn, CG, by email (Re: John Carter Report) to Charles Francis, March 1, 2021.

7. The Civil War and Its Aftermath," Britannica, accessed April 21, 2023, https://www.britannica.com/place/Alabama-state/The-Civil-War-and-its-aftermath.

8. Interview with Carter Sr., "Nearly a Centenarian."

9. Andrew Solomon, *Far from the Tree: Parents, Children and the Search for Identity* (New York: Scribner, 2012).

10. Evelyn Miller Crowell, *Men of Achievement: Texas Edition* (Dallas: John Moranz Associates, 1948), 178–79.

11. "Pegasus" and Magnolia Petroleum, Texas Historical Commission Facebook post, April 11, 2020, https://www.facebook.com/Texas-HistoricalCommission/photos/the-magnolia-petroleum-companys-pegasus-a-forty-foot-long-and-thirty-foot-high-r/2764607270318727/.

12. Charlie Francis, "one of the heroic figures in the Texas oil industry"; Robert Caro, *Master of the Senate*, vol. 3 of *The Years of Lyndon Johnson* (New York: Knopf, 2002), 663.

13. Pauline Bren, *The Barbizon: The Hotel that Set Women Free* (New York: Simon & Schuster, 2021).

14. Ruth Altshuler, note to Charles Francis, 1992.

15. Sarah Bean Apmann, "Café Society, The Wrong Place for the Right People," Off the Grid (blog), December 30, 2015, https://www.villagepreservation.org/2015/12/30/cafe-society-the-wrong-place-for-the-right-people/.

16. Altshuler, note to Francis.

17. H. Keith Melton and Robert Wallace, *The Official CIA Manual of Trickery and Deception* (New York: William Morrow, 2009), vii.

18. Samuel J. Ayers, *Tex Robertson: Attaway-to-Go!* (Lubbock: Lubbock Christian University, 2002).

19. Richard Rodgers and Oscar Hammerstein II, "Pore Jud Is Daid," in *Oklahoma!*, 1943.

20. Dark secret: The tune of "Hail to the Campfire Lighter" is a direct lift from "Hail to the Victor," the University of Michigan fight song. Tex Robertson was a champion swimmer at Michigan.

21. Chow chow is a spiced, hot, green-tomato relish that goes great with black-eyed peas.

22. Larry L. King, *True Facts, Tall Tales, and Pure Fiction* (Austin: University of Texas Press, 1997); King passed away in Washington, "DeeCee," but left his papers, all 245 pounds of them, to Texas State University in San Marcos.

23. Paul Crume, "Two Ghosts in Dallas Plaza," Big D, *Dallas Morning News*, July 27, 1964, in *The World of Paul Crume*, with Marion Crume (Dallas: SMU Press, 1980), 191.

24. Mike Rawlings, interview with Charles Francis, April 1, 2022.

25. William Waybourn, email memories of Ruth Altshuler to Charles Francis, May 3, 2023.

26. Glenn Hunter, "Ruth Altshuler, R.I.P.," *D Magazine*, December 10, 2017.

27. Roger Staubach, "JFK Remembered," ESPN interview, November 21, 2013.

28. Crume, "Two Ghosts in Dallas Plaza," 191.

29. Jacquelynn Floyd, "Dallas Struck Pitch-Perfect Note in First Observance of JFK Assassination Anniversary," *Dallas Morning News*, November 22, 2013.

30. Walt Whitman, "In Paths Untrodden" (1860), in *Leaves of Grass and Selected Prose* (New York: Modern Library College Edition, 1981), Calamus, 93.

Chapter 2

1. Daphne White, "Digitization Project Reveals Unseen 'Guerilla' Footage that Revolutionized TV," *Berkeleyside*, July 18, 2018; quoting Deidre Boyle, *Radical Light: Alternative Films & Video in the SF Bay Area, 1945–2000* (Berkley: University of California Press, 2010).

2. *Lord of the Universe*, directed by Michael Shamberg, produced by TVTV (Top Value Television), aired February 2, 1974 on PBS; the documentary was filmed using Portapak video cameras in 1973 at the Houston Astrodome.

3. Jonny Coleman, "White Men Only: The Troubled Past of Studio One, a Historic Gay Disco," *LAist*, March 13, 2017.

4. E. B. White, *Here Is New York* (New York: Harper & Bros., 1949), 1.

5. Ralph Waldo Emerson, "On Self Reliance" (1841), in *American Literature, Tradition and Innovation*, ed. Harrison T. Meserole, Walter Sutton, and Brom Weber, vol. 2, *Ralph Waldo Emerson to Sidney Lanier* (Lexington, MA: D. C. Heath, 1969), 976.

6. "Proclamation of Sam Houston, Commander-in-Chief of the Army of Texas," December 12, 1835, Dolph Briscoe Center for American History, University of Texas, https://digitalcollections.briscoecenter.org/item/419743?solr_nav%5Bid%5D=c818c636334e4e6dfd-6c&solr_nav%5Bpage%5D=0&solr_nav%5Boffset%5D=2.

Chapter 3

1. Mike Bloomberg, "Mike Bloomberg on the Passing of David Rockefeller," MikeBloomberg.com, March 20, 2017, https://www.mike-bloomberg.com/news/mike-bloomberg-passing-david-rockefeller/.

2. Fraser Seitel, note to Charles Francis, September 12, 1980.

3. Irving Long and Bill Van Haintze, "Bank Boxes Looted in Roslyn Burglary," *Newsday*, January 20, 1981.

4. Long and Van Haintze, "Bank Boxes Looted."

5. "U.S. Banks Trim Prime to 19 ½%," *New York Herald Tribune*, February 3, 1981.

6. Joseph Verner Reed Papers, Beinecke Library, Archives at Yale, 46 boxes, including "Shah of Iran," which contains information on Rockefeller's role in gaining permission for the exiled shah of Iran to undergo medical treatment in the United States in 1980.

7. David Kirkpatrick, "How a Chase Chairman Helped the Deposed Shah of Iran Enter the US," *New York Times,* December 29, 2019.

8. John Goshko, "Banker Who Aided Shah Up for Ambassadorship," *Washington Post,* May 30, 1981.

9. Kirkpatrick, "How a Chase Chairman Helped the Deposed Shah."

10. Mark A. Greene, "A Critique of Social Justice as an Archival Imperative: What Is It We're Doing That's All That Important?," *American Archivist* 76, no. 7 (Fall/Winter 2013), 324.

11. Joseph Reed, note to Charles Francis, April 21, 1981.

Chapter 4

1. Robert Rosenblatt and Ronald J. Ostrow, "Robert Gray, Capital's King of Clout," *Los Angeles Times*, May 13, 1984.

2. Bernard Gwertzman, "A Moroccan Libyan 'Union' Jolts U.S.," *New York Times*, August 26, 1984.

3. Bob Gray, interview by Charles Francis, May 19, 2012.

4. Alan Bennett, *The History Boys*, Faber & Faber (New York: Farrar, Straus and Giroux, 2004), 74.

5. T. E. Lawrence, *Seven Pillars of Wisdom* (London: Jonathan Cape, 1935), 31.

Chapter 5

1. Fred C. Shapiro, "Mediator," *New Yorker*, July 30, 1970.

2. Steven Greenhouse, "Theodore W. Kheel, Mediator, Dies at 96," *New York Times*, November 15, 2010.

3. Conversation reported by William Safire, "Cast of Character," *New York Times*, January 18, 1999.

4. Safire, "Cast of Character."

5. Tom Scarbrough, Investigator, "What to Do during Registration Drives," May 5, 1964, Mississippi State Sovereignty Commission (MSSC), Paul B. Johnson Family Papers, University of Southern Mississippi, Hattiesburg, MS (hereafter cited as Johnson Family Papers).

6. Frank Mankiewicz, "In Which I Watch Orson Welles Rehearse Live Radio Broadcasts and Develop a Love for Radio That Later Shapes Much of Today's NPR," chap. 3, in *So As I Was Saying: My Somewhat Eventful Life*, with Joel L. Swerdlow (New York: St. Martin's Press, 2016), 26.

7. Marjorie Williams, "Clark Clifford: The Rise of a Reputation" and "The Man Who Banked on His Good Name," *Washington Post*, May 9, 1991.

Chapter 6

1. Richard Farina, *Been Down So Long It Looks Like Up to Me* (New York: Random House, 1966).

2. Frank Bruni, "Bush in Reversal to Meet with Gay Group," *New York Times*, August 8, 2020.

3. "I look forward to learning . . ."; note from George W. Bush to Charles Francis, April 8, 1998, Charles C. Francis Papers, 1911–2013, University of North Texas Libraries Special Collections, Denton, TX (hereafter cited as Francis Papers).

4. Richard Berke, "High in the Polls and Close to Home, Bush Navigates by the Center Line," *New York Times*, April 9, 1999.

5. Fax from Francis to Governor Bush and Karen Hughes, April 8, 1999, Francis Papers.

6. Frank Bruni, *Ambling into History: The Unlikely Odyssey of George W. Bush* (Waterville, ME: Thorndike Press, 2002).

7. Richard Gooding, "The Trashing of John McCain," *Vanity Fair*, November 2004.

8. Karen Hughes, *Ten Minutes from Normal* (New York: Viking/Penguin 2004).

9. Log Cabin Republicans, News Release, September 8, 2004; and Alison Mitchell, "I Am a Better Person," *New York Times*, April 14, 2000.

10. "It's important for the next president to listen to people's real life stories," he said; Associated Press, "Governor Bush Meets with Gays," April 14, 2000; "Bush Talks to Gays and Calls It Beneficial," *New York Times*, April 14, 2000; "Meeting Pleases Bush, Gay Supporters," *Dallas Morning News*, April 14, 2000.

11. Rove note to Francis, April 8, 2000, Francis Papers; Bush note to Francis, May 18, 2000, Francis Papers.

12. Gunderson, "Behind the Scenes at a Bush 'Sensitivity Session,'" *Newsweek*, April 24, 2000, p. 43, Francis Papers.

13. In November 2000 an estimated one million gay and lesbian voters voted for Governor Bush. In Florida, approximately 50,000 gay-identified voters supported Bush's 537-vote win in Florida; "Gay Republican Group Won't Endorse Bush," NBC News, September 8, 2004.

14. Allan Lengel, "Thousands Mourn Student's Death," *Washington Post*, October 15, 1998.

15. Amici curiae brief of the Republican Unity Coalition, Lawrence v. Texas, 539 US 558 (2003).

16. President Gerald Ford letter to Francis, March 6, 2003, Francis Papers.

17. Mary J. Matalin email to Francis, August 21, 2002, Francis Papers.

18. John Cloud, "The New Face of Gay Power," *Time*, October 13, 2003.

19. "High Noon Rally for Liberty," Log Cabin Republican ad, Saturday, June 13, 1998.

20. "The Lone Pilgrimage of Rev. Otwell," *D Magazine*, January 17, 1987.

21. Letter from Francis to Governor Bush, June 8, 1998, Francis Papers.

22. Todd J. Gillman, "Gay Republicans Protest Convention Treatment," *Dallas Morning News*, June 9, 1998.

23. "Statement did go out on Associated Press wire. . . . Thanks for your help!"; fax from Hughes to Francis, June 10, 1998, Francis Papers.

24. Frank Rich, "The Fire Next Time," *New York Times*, June 20, 1998.

25. Will Maddox, "The Grand Story of Loryland," *D Magazine*, July 13, 2022.

26. Eric Neugeboren, "'We Failed': Gay Republicans Who Fought for Acceptance in the Texas GOP See Little Progress," *Texas Tribune*, July 24, 2022.

27. Dale Carpenter, *Flagrant Conduct: The Story of* Lawrence v. Texas*: How a Bedroom Arrest Decriminalized Gay America*, (New York: W. W. Norton, 2013), xii

28. Carpenter, *Flagrant Conduct*, 8.

29. Amici brief, Republican Unity Coalition, *Lawrence*, 539 US 558.

30. Alan Simpson, "Lawrence v. Texas," *Wall Street Journal,* March 26, 2003.

31. Letter from President Ford to Francis, March 6, 2003, Francis Papers.

32. Carpenter, *Flagrant Conduct*, 318n35.

33. *Loving v. Virginia*, 388 US 1 (1967).

34. Linda Greenhouse, "Justices 6–3, Legalize Gay Sexual Conduct," *New York Times*, June 27, 2003.

35. Sasha Issenberg, *The Engagement: America's Quarter-Century Struggle over Same-Sex Marriage* (New York: Random House, 2022), 372.

36. Carolyn Lochhead, "How Gay GOP Group Lost Its Faith in Bush," *San Francisco Chronicle*, October 10, 2004.

37. Truth Wins Out, "TWO's Wayne Besen Interviews Randy Thomas, Former 'Ex-Gay' Exodus Leader," November 24, 2020, YouTube video, 30:40 and 31:20, https://www.youtube.com/watch?v=Z-krkZaTzcE.

38. Wayne Slater, "Rove Says He Didn't Engineer Anti-Gay Marriage Amendments. He Did," *Dallas Morning News*, August 26, 2010; and

Stuart Stevens, *It Was All a Lie: How the Republican Party Became Donald Trump* (New York: Doubleday, 2020).

39. Isaac Chotiner, "Why Stuart Stevens Wants to Defeat Donald Trump," *New Yorker*, August 3, 2020.
40. "As flies to wanton boys are we to the Gods. They kill us for their sport"; William Shakespeare, *King Lear*, in *William Shakespeare: The Complete Works,* ed. Alfred Harbage (Baltimore: Penguin Books, 1969), act 4, scene 2.
41. "Our nation must defend the sanctity of marriage," he continued; Gerson, State of the Union address, January 20, 2004, https://georgewbush-white-house.archives.gov/news/releases/2004/01/20040120-7.html.
42. Gerson, "How the Gay Rights Movement Found Such Stunning Success," *Washington Post*, June 13, 2022.
43. Donald Loren Hardy, *Shooting from the Lip: The Life of Senator Al Simpson* (Norman: University of Oklahoma Press, 2011), 444n1. Hardy served as Senator Simpson's chief of staff. This footnote is the only mention in the biography of Alan Simpson's extensive advocacy on behalf of LGBTQ Americans.
44. Alan Simpson, "Missing the Point on Gays," *Washington Post*, September 5, 2003.
45. Oscar Wilde, *A Woman of No Importance* (Melbourne: Bloom Publishing, 2022), act 3, scene 1.
46. Sean Loughlin, "Santorum under Fire for Comments on Homosexuality," CNN, April 22, 2003.
47. Alan Cooperman, "Frist and Specter Defend Santorum," *Washington Post*, April 24, 2003.
48. "A Republican Group Demands That Senator Apologize to Gays," *New York Times*, April 24, 2003.
49. Dana Milbank and Alan Cooperman, "White House Defends Santorum," *Washington Post*, April 26, 2003.
50. Mary Matalin and James Carville, *Meet the Press*, transcript, May 11, 2003, p. 27, Francis Papers.
51. Matalin and Carville, *Meet the Press* transcript, p. 28, Francis Papers.
52. David Mixner, *Stranger among Friends* (New York: Bantam Books, 1996), 331.
53. Mark Twain, *The Adventures of Huckleberry Finn* (Mineola, NY: Dover, 2005), 256.
54. See Leslie Fiedler, "Come Back to the Raft Ag'in, Huck Honey," *Partisan Review*, June 1948.

Chapter 7

1. "The Troubles of Bus Boycott's Forgotten Woman," *Jet*, July 14, 1960.
2. James Baldwin, "The White Man's Guilt," *Ebony*, August 1965.
3. William Eskridge, Remarks at Kameny's memorial service, Cannon Caucus Room, Washington, DC, November 17, 2011.
4. Thomas Mallon, *Fellow Travelers* (New York: Pantheon Books, 2007).
5. Stephen Bottum, "Fellow Travelers Book Party," *Band of Thebes* (blog), May 16, 2007, https://bandofthebes.typepad.com/bandofthebes/2007/05/fellow_traveler.html.
6. Sterlingmanor, "Anyone Know the Band of Thebes Blog?," Reddit.com, December 1, 2019, https://www.reddit.com/r/gaybrosbookclub/comments/e4q5q6/anyone_know_the_band_of_thebes_blog/.
7. Dudley Clendinen and Adam Nagourney, *Out for Good: The Struggle to Build a Gay Rights Movement in America* (New York: Simon & Schuster, 1999), 113.
8. See Claudia Kalb, *Andy Warhol Was a Hoarder: Inside the Minds of History's Great Personalities* (Washington, DC: National Geographic Books, 2016), 59–66.
9. Jose Antonio Vargas, "Signs of Progress," *Washington Post,* July 23, 2005.
10. National Museum of American History, "Beyond the Ballot," part of the permanent exhibit *American Democracy: A Great Leap of Faith*, accessed April 27, 2023, https://americanhistory.si.edu/democracy-exhibition/beyond-ballot.
11. Gail Fineberg, "Library of Congress Acquires Papers of Gay Rights Pioneer," *Library of Congress Bulletin*, November 2006.
12. Frank Kameny letter to Tom Brokaw, November 26, 2007, Kameny Papers Project, http://www.kamenypapers.org/boomletter.htm.
13. Jean Edward Smith, *Eisenhower: In War and Peace* (New York: Random House, 2012); Jim Newton, *Eisenhower: The White House Years* (New York: Doubleday, 2011); and Evan Thomas, *Ike's Bluff: President Eisenhower's Secret Battle to Save the World* (New York: Little, Brown, 2012).
14. "Frank Kameny, an American Hero," editorial, *Washington Post,* October 12, 2011.
15. Frank Kameny, *Petition Denied, Revolution Begun: Frank Kameny Petitions the Supreme Court*, ed. Charles Francis, (self-pub., Amazon Digital Services, 2011), Kindle.

16. Brett Zongker, "Asteroid Named for Gay Rights Pioneer Frank Kameny," NBC News, July 10, 2012, https://www.nbcnews.com/id/wbna48142044.

17. Eric Cervini, *The Deviant's War: The Homosexual vs. the United States of America* (New York: Farrar, Strauss and Giroux, 2020), 385.

18. Richard Ovenden, *Burning the Books: A History of the Deliberate Destruction of Knowledge* (Cambridge, MA: Belknap Press of Harvard University Press, 2020), 3.

19. Simon Schama, "Who Controls the Past?," Life & Arts, *Financial Times,* May 7, 2022. Schama is an *FT* contributing editor, historian, and author.

Chapter 8

1. "how do you like your blueeyed boy / Mister Death"; e. e. Cummings, "[Buffalo Bill 's]," in *e.e. cummings Complete Poems, 1904–1962,* edited by George J. Firmage (New York: Liveright, 2016), 98.

2. Allan Bérubé, *My Desire for History: Essays in Gay, Community, & Labor History* (Chapel Hill: University of North Carolina Press, 2011).

3. Jonathan Katz, *Gay American History: Lesbians & Gay Men in the USA: A Documentary* (New York: Crowell, 1976; New York: Harper & Row, 1985).

4. John D'Emilio (b. 1948) is professor emeritus of history and women's and gender studies at the University of Illinois, Chicago; a pioneer in the field of gay history, he is author of six books, including the definitive *Sexual Politics, Sexual Communities: The Making of a Homosexual Minority in the United States,* 2nd ed. (Chicago: University of Chicago Press, 1998).

5. John D'Emilio letter to Franklin E. Kameny, May 22, 1978; Correspondence, Folder D; Kameny Papers, Manuscript Division, Library of Congress, Washington, DC (hereafter cited as Kameny Papers).

6. Gerard Koskovich, "The History of Queer History: One Hundred Years of the Search for Shared Heritage," article 4 in *LGBTQ America: A Theme Study of Lesbian, Gay, Bisexual, Transgender, and Queer History* (Washington, DC: National Park Service, 2016); also chap. 2 in Katherine Crawford-Lackey and Megan E. Springate, eds., *Preservation and Place: Historic Preservation by and of LGBTQ Communities in the United States* (New York: Berghahn Books, 2019).

7. Koskovich, "History of Queer History," 3.

8. "Expanded 'Don't Say Gay' Law in Florida is a 'Flagrant Escalation' of Censorship in Schools," PEN America press release, April 19, 2023; a similarly expanded "Don't Say Gay" law covering all grades in Texas was passed by the Texas Senate, May 23, 2023.

9. Charles Francis, remarks to the LGBTQ Section of the Special Libraries Association, June 16, 2009; see also Omar G. Encarnación, "Digging Up a Painful Past: Archive Activism," chap. 2 in *The Case for Gay Reparations* (New York: Oxford University Press, 2021).

10. Encarnación, *Case for Gay Reparations*, 56.

11. Dale Carpenter, "Windsor Products, Equal Protection from Animus," *Supreme Court Review* 183 (2013): 188; "The government acts on animus when, to a material degree, it aims 'to disparage and to injure' a person or group of people," 186.

12. Steele, "Homosexuality and Government Employment," Suitability Files; RG 146; NACP.

13. Matt Apuzzo, "Uncovered Papers Show Past Government Efforts to Drive Gays from Jobs," *New York Times*, May 20, 2014.

14. Daniel Jonah Goldhagen, *Hitler's Willing Executioners: Ordinary Germans and the Holocaust* (New York: Random House, 1996), 38.

15. Latin proverb on the official Seal of the National Archives, https://www.ecfr.gov/current/title-36/chapter-XII/subchapter-A/part-1200/subpart-B.

16. Winfred Ernest Garrison, "The Breton Fisherman's Prayer," https://oneragamuffin.com/2020/05/25/breton-fishermans-prayer/.

17. Chief Justice John Roberts , Dissent, U.S. v. Windsor, challenging the Defense of Marriage Act (2013), "snippets of history to tar the political branches with the brush of bigotry"

18. John Macy, director, US Civil Service Commission, letter to The Mattachine Society of Washington, DC, February 25, 1966; Boxes 41, 42; Kameny Papers.

19. L. V. Meloy, General Counsel, Letter to John Macy, Civil Service Commission Director, September 21, 1962; Suitability Files; RG 146; NACP.

20. Burton McDonald, Civil Service Commission General Counsel, letter to Justice Department, June 29, 1973; folder 10, doc. 1; Suitability Files; RG 146; NACP.

21. Mike Isikoff, dir., "1: The Betrayal," 1:30 in "Uniquely Nasty: The US Government's War on Gays," June 18, 2015, YouTube video, https://www.youtube.com/watch?v=Ouj-95lNF8M.

22. Kennicott, "Culture of Animus."
23. Amicus brief of the Mattachine Society, *Obergefell*, 576 US 644.
24. Kennicott, "Culture of Animus."
25. Isikoff, "Uniquely Nasty."

Chapter 9

1. Emily Langer, "Lilli Vincenz, Early Activist in Gay Rights Movement, Dies at 85," *Washington Post*, June 30, 2023; and Lou Chibbaro, "Celebrating the Life of Lilli Vincenz," *Washington Blade*, July 6, 2023.
2. In 2001 Lilli Vincenz permitted extended excerpts of *Second Largest Minority* to be used in the documentary *Gay Pioneers*, directed by Glenn Holsten and produced by the Equality Forum in collaboration with Philadelphia PBS affiliate WHYY, including an interview with Vincenz herself.
3. ONE, Inc. v. Olesen, Postmaster of Los Angeles, 355 US 371 (1958).
4. For CBS News and homosexuality, see Steve Hartman, "A Look at CBS News' 1967 Documentary: 'The Homosexuals,'" CBS Evening News, June 26, 2015, https://www.cbsnews.com/news/how-far-weve-come-since-the-1967-homosexuals-documentary/. This report offers a retrospective on Mike Wallace's "CBS Reports: The Homosexuals," from 1967, two years before Stonewall.
5. Monica Hesse, "What Lilli Saved," *Washington Post*, July 25, 2013.
6. Mike Mashon, "Lilli Vincenz and the Power of PRIDE," *Now See Hear!*, Library of Congress National Audio-Visual Conservation Center blog, June 5, 2014, https://blogs.loc.gov/now-see-hear/2014/06/lilli-vincenz/.
7. "Gay and Proud: Lilli's Legacy," produced and directed by Patrick Sammon for the Mattachine Society of Washington, DC, June 21, 2019, YouTube video, https://www.youtube.com/watch?v=b8Zbr3PUy9k&t=31s.
8. Senator Tammy Baldwin (D-WI), "Gay and Proud," 1:45.

Chapter 10

1. Charles Francis, "Freedom Summer 'Homos': An Archive Story," *American Historical Review* 124, no. 4 (October 2019): 1351–63.
2. District Court Judge Carlton Reeves Opinion striking down Mississippi ban on same-sex marriage, Campaign for Southern Equality v. Bryant, 64 F. Supp. 3d 906 (S.D. Miss. 2014).

3. District Judge Carlton Reeves Opinion in Dobbs v. Jackson Women's Health Organization 379 F. Supp. 3d 549 (S.D. Miss. 2019).

4. Reynolds Holding, "The Judge Who Told the Truth about the Mississippi Abortion Ban," *Atlantic*, November 30, 2021.

5. Scarbrough, "What to Do during Registration Drives," May 5, 1964, MSSC, Johnson Family Papers.

6. Scarbrough, "What to Do during Registration Drives," May 5, 1964, MSSC, Johnson Family Papers.

7. Bill Luckett died in 2021. His memorial celebration was held at the Ground Zero Blues Club in Clarksdale.

8. Dr. Earnest Smith, oral history, recorded by Roy DeBerry Jr. and Les McLemore, in Yazoo City, MS, 2003.

9. Tom Scarbrough, Investigator, "Marshall County (Rust College)," June 30, 1964.

10. Scarbrough, "Marshall County (Rust College)."

11. Lelie Burl McLemore, interview by Charles Francis at McLemore's home in Walls, MS, 2015.

12. Gloria Clark, interview by Francis, December 2, 2015.

13. McLemore, interview.

14. Frank Moorer, interview by Francis at Moorer's home in Montgomery, AL, September 12, 2018.

15. Moorer interview.

16. African American Civil War Museum homepage, accessed April 28, 2023, https://www.afroamcivilwar.org.

17. Frank Smith, executive director of the African American Civil War Museum, interview by Francis, Washington, DC, December 9, 2015.

18. Jacques Derida, *Archive Fever: A Freudian Impression* (Chicago: University of Chicago Press, 1995), 2.

19. Scarbrough, Memorandum to Office of Governor, February 11, 1965, Johnson Family Papers.

20. Francis, "Freedom Summer 'Homos.'"

21. Alex Lichtenstein, "In This Issue," *American Historical Review* 124, no. 4 (October 2019): xii.

22. Scarbrough, "What to Do during Registration Drives," May 5, 1964, MSSC, Johnson Family Papers.

23. Judge Reeves Opinion, Jackson Women's Health Organization v. Mary Currier, 349 F. Supp. 3d 536 (S.D. Miss. 2018), 12n40.

24. *Dobbs v. Jackson Women's Health Organization*, the case that overruled *Roe v. Wade* and *Planned Parenthood v. Casey,* eliminating the constitutional right to abortion.

25. For more on Mattachine and *vergangenheitsbewältigung*, see Giambrone "Asylum Seekers, Traumatic Treatments LGBT People Suffered at St. Elizabeths," *Washington City Paper*, May 31, 2018.

Chapter 11

1. John Dowdy Statement on the Mattachine Society of Washington, DC, July 5, 1963, Congressional Record, A 4211, pp. 14836–44. Dowdy was elected to ten Congresses (1952–1973), beginning with representing the Seventh Congressional District of Texas from 1952–1967. At the time of his attack on Mattachine, Texas's Seventh was in Central Texas, including Waco. In 1966 the district moved into Harris County, west of Houston.
2. John Kyle Day, *The Southern Manifesto: Massive Resistance and the Fight to Preserve Segregation* (Jackson: University Press of Mississippi, 2014), 3.
3. Dowdy Statement on the Mattachine Society, July 5, 1963.
4. Zona Hostetler, oral history conducted by Dr. Eric Cervini for the Mattachine Society of Washington, DC, 2018.
5. Hostetler, oral history.
6. Hostetler, oral history.
7. Cervini, "The Congressman," chap. 9 in *Deviant's War*, 136–54.
8. Hostetler, oral history.
9. UPI photo credit, "Representative John Dowdy, a Texan with 19 years in Congress, leaves U.S. District Court 12/30/71 after being found guilty of accepting a $25,000 bribe to influence Justice Department fraud investigation of a Washington, D.C. home improvement firm."
10. The Papers of John V. Dowdy, Baylor University Libraries, Introduction, concludes, "Dowdy may have been set up by those who opposed his conservative stance on urban renewal"; https://www.baylor.edu/library/index.php?id=974745.

Chapter 12

1. Presidential Records (44 U.S.C. Chapter 22), §2201.2, https://www.archives.gov/about/laws/presidential-records.html.
2. See Department of Justice Archives, FOIA Guide, Exemption 5, Guidance 22.
3. Email response to Charles Francis from GWBush.Library@nara.gov, September 6, 2022.

4. Nick Schwellenbach and Sean Moulton, "The Most Abused FOIA Exemption (P5) Still Needs to Be Reined In," *Washington Post,* February 6, 2020.

5. Dr. James Dobson, letter to Karl Rove, July 22, 2002, George W. Bush Presidential Library. Maybe you can find it?

6. Dale Olson telegram to Mark Weinberg, Reagan White House, July 24, 1985; "hospitals/insurance/medical" file sequence; Ronald Reagan Presidential Library, Simi Valley, CA; discovered by Reagan Library curator at request of the Mattachine Society of Washington, DC.

7. Chris Geidner, "Nancy Reagan Turned Down Rock Hudson's Plea for Help Nine Weeks before He Died," *BuzzFeed News*, February 2, 2015, https://www.buzzfeednews.com/article/chrisgeidner/nancy-reagan-turned-down-rock-hudsons-plea-for-help-seven-we.

8. Karen Tumulty, *The Triumph of Nancy Reagan* (New York: Simon & Schuster, 2021), 417.

9. Alexandra Topping, "Nancy Reagan Refused to Help Dying Rock Hudson Get AIDs Treatment," *Guardian*, February 3, 2015.

10. Stephen Kijak, dir., *Rock Hudson: All That Heaven Allowed* (HBO Documentary Films, 2023).

11. When Johnson dedicated the LBJ Presidential Library in 1971, he said, "It's all here, the story of our time—with the bark off"; https://www.lbjlibrary.org/object/text/remarks-president-johnson-lbj-library-dedication-05-22-1971.

12. LBJ librarian Claudia Anderson, email to Charles Francis, August 10, 2015.

13. Mildred Stegall, "LBJ as I Know Him," January 13, 2016, Aides Files of Mildred Stegall, Oral History Transcript [NAID 24617781], LBJ Presidential Library, Austin, TX (hereafter cited as Stegall Files).

14. Prepared memorandum to be signed by Walter Jenkins, October 1964, Stegall Files.

15. Jenkins memorandum, Stegall Files; this document was held by Mildred Stegall until released to Mattachine in 2016.

16. James Kirchick, "A Long Way from Arp," in *Secret City: The Hidden History of Gay Washington* (New York: Henry Holt and Company, 2022), 297–312.

17. Kirchick, "Acknowledgment," in *Secret City*, 658.

18. Vice President Hubert Humphrey, letter to Franklin Kameny, June 6, 1965, Kameny Papers.

19. Macy, letter to Mattachine Society, February 25, 1966, Kameny Papers.

20. Kennicott, "Culture of Animus."

21. "Talent Scout," *Time*, May 7, 1965.

22. Gift of Papers and Other Historical Materials of John W. Macy Jr. to the Lyndon Baines Johnson Library, Agreement signed December 8, 1980; LBJ Library.

23. Macy Gift Agreement with LBJ Library, December 8, 1980, paragraph 4(b); LBJ Library.

24. Kennicott, "Culture of Animus."

25. "The winds of change are blowing, Mr. Macy"; Cervini, *Deviant's War*, 74–75.

26. Scott v. Macy, 349 F.2d 182 (D.C. Cir. 1965); Scott v. Macy, 402 F.2d 644 (D.C. Cir. 1968); Norton v. Macy, 417 F.2d 1161 (D.C. Cir. 1969).

27. Memo to Pellerzi, February 14, 1966; Personal Papers of John W. Macy; Reading File, Jan–March 1966, Box 15; LBJ Library.

28. John W. Macy, Memorandum for Mr. W. J. Oganovic, August 17, 1965; Personal Papers of John W. Macy, Jr.; Box 16; LBJ Library.

29. John W. Macy Jr., *Public Service: The Human Side of Government* (New York: Harper & Row, 1971), 65.

30. Kennicott, "Culture of Animus," regarding Bill Moyers.

Chapter 13

1. Rev. John Smid, *Love in Action Handbook*, Archives Center, Smithsonian National Museum of American History, Washington, DC.

2. Garrard Conley, "Author's Note," in *Boy Erased: A Memoir of Identity, Faith, and Family* (New York: Penguin Random House, 2016).

3. Conley, *Boy Erased*, 336.

4. See American Psychological Association Resolution on Sexual Orientation Change Efforts (SOCE), February 2021, apa.og/about/policy/resolution-sexual-orientation-change-efforts.pdf.

5. Conley, *Boy Erased*, 320.

6. See Alex Williams, "Gay Teenager Stirs a Storm," *New York Times*, June 17, 2005.

7. Joel Edgerton, dir., *Boy Erased* (Universal City, CA: Focus Features, 2018).

8. "Born Again" and "Ministries Try to Turn Gays Straight," *San Francisco Chronicle*, September 19, 1990.

9. National Museum of American History, Press Release, "National Museum of American History Acquires Archival Collection Related to LGBT Conversion Therapy," October 16, 2017.

10. Conley, "Author's Note," *Boy Erased*.

11. McDermott Will & Emery, "The Pernicious Myth of Conversion Therapy: How Love in Action Perpetrated a Fraud on America," October 12, 2018, white paper, https://stopconversiontherapy.org/wp-content/uploads/2019/07/Mattachine-Society-Conversion-Therapy-White-Paper-Redacted.pdf?6bfec1&6bfec1.

12. Smid, interview with Lisa Linksky, December 29, 2017.

13. McDermott, "Pernicious Myth of Conversion Therapy," 31.

14. Jad Abumrad, "UnErased: Smid," Novemer 27, 2018, radiolab.org/episodes/unerased-smid; see also the transcript, https://radiolab.org/podcast/unerased-smid/transcript.

15. Conley, *Boy Erased*, 327.

16. "Mattachine and Me," produced and directed by Patrick Sammon, featuring Garrard Conley, October 8, 2018, YouTube video, https://www.youtube.com/watch?v=L3DOHE9oc0c.

17. Pryor Center for Arkansas Oral and Visual History, "The Mission," accessed April 27, 2023, https://pryorcenter.uark.edu/about.php#mission.

18. "Welcome, Garrard," produced by Mattachine Society of Washington, DC, October 8, 2018, YouTube video, https://www.youtube.com/watch?v=o5CbjaDy3N8.

19. Interview with Martha Caudill Conley by Scott Lunsford, Pryor Center, University of Arkansas Memories Project, January 23, 2018.

20. "Mattachine and Me."

Chapter 14

1. Giambrone, "Asylum Seekers."

2. Sarah A. Leavitt, *St. Elizabeths in Washington, DC: Architecture of an Asylum* (Charleston, SC: History Press, 2019).

3. Giambrone, "Asylum Seekers," 9.

4. The DC Sexual Psychopath Act of 1948, chap. 38, Sexual Psychopath, §22-3809. A law that provided "the Court shall appoint two qualified psychiatrists to make a personal examination of the patient and thereafter to file written reports, including conclusions as to whether the patient is a sexual psychopath."

5. Saidiya Hartman, *Wayward Lives, Beautiful Experiments: Intimate Histories of Riotous Black Girls, Troublesome Women and Queer Radicals* (New York: W. W. Norton, 2020).

6. Scope of Collection description, Benjamin Karpman Papers, Jean Nickolaus Tretter Collection in GLBT Studies, University of

Minnesota Libraries, Minneapolis, MN (hereafter cited as Karpman Papers).

7. Benjamin Karpman, Memorandum, 1954, box 9, folder 1, Karpman Papers.
8. Giambrone, "Asylum Seekers."
9. Glass lantern teaching slides, St. Elizabeths Hospital Collection, 1861–1990, Otis Historical Archives 293.25, National Museum of Health and Medicine, Silver Spring, MD.
10. Nitasha Tiku, "AI Opens New Frontiers in Disinformation," *Washington Post*, September 29, 2022.
11. Robert Bell, "Frederick Douglass Has Gone Viral on Social Media. Here's Why," *Rochester Democrat and Chronicle*, March 2, 2021, https://www.democratandchronicle.com/story/news/2021/03/02/frederick-douglass-trending-social-media-heres-why-deep-nostalgia-myheritage-com/6883174002/.
12. LaMarr Jurelle Bruce (@Afromanticist), "Brace yourself and press play," Twitter, February 28, 2021, https://twitter.com/Afromanticist/status/1365927680923881472.
13. Slides in the video "The Acknowledgment"(13:49), directed by Patrick Sammon for the Mattachine Society of Washington, DC, at YouTube Mattachine Society of Washington, DC. St. Elizabeths Hospital begins at 7:00.
14. See *Queering the Medical Model*, June 23, 2022, zine by Texas artist Wes Holloway at https://mattachinesocietywashingtondc.org/2022/06/23/queering-st-elizabeths/.
15. Jillian Eugenios, "'I am a homosexual. I am a psychiatrist': How Dr. Anonymous Changed History," NBC News.com, May 2, 2022, https://www.nbcnews.com/nbc-out/out-news/-homosexual-psychiatrist-dr-anonymous-changed-history-rcna26836#.
16. The *Diagnostic and Statistical Manual of Mental Disorders*, the American Psychiatric Association's "bible" of psychiatry.
17. Patrick Sammon and Bennett Singer, dirs., *Cured* (PBS / Independent Lens, 2022).
18. "Gay, Proud and Healthy" leaflet, 1972, Kameny Papers.
19. Kameny, letter to Dr. Frank S. Caprio, May 30, 1972, Kameny Papers.
20. David Reddish, "Doctors Once Considered Homosexuality an Illness: *Cured* Celebrates Heroes Who Proved Otherwise," *Queerty*, August 23, 2020, https://www.queerty.com/doctors-considered-homosexuality-illness-cured-celebrates-heroes-proved-otherwise-20200823.

Chapter 15

1. Dewilda N. Harris, "My Job in Germany, 1945-1954," quoted in Atina Grossman, *Jews, Germans and Allies: Close Encounters in Occupied Germany* (Princeton, NJ: Princeton University Press, 2007), 15.

2. "Remembering the Battle of Berlin: The Soviet War Memorial at Tiergarten," National World War II Museum: New Orleans, May 2, 2020, https://www.nationalww2museum.org/war/articles/battle-of-berlin-memorial-tiergarten.

3. Larry Kramer, *The American People*, vol. 1, *Search for My Heart* (New York: Farrar, Straus and Giroux, 2015), 210.

4. Ned Rorem, *Knowing When to Stop: A Memoir* (New York: Open Road Media, 2013), chap. 8.

5. Walter Laqueur and Richard Breitman, *Breaking the Silence: The German Who Exposed the Final Solution* (Hanover, MA: Brandeis University Press, 1994), 233–34.

6. OMGUS files, 1946–1947 (OMGUS files); Records of Public Safety Branch files, Box 893 (Box 893); Records of U.S. Occupation Headquarters WW II, RG 260 (RG 260); NACP.

7. Rorem, *Knowing When to Stop*, chap. 8.

8. Douglas Waller, *Wild Bill Donovan: The Spymaster Who Created the OSS and Modern American Espionage* (New York: Simon & Schuster, 2011), 132.

9. Letter to Robert D. Murphy, US Political Advisor, Department of State, from C. W. Whittemore, National Labor Relations Board, October 7, 1947; OMGUS files; Box 893; RG 260; NACP.

10. Richard Bessel, Germany 1945: From War to Peace (New York: HarperCollins, 2009), 178, the Supreme Headquarters Allied Expeditionary Force (SHAEF) Handbook, policy no. 629.

11. State Department Review of Thomas B. Stauffer, Cairo, January 1949, marked "Declassified," donated to Mattachine Society of Washington, DC, by Stauffer family.

12. Thomas Stauffer, "Night Masque," summer 1940, handwritten, unpublished poem, Thomas Stauffer Papers, including correspondence, photographs and other documents, donated in 2016 to Mattachine Society of Washington, DC, by Stauffer family.

13. Memorandum to Leave Section, Mr. Howard from D. L. Wood, September 8, 1950; Authorized by Foreign Service, File 5, declassified in 1973; Stauffer Papers; NACP.

14. Letter from Carlisle H. Humelsine, Deputy Undersecretary of State, to Thomas Baer Stauffer, March 4, 1951; declassified in 1973; Stauffer Papers; NACP.

15. Reply of Thomas Baer Stauffer to interrogatory of Loyalty Review Board, February 8, 1950; Stauffer Papers; NACP.

16. Letter to Thomas Stauffer from Elbridge Durbrow, Chief Division of Foreign Service Personnel, September 13, 1951; Stauffer Papers; NACP.

17. Department of State, Memorandum of Conversation re: Thomas B. Stauffer, FSO, between Laurence A. Knapp, Attorney, and Robert J. Ryan, September 5, 1951.

18. Carlisle H. Humelsine, memorandum to Mr. Webb, "Problem of Homosexuals and Sex Perverts in the Department of State," June 23, 1950; Sex Perversion [investigations of Federal employees] (Sex Perversion); Confidential Subject Files, 1945–1953 (CSF); Confidential Files (Truman Administration), 1938–1953 (HST-CF); NACP.

19. Durbrow, letter to Stauffer, September 13, 1951; Stauffer Papers; NACP.

20. Loyalty Review Board hearings were November 9, 1950, and September 10 and 11, 1951; Lawrence Knapp, attorney for Thomas Stauffer.

21. Stauffer Loyalty Review Board Hearing, September 11, 1951 (transcript declassified 2017); "one further point," p. 161.

22. Stauffer, letter to father, February 7, 1951, Stauffer Papers, Mattachine Society.

23. Richard Harris Smith, *OSS: The Secret History of America's First Central Intelligence Agency* (Guilford, CT: Lyon Press, 2005), 1.

24. Records of the Office of Strategic Services, RG 226; NACP.

25. Waller, *Wild Bill Donovan*, 355.

26. Smith, *OSS*, xii.

27. Humelsine to Webb, "Problem of Homosexuals"; Sex Perversion; CSF; HST-CF; NACP.

28. David K. Johnson, "The Shameful History of the Lavender Scare Echoes Today," *Washington Post*, April 27, 2023.

29. US Senate Resolution 275, Acknowledging and Apologizing for the Mistreatment of, and Discrimination against, LGBT Individuals, 1st Session, 117th Congress, Senators Kaine (D-VA) and Baldwin (D-WI).

30. Testimony of Carlisle H. Humelline, Acting Deputy Under Secretary of State, to the Investigations Subcommittee, Committee on Expenditures in the Executive Departments, Senator Clyde R. Hoey chairman, July 19, 1950, p. 2201.

31. "We see your sacrifices. We acknowledge what you lost . . ."; Joseph R. Biden Jr., "A Proclamation on the 70th Anniversary of the Lavender Scare," April 26, 2023, https://www.whitehouse.gov/briefing-room/presidential-actions/2023/04/26/a-proclamation-on-the-70th-anniversary-of-the-lavender-scare/.

Chapter 16

1. "Transgender at the CIA," *New York Times*, May 11, 2015.
2. Admiral Roscoe Hillenkoetter, closed proceeding testimony in executive session before the Senate Investigations Subcommittee, Clyde Hoey, Chairman of the Subcommittee presiding, "Employment of Homosexuals and Other Sex Perverts in Government," July 1950. This was the same Investigations subcommittee hearing with Carlisle Humelsine.
3. Frank Gardner, "MI6 Chief Apologises for Past Ban on LGBT Staff," BBC News, February 19, 2021.
4. Exhibition program, "Nazi Persecution of Homosexuals 1933–1945," United States Holocaust Memorial Museum, Washington, DC, 2002.
5. Elizabeth Olson, "Gay Focus at the Holocaust Museum," *New York Times,* July 4, 2003.
6. Encarnación, *Case for Gay Reparations*, chap. 3.
7. Julia Lutsky, "Political Prisoners in Spain," Prison Legal News, December 13, 2022.
8. Omar Encarnacion, *Out in the Periphery: Latin America's Gay Rights Revolution* (New York: Oxford University Press, 2016), 92.
9. Greene, "Critique of Social Justice," 324.

Chapter 17

1. Priscilla Hayner, *Unspeakable Truths: Facing The Challenge of Truth Commissions* (New York: Routledge, 2011), 1.
2. Catechism of the Catholic Church, paragraphs 2357–59, accessed April 24, 2023, https://www.usccb.org/beliefs-and-teachings/what-we-believe/catechism/catechism-of-the-catholic-church.
3. Guy Faulconbridge, "Britain's MI6 Spy Master Apologises for Historic Discrimination against LGBT+ People," Reuters, February, 19, 2021.
4. Vin Gurrieri, "FBI Loses FOIA Suit over Program to Fire Gay Employees," Law360.com, July 31, 2017, https://www.law360.com/aerospace/articles/949515/fbi-loses-foia-suit-over-program-to-fire-gay-employees;

Mattachine Society of Washington, DC v. US Department of Justice, 406 F. Supp. 3d 64 (D.D.C. 2019).

5. Eric Tucker, "Suit Seeks Records Tied to Ike's Anti-Gay Order," AP, April 27, 2016.

6. Lamberth, Opinion, *Mattachine*, 406 F. Supp. 3d 64, III Analysis/A. The FBI's search was not adequate.

7. Ann E. Morrow and Carol D. Leonig, "Royce Lamberth Steps Down from Court Post," *Washington Post*, July 16, 2013.

8. McDermott Will & Emery, "McDermott, Mattachine Society Call for US Government to Apologize for Seven Decade-Long Federal Assault on LGBT Americans: White Paper Report Offers Evidentiary History of Tens of Thousands of Destroyed Lives," June 17, 2021, https://www.mwe.com/media/mcdermott-mattachine-society-call-for-us-government-to-apologize-for-seven-decade-long-federal-assault-on-lgbt-americans/.

9. Strom Thurmond attack on Bayard Rustin, Congressional Record, 88th Congress, Vol. 109, pt. 11, pp. 14837–38.

10. For more on Thurmond and Rustin, see John D'Emilio, *Lost Prophet: The Life and Times of Bayard Rustin* (New York: Free Press, 2003).

11. Jonathan Capehart, "What Pete Buttigieg Really Said about Being Gay, Prejudice and Blacks," *Washington Post,* December 3, 2019.

12. John Lewis, "At a Crossroads on Gay Unions," *Boston Globe*, October 25, 2003.

13. "Senators Call for the Federal Government to Apologize for Past Anti-LGBTQ Policies," LGBTQ Nation, June 20, 2021, https://www.lgbtqnation.com/2021/06/senators-call-federal-government-apologize-past-anti-lgbtq-policies/.

14. "The Acknowledgment," directed by Patrick Sammon, produced by the Mattachine Society of Washington, DC, and Patrick Sammon, September 8, 2021, YouTube video, https://www.youtube.com/watch?v=YBTfWAGCkAE.

15. John Gallagher, "An American Apology Long Overdue," *LGBTQ Nation*, February 5, 2022.

16. Encarnación, *Case for Gay Reparations*, 149.

17. Encarnación, *Case for Gay Reparations*, 151.

18. Lou Chibbaro Jr., "US Senate to Consider Apology for Past Anti-LGBTQ Discrimination," *Washington Blade*, June 17, 2021.

19. Senate impeachment trial of Donald J. Trump, day one House managers video presentation @ 19:50, "House Impeachment Managers Play Video of Capitol Riot," NBC News, February 9, 2021, YouTube video, https://www.youtube.com/watch?v=ERIbhsCzZwk.

Chapter 18

1. Remy Tumin, "Same-Sex Couple Households in U.S. Surpass One Million," *New York Times*, December 2, 2022.
2. US District Court Judge Vaughn Walker, Opinion, Hollingsworth v. Perry, 133 S. Ct. 2652 (2013), Findings of Fact (74.C).
3. Homer Trails Alliance, accessed July 6, 2023, www.homertrailsalliance.org.
4. The "Bitter Queens" are, in fact, Iliamna, Redoubt, and Augustine volcanoes, visible on the drive south from Anchorage to Homer, Alaska.

Chapter 19

1. William D. Brannon, President, J. Edgar Hoover Foundation, to Linda Harper, Chairperson, Association for the Preservation of Historic Congressional Cemetery, October 7, 2007.
2. J. Edgar Hoover, "re: Sex Deviates in Government Service," June 20, 1951, https://mattachinesocietywashingtondc.files.wordpress.com/2020/05/4.1-hoover-memo-6.20.1951.pdf.
3. "Thanks to New York Times reporter Matt Apuzzo and Charles Francis for sharing this document, which the FBI had not previously released"; Douglas M. Charles, *Hoover's War on Gays: Exposing the FBI's "Sex Deviates" Program* (Lawrence: University Press of Kansas, 2015), 385n106.
4. Matt Apuzzo, "Uncovered Papers Show Past Government Efforts to Drive Gays from Jobs," *New York Times*, May 20, 2014.
5. Betty Medsger, *The Burglary: The Discovery of J. Edgar Hoover's Secret FBI* (New York: Alfred A. Knopf, 2014), 343.
6. See Tim Weiner's *Enemies: A History of the FBI* (New York: Random House, 2012), 176.
7. Dudley Clendinen, "J. Edgar Hoover, 'Sex Deviates' and My Godfather," Opinion page, *New York Times,* November 27, 2011.
8. Richard Nixon, Eulogy Delivered at Funeral Services for J. Edgar Hoover, Washington National Cathedral, May 4, 1972, American Presidency Project, UC Santa Barbara, https://www.presidency.ucsb.edu/documents/eulogy-delivered-funeral-services-for-j-edgar-hoover.
9. Beverly Gage, *G-Man: J. Edgar Hoover and the Making of the American Century* (New York: Viking, 2022), 416–17.
10. Amicus brief of the Mattachine Society, *Obergefell*, 576 US 644.
11. Interview with Bobby Baker at his Florida assisted living facility, November 2017.

12. "Dining," Mayflower Hotel, accessed April 22, 2023, https://www. themayflowerhotel.com/dining/.
13. "Tolson Restaurant," Mayflower Hotel, accessed April 22, 2023, https://www.themayflowerhotel.com/tolson-restaurant-preview/.
14. 9.8% LGBT; Kerith J. Conron and Shoshana K. Goldberg, *Adult LGBT Population in the United States*, UCLA School of Law, Williams Institute, July 2020, https://williamsinstitute.law.ucla.edu/wp-content/uploads/LGBT-Adult-US-Pop-Jul-2020.pdf.
15. "The National Commission on Renaming the J. Edgar Hoover FBI Headquarters Building Act," introduced by Rep. Gerry Connolly (VA).
16. James Kirchick, "The Founding Myth of Stonewall," *UnHerd*, July 1, 2022.

Chapter 20

1. Charles Dickens, *A Christmas Carol* (New York: Harper Brothers, New York, 1876), 37.
2. Baldwin, "White Man's Guilt."
3. Re: "Martin Luther Queen," see Thomas Chatterton Williams, "Breaking into James Baldwin's House," *New Yorker*, October 28, 2015.

Conclusion

1. Louis L'Amour, *Lonely on the Mountain* (New York: Bantam Books, 1980), 1.
2. Justin McCarthy, "Same-Sex Marriage Support Inches Up to New High of 71%," Gallup, June 1, 2022, https://news.gallup.com/poll/393197/same-sex-marriage-support-inches-new-high.aspx.
3. US Census Bureau, "Relationship to Householder Question," US Department of Commerce, 2019.
4. Chris Geidner, email response to the author, January 8, 2023; Geidner is an MSNBC columnist and Supreme Court blogger, "The Law Dork."
5. Allan Bérubé, *Coming Out Under Fire* (New York: Free Press, 1990).
6. Geidner email to Francis.
7. Invisible Histories Project, accessed April 21, 2023, https://invisiblehistory.org/qhs/.
8. "LGBTQ Heritage," National Park Service, 2016, https://www.nps.gov/subjects/tellingallamericansstories/lgbtqheritage.htm.
9. ALA News press release, "American Library Association Reports Record Number of Demands to Censor Library Books and Materials

in 2022," American Library Association, March 22, 2023, https://www.
ala.org/news/press-releases/2023/03/record-book-bans-2022.

10. ALA News, "Record Number of Demands."

11. Nobel Peace Prize 2022 to Ales Bialiatski, "Memorial" archive, Center for
Civil Liberties, which was forcibly dissolved after the Russian invasion of
Ukraine.

12. "McDermott Continues Partnership with the Mattachine Society,"
McDermott Will & Emery, June 11, 2018, YouTube video, https://
www.youtube.com/watch?v=4BKSdOKHbjM.

13. Gregory Samantha Rosenthal, *Living Queer History: Remembrance
and Belonging in a Southern City* (Chapel Hill: University of North
Carolina Press, 2021), 10.

14. Twain, *Huckleberry Finn*, 256.

15. Romer v. Evans, 517 U.S. 620 (1996), opinion written by Justice
Kennedy.

16. "Stonewall's 50th Anniversary Gala," Stonewall National Museum,
Archives, and Library, accessed April 22, 2023, https://stonewall-
museum.org/50-anniversary-gala/.

Bibliography

Archives

Aides Files of Mildred Stegall. LBJ Presidential Library, Austin, TX.

Archives Center. Smithsonian National Museum of American History, Washington, DC

Benjamin Karpman Papers. Jean Nickolaus Tretter Collection in GLBT Studies. University of Minnesota Libraries, Minneapolis, MN.

Charles C. Francis Papers 1911–2013. University of North Texas Libraries Special Collections, Denton, TX.

Frank Kameny Papers. Manuscript Division. Library of Congress, Washington, DC.

Joseph Verner Reed Papers. Beinecke Library. Archives at Yale University, New Haven, CT.

LBJ Presidential Library, Austin, TX.

National Archives Building, Washington, DC.

National Archives at College Park, MD.

Paul B. Johnson Family Papers. University of Southern Mississippi, Hattiesburg, MS.

Ronald Reagan Presidential Library, Simi Valley, CA.

St. Elizabeths Hospital Collection, 1861–1990. Otis Historical Archives. National Museum of Health and Medicine, Silver Spring, MD.

Articles and Essays

Apmann, Sarah Bean. "Café Society, The Wrong Place for the Right People." *Off the Grid* (blog), December 30, 2015. https://www.villagepreservation.org/2015/12/30/cafe-society-the-wrong-place-for-the-right-people/.

Apuzzo, Matt. "Uncovered Papers Show Past Government Efforts to Drive Gays from Jobs." *New York Times*, May 20, 2014.

Associated Press. Interview with Rick Santorum. April 7, 2003. https://usatoday30.usatoday.com/news/washington/2003-04-23-santorum-excerpt_x.htm.

Baldwin, James. "The White Man's Guilt." *Ebony*, August 1965.

Bell, Robert. "Frederick Douglass Has Gone Viral on Social Media. Here's Why." *Rochester Democrat and Chronicle*, March 2, 2021. https://www.democratandchronicle.com/story/news/2021/03/02/

frederick-douglass-trending-social-media-heres-why-deep-nostalgia-my-heritage-com/6883174002/.

Berke, Richard. "High in the Polls and Close to Home, Bush Navigates by the Center Line." *New York Times*, April 9, 1999.

Bloomberg, Mike. "Mike Bloomberg on the Passing of David Rockefeller." MikeBloomberg.com, March 20, 2017. https://www.mikebloomberg.com/news/mike-bloomberg-passing-david-rockefeller/.

Bottum, Stephen. "Fellow Travelers Book Party." *Band of Thebes* (blog), May 16, 2007. https://bandofthebes.typepad.com/bandofthebes/2007/05/fellow_traveler.html.

Bruni, Frank. "Bush in Reversal to Meet with Gay Group." *New York Times*, August 8, 2020.

Capehart, Jonathan. "What Pete Buttigieg Really Said about Being Gay, Prejudice and Blacks." *Washington Post*, December 3, 2019.

Carpenter, Dale Carpenter. "Windsor Products, Equal Protection from Animus." *Supreme Court Review* 183 (2013): 183–285.

Carter, Charles Franklin. Obituary. "Pioneer of Dallas Claimed by Death: Citizen Prominently Identified with Early Growth of Dallas Passes Peacefully." *Dallas Morning News*, November 18, 1912.

Carter, Charles Sr. Interview. "Nearly a Centenarian Mr. Charles Carter of Alabama Tells of the Past." *Dallas Morning News*, September 18, 1892.

Chibbaro, Lou, Jr. "US Senate to Consider Apology for Past Anti-LGBTQ Discrimination." *Washington Blade*, June 17, 2021.

Chotiner, Isaac. "Why Stuart Stevens Wants to Defeat Donald Trump." *New Yorker*, August 3, 2020.

Clendinen, Dudley. "J. Edgar Hoover, 'Sex Deviates' and My Godfather." Opinion page. *New York Times*, November 27, 2011.

Cloud, John. "The New Face of Gay Power." *Time*, October 13, 2003.

Coleman, Jonny. "White Men Only: The Troubled Past of Studio One, a Historic Gay Disco." *LAist*, March 13, 2017.

Cooperman, Alan. "Frist and Specter Defend Santorum." *Washington Post*, April 24, 2003.

D Magazine. "The Lone Pilgrimage of Rev. Otwell." January 17, 1987.

Eugenios, Jillian. "'I am a homosexual. I am a psychiatrist': How Dr. Anonymous Changed History." *NBC News*, May 2, 2022. https://www.nbcnews.com/nbc-out/out-news/-homosexual-psychiatrist-dr-anonymous-changed-history-rcna26836#.

Faulconbridge, Guy. "Britain's MI6 Spy Master Apologises for Historic Discrimination against LGBT+ People." Reuters, February, 19, 2021.

Fiedler, Leslie. "Come Back to the Raft Ag'in, Huck Honey." *Partisan Review*, June 1948.

Fineberg, Gail. "Library of Congress Acquires Papers of Gay Rights Pioneer." *Library of Congress Bulletin*, November 2006.

Floyd, Jacquelyn. "Dallas Struck Pitch-Perfect Note in First Observance of JFK Assassination Anniversary." *Dallas Morning News*, November 22, 2013.

Francis, Charles. "Freedom Summer 'Homos': An Archive Story." *American Historical Review* 124, no. 4 (October 2019): 1351–63.

Francis, Charles. "Homosexuality: An 'Inherently Divisive Concept' at UVA." *Washington Blade*, March 11, 2022.

Gallagher, John. "An American Apology Long Overdue." *LGBTQ Nation*, February 5, 2022.

Gardner, Frank. "MI6 Chief Apologises for Past Ban on LGBT Staff." *BBC News*, February 19, 2021.

Geidner, Chris. "Nancy Reagan Turned Down Rock Hudson's Plea for Help Nine Weeks before He Died." *BuzzFeed News*, February 2, 2015. https://www.buzzfeednews.com/article/chrisgeidner/nancy-reagan-turned-down-rock-hudsons-plea-for-help-seven-we.

Gerson, Michael. "How the Gay Rights Movement Found Such Stunning Success." *Washington Post*, June 13, 2022.

Giambrone, Andrew. "Asylum Seekers, Traumatic Treatments LGBT People Suffered at St. Elizabeths." *DC City Paper*, 2018.

Gillman, Todd J. "Gay Republicans Protest Convention Treatment." *Dallas Morning News*, June 9, 1998.

Gooding, Richard. "The Trashing of John McCain." *Vanity Fair*, November 2004.

Goshko, John. "Banker Who Aided Shah Up for Ambassadorship." *Washington Post*, May 30, 1981.

Greene, Mark A. "A Critique of Social Justice as an Archival Imperative: What Is It We're Doing That's All That Important?" *American Archivist* 76, no. 2 (Fall/Winter 2013): 302–34.

Greenhouse, Linda. "Justices 6–3, Legalize Gay Sexual Conduct." *New York Times*, June 27, 2003.

Greenhouse, Steven. "Theodore W. Kheel, Mediator, Dies at 96." *New York Times*, November 15, 2010.

Gurrieri, Vin. "FBI Loses FOIA Suit over Program to Fire Gay Employees." Law360.com, July 31, 2017. https://www.law360.com/aerospace/articles/949515/fbi-loses-foia-suit-over-program-to-fire-gay-employees.

Gwertzman, Bernard. "A Moroccan Libyan 'Union' Jolts U.S." *New York Times*, August 26, 1984.

Hartman, Steve. "A Look at CBS News' 1967 Documentary: 'The Homosexuals.'" CBS Evening News, June 26, 2015. https://www.cbsnews.com/news/how-far-weve-come-since-the-1967-homosexuals-documentary/.

Hesse, Monica. "What Lilli Saved." *Washington Post*, July 25, 2013.

Holding, Reynolds. "The Judge Who Told the Truth about the Mississippi Abortion Ban." *Atlantic*, November 30, 2021.

Hunter, Glenn. "Ruth Altshuler, R.I.P." *D Magazine*, December 10, 2017.

Jet. "The Troubles of Bus Boycott's Forgotten Woman." July 14, 1960.

Johnson, David K. "The Shameful History of the Lavender Scare Echoes Today." *Washington Post*, April 27, 2023.

Kennicott, Philip. "In America's Past, a Culture of Animus against Federal Workers." *Washington Post*, April 27, 2015.

Kirchick, James. "The Founding Myth of Stonewall." *UnHerd*, July 1, 2022.

Kirchick, James. "The Long War against a Gay Cure." *New York Review of Books*, January 10, 2019.

Kirkpatrick, David. "How a Chase Chairman Helped the Deposed Shah of Iran Enter the US." *New York Times*, December 29, 2019.

Koskovich, Gerard. "The History of Queer History: One Hundred Years of the Search for Shared Heritage." Article 4 in *LGBTQ America: A Theme Study of Lesbian, Gay, Bisexual, Transgender, and Queer History*. (Washington, DC: National Parks Service, 2016).

Lengel, Allan. "Thousands Mourn Student's Death." *Washington Post*, October 15, 1998.

Levitan, Corey. "J. Edgar's LaJolla, Remembering the Hotel Del Charro." *LaJolla Light*, June 16, 2018.

Lewis, John. "At a Crossroads on Gay Unions." *Boston Globe*, October 25, 2003.

Lichtenstein, Alex. "In This Issue." *American Historical Review* 124, no. 4 (October 2019): x–xiii.

Lochhead, Carolyn. "How Gay GOP Group Lost Its Faith in Bush." *San Francisco Chronicle*, October 10, 2004.

Long, Irving, and Bill Van Haintze. "Bank Boxes Looted in Roslyn Burglary." *Newsday*, January 20, 1981.

Loughlin, Sean. "Santorum under Fire for Comments on Homosexuality." *CNN*, April 22, 2003.

Lutsky, Julia. "Political Prisoners in Spain." *Prison Legal News*, December 13, 2022.

Maddox, Will. "The Grand Story of Loryland." *D Magazine*, July 13, 2022.

Mashon, Mike, "Lilli Vincenz and the Power of PRIDE." *Now See Hear!* Library of Congress National Audio-Visual Conservation Blog. June 5, 2015. https://blogs.loc.gov/now-see-hear/2014/06/lilli-vincenz/.

McCarthy, Justin. "Same-Sex Marriage Support Inches Up to New High of 71%." *Gallup*, June 1, 2022. https://news.gallup.com/poll/393197/same-sex-marriage-support-inches-new-high.aspx.

Milbank, Dana, and Alan Cooperman. "White House Defends Santorum." *Washington Post*, April 26, 2003.

Mitchell, Alison. "I Am a Better Person." *New York Times*, April 14, 2000.

Morrow, Ann E., and Carol D. Leonig. "Royce Lamberth Steps Down from Court Post." *Washington Post*, July 16, 2013.

NBC News. "Gay Republican Group Won't Endorse Bush." September 8, 2004.

Neugeboren, Eric. "'We Failed': Gay Republicans Who Fought for Acceptance in the Texas GOP See Little Progress." *Texas Tribune*, July 24, 2022.

New York Herald Tribune. "U.S. Banks Trim Prime to 19 ½%." February 3, 1981.

New York Times. "A Republican Group Demands that Senator Apologize to Gays." April 24, 2003.

New York Times. "Transgender at the CIA." May 11, 2015.

New York Times. "Young Pianist Heard." August 10, 1953.

Olson, Elizabeth. "Gay Focus at the Holocaust Museum." *New York Times*, July 4, 2003.

Reddish, David. "Doctors Once Considered Homosexuality an Illness: *Cured* Celebrates Heroes Who Proved Otherwise." *Queerty*, August 23, 2020. https://www.queerty.com/doctors-considered-homosexuality-illness-cured-celebrates-heroes-proved-otherwise-20200823.

Rich, Frank. "The Fire Next Time." *New York Times*, June 20, 1998.

Rosenblatt, Robert, and Ronald J. Ostrow. "Robert Gray, Capital's King of Clout." *Los Angeles Times*, May 13, 1984.

Safire, William. "Cast of Character." *New York Times*, January 18, 1999.

San Francisco Chronicle. "Born Again." September 19, 1990.

San Francisco Chronicle. "Ministries Try to Turn Gays Straight." September 19, 1990.

Schama, Simon. "Who Controls the Past?" Life & Arts. *Financial Times*, May 7, 2022.

Schwellenbach, Nick, and Sean Moulton. "The Most Abused FOIA Exemption (P5) Still Needs to Be Reined In." *Washington Post*, February 6,
2020.

Shapiro, Fred C. "Mediator." *New Yorker*, July 30, 1970.

Simpson, Alan. "Lawrence v. Texas." *Wall Street Journal*, March 26, 2003.

Simpson, Alan. "Missing the Point on Gays." *Washington Post*, September 5,
2003.

Slater, Wayne. "Rove Says He Didn't Engineer Anti-Gay Marriage Amendments. He Did." *Dallas Morning News*, August 26, 2010.

Staubach, Roger. "JFK Remembered." *ESPN* interview, November 21, 2013.

Stolberg, Sheryl Gay. "A Republican Group Demands that Senator Apologize
to Gays." *New York Times*, April 4, 2003.

Tiku, Nitasha. "AI Opens New Frontiers in Disinformation." *Washington
Post*, September 29, 2022.

Time. "Talent Scout." May 7, 1965.

Topping, Alexandra. "Nancy Reagan Refused to Help Dying Rock Hudson
Get AIDs Treatment." *Guardian*, February 3, 2015.

Tucker, Eric. "Suit Seeks Records Tied to Ike's Anti-Gay Order." Associated
Press, April 27, 2016.

Vargas, Jose Antonio. "Signs of Progress." *Washington Post*, July 23, 2005.

Washington Post. "Frank Kameny, an American Hero." Editorial. October 12,
2011.

White, Daphne. "Digitization Project Reveals Unseen 'Guerilla' Footage that
Revolutionized TV." *Berkeleyside*, July 18, 2018.

Williams, Alex. "Gay Teenager Stirs a Storm." *New York Times*, July 17,
2005.

Williams, Marjorie. "Clark Clifford: The Rise of a Reputation." *Washington
Post*, May 9, 1991.

Williams, Marjorie. "The Man Who Banked on His Good Name." *Washington
Post*, May 9, 1991.

Williams, Thomas Chatterton. "Breaking into James Baldwin's House."
New Yorker, October 28, 2015.

Wilonsky, Robert. "Dallas Radio Has Lost a Legend, Linwood Henderson."
Dallas Observer, July 1, 2011.

Zongker, Brett. "Asteroid Named for Gay Rights Pioneer Frank Kameny."
NBC News, July 10, 2012. https://www.nbcnews.com/id/wbna48142044.

Books and Plays

Ayers, Samuel J. *Tex Robertson: Attaway-to-Go!* Lubbock: Lubbock Christian University, 2002.

Bennett, Alan. *The History Boys*. Faber & Faber. New York: Farrar, Straus and Giroux, 2004.

Bérubé, Allan. *Coming Out Under Fire*. New York: Free Press, 1990.

Bérubé, Allan. *My Desire for History: Essays in Gay, Community, & Labor History*. Chapel Hill: University of North Carolina Press, 2011.

Bren, Pauline. *The Barbizon: The Hotel that Set Women Free*. New York: Simon & Schuster, 2021.

Bruni, Frank. *Ambling into History: The Unlikely Odyssey of George W. Bush*. Waterville, ME: Thorndike Press, 2002.

Caro, Robert. *Master of the Senate*. Vol. 3 of *The Years of Lyndon Johnson*. New York: Knopf, 2002.

Carpenter, Dale. *Flagrant Conduct: The Story of* Lawrence v. Texas: *How a Bedroom Arrest Decriminalized Gay America*. New York: W. W. Norton, 2013.

Cervini, Eric. *The Deviant's War: The Homosexual vs. the United States of America*. New York: Farrar, Straus and Giroux, 2020.

Charles, Douglas M. *Hoover's War on Gays: Exposing the FBI's "Sex Deviates" Program*. Lawrence: University Press of Kansas, 2015.

Clendinen, Dudley, and Adam Nagourney. *Out for Good: The Struggle to Build a Gay Rights Movement in America*. New York: Simon & Schuster, 1999.

Clifford, Clark. *Counsel to the President: A Memoir*. New York: Random House, 1990.

Conley, Garrard. *Boy Erased: A Memoir of Identity, Faith, and Family*. New York: Penguin Random House, 2016.

Crowell, Evelyn Miller. *Men of Achievement: Texas Edition*. Dallas: John Moranz Associates, 1948.

Crume, Paul. *The World of Paul Crume*. With Marion Crume. Dallas: SMU Press, 1980.

Davis, Ellis, and Edwin H. Grobe. *The Encyclopedia of Texas*. Vol. 1, *Short Biographies of Prominent Texans*. Dallas: Texas Development Bureau, 1922.

Day, John Kyle. *The Southern Manifesto: Massive Resistance and the Fight to Preserve Segregation*. Jackson: University Press of Mississippi, 2014.

D'Emilio, John. *Lost Prophet: The Life and Times of Bayard Rustin*. New York: Free Press, 2003.

D'Emilio, John. *Sexual Politics, Sexual Communities: The Making of a Homosexual Minority in the United States*. 2nd ed. Chicago: University of Chicago Press, 1998.

D'Emilio, John, William B. Turner, and Urvashi Vaid, eds. *Creating Change: Sexuality, Public Policy, and Civil Rights*. New York: St. Martin's Press, 2000.

Derida, Jacques. *Archive Fever: A Freudian Impression*. Chicago: University of Chicago Press, 1995.

Dickens, Charles. *A Christmas Carol*. New York: Harper Brothers, 1876.

Encarnación, Omar G. *The Case for Gay Reparations*. New York: Oxford University Press, 2021.

Encarnación, Omar. *Out in the Periphery: Latin America's Gay Rights Revolution*. New York: Oxford University Press, 2016.

Farina, Richard. *Been Down So Long It Looks Like Up to Me*. New York: Random House, 1996.

Gage, Beverly. *G-Man: J. Edgar Hoover and the Making of the American Century*. New York: Viking, 2022.

Goldhagen, Daniel Jonah. *Hitler's Willing Executioners: Ordinary Germans and the Holocaust*. New York: Random House, 1996.

Grossman, Atina. *Jews, Germans and Allies: Close Encounters in Occupied Germany*. Princeton, NJ: Princeton University Press, 2007.

Hardy, Donald Loren. *Shooting from the Lip: The Life of Senator Al Simpson*. Norman: University of Oklahoma Press, 2011.

Hartman, Saidiya. *Wayward Lives, Beautiful Experiments: Intimate Histories of Riotous Black Girls, Troublesome Women and Queer Radicals*. New York: W. W. Norton, 2020.

Hayner, Priscilla. *Unspeakable Truths: Facing the Challenge of Truth Commissions*. New York: Routledge, 2011.

Hughes, Karen. *Ten Minutes from Normal*. New York: Viking/Penguin, 2004.

Issenberg, Sasha. *The Engagement: America's Quarter-Century Struggle over Same-Sex Marriage*. New York: Random House, 2022.

Kalb, Claudia. *Andy Warhol Was a Hoarder: Inside the Minds of History's Great Personalities*. Washington, DC: National Geographic Books, 2016.

Kameny, Frank. *Petition Denied, Revolution Begun: Frank Kameny Petitions the Supreme Court*. Edited by Charles Francis. Self-published. Amazon Digital Services, 2011. Kindle.

Katz, Jonathan. *Gay American History: Lesbians & Gay Men in the USA: A Documentary*. New York: Crowell, 1976; New York: Harper & Row, 1985.

King, Larry L. *True Facts, Tall Tales, and Pure Fiction*. Austin: University of Texas Press, 1997.

Kirchick, James. *Secret City: The Hidden History of Gay Washington*. New York: Henry Holt and Company, 2022.

Kramer, Larry. *The American People*. Vol. 1, *Search for My Heart*. New York: Farrar, Straus and Giroux, 2015.

L'Amour, Louis. *Lonely on the Mountain*. New York: Bantam Books, 1980.

Laqueur, Walter, and Richard Breitman. *Breaking the Silence: The German Who Exposed the Final Solution*. Hanover, MA: Brandeis University Press, 1994.

Lawrence, T. E. *Seven Pillars of Wisdom*. London: Jonathan Cape, 1935.

Leavitt, Sarah A. *St. Elizabeths in Washington, DC: Architecture of an Asylum*. Charleston, SC: History Press, 2019.

Lopez, Barry, ed. *Home Ground, Language for an American Landscape*. Trinity University Press, San Antonio, 2006.

Macy, John W., Jr. *Public Service: The Human Side of Government*. New York: Harper & Row, 1971.

Mallon, Thomas. *Fellow Travelers*. New York: Pantheon Books, 2007.

Mankiewicz, Frank. *So As I Was Saying: My Somewhat Eventful Life*. With Joel L. Swerdlow. New York: St. Martin's Press, 2016.

Medsger, Betty. *The Burglary: The Discovery of J. Edgar Hoover's Secret FBI*. New York: Alfred A. Knopf, 2014.

Melton, H. Keith, and Robert Wallace. *The Official CIA Manual of Trickery and Deception*. New York: William Morrow, 2009.

Meserole, Harrison T., Walter Sutton, and Brom Weber, eds. *American Literature, Tradition and Innovation*. Vol. 2, *Ralph Waldo Emerson to Sidney Lanier*. Lexington, MA: D. C. Heath, 1969.

Mixner, David. *Stranger among Friends*. New York: Bantam Books, 1996.

Morris, Edmund. *Edison*. New York: Random House, 2019.

Murphy, Robert. *Diplomat among Warriors: The Unique World of a Foreign Service Expert*. New York: Doubleday, 1964.

Newton, Jim. *Eisenhower: The White House Years*. New York: Doubleday, 2011.

Ovenden, Richard. *Burning the Books: A History of the Deliberate Destruction of Knowledge*. Cambridge, MA: Belknap Press of Harvard University Press, 2020.

Rorem, Ned. *Knowing When to Stop: A Memoir*. New York: Open Road Media, 2013.

Rosenthal, Gregory Samantha. *Living Queer History: Remembrance and Belonging in a Southern City*. Chapel Hill: University of North Carolina Press, 2021.

Santayana, George. *The Life of Reason*. Vol. 1, *Reason in Common Sense*. New York: Scribner, 1905.

Schutze, Jim. *The Accommodation, the Politics of Race in an American City.* Deep Vellum Publishing, 1986.

Shakespeare, William. *King Lear.* In *William Shakespeare: The Complete Works.* Edited by Alfred Harbage. Baltimore: Penguin Books, 1969.

Smith, Jean Edward. *Eisenhower: In War and Peace.* New York: Random House, 2012.

Smith, Richard Harris. *OSS: The Secret History of America's First Central Intelligence Agency.* Guilford, CT: Lyon Press, 2005.

Solomon, Andrew. *Far from the Tree: Parents, Children and the Search for Identity.* New York: Scribner, 2012.

Stevens, Stuart. *It Was All a Lie: How the Republican Party Became Donald Trump.* New York: Doubleday, 2020.

Thomas, Evan. *Ike's Bluff: President Eisenhower's Secret Battle to Save the World.* New York: Little, Brown, 2012.

Tumulty, Karen. *The Triumph of Nancy Reagan.* New York: Simon & Schuster, 2021.

Twain, Mark. *The Adventures of Huckleberry Finn.* Mineola, NY: Dover, 2005.

Waller, Douglas. *Wild Bill Donovan: The Spymaster Who Created the OSS and Modern American Espionage.* New York: Simon & Schuster, 2011.

Weiner, Tim. *Enemies: A History of the FBI.* New York: Random House, 2012.

White, E. B. *Here Is New York.* New York: Harper & Bros., 1949.

Whitman, Walt. *Leaves of Grass and Selected Prose.* New York: Modern Library College Edition, 1981.

Wilde, Oscar. *A Woman of No Importance.* Melbourne: Bloom Publishing, 2022.

Video

"The Acknowledgment." Directed by Patrick Sammon. Produced by the Mattachine Society of Washington, DC, and Patrick Sammon. September 8, 2021. YouTube video. https://www.youtube.com/watch?v=YBTfWAGCkAE.

Edgerton, Joel, dir. *Boy Erased.* Universal City, CA: Focus Features, 2018.

"Gay and Proud: Lilli's Legacy." Produced and directed by Patrick Sammon for the Mattachine Society of Washington, DC. June 21, 2019. YouTube video. https://www.youtube.com/watch?v=b8Zbr3PUy9k&t=31s.

Holsten, Glenn, dir. *Gay Pioneers.* Equality Forum, in collaboration with Philadelphia PBS affiliate WHYY. 2001.

Isikoff, Mike, dir. "Uniquely Nasty: The US Government's War on Gays." June 18, 2015. YouTube video. https://www.youtube.com/watch?v=Ouj-95lNF8M.

Kijak, Stephen, dir. *Rock Hudson: All That Heaven Allowed*. HBO Documentary Films, 2023.

"Mattachine and Me." Produced and directed by Patrick Sammon. Featuring Garrard Conley. October 8, 2018. YouTube video. https://www.youtube.com/watch?v=L3DOHE9oc0c.

"McDermott Continues Partnership with the Mattachine Society." McDermott Will & Emery. June 11, 2018. YouTube video. https://www.youtube.com/watch?v=4BKSdOKHbjM.

NBC News. "House Impeachment Managers Play Video of Capitol Riot." February 9, 2021. YouTube video. https://www.youtube.com/watch?v=ERIbhsCzZwk.

Sammon, Patrick, and Bennett Singer, dirs. *Cured*. PBS / Independent Lens, 2022.

Shamberg, Michael, dir. *Lord of the Universe*. Produced by TVTV. Aired February 2, 1974, on PBS.

Truth Wins Out. "Former 'Ex-Gay' Lobbyist to 'Marry a Dude': The Randy Thomas Story." November 24, 2020. YouTube video. https://www.youtube.com/watch?v=Hb1IylOTjxU.

Truth Wins Out. "TWO's Wayne Besen Interviews Randy Thomas, Former 'Ex-Gay' Exodus Leader." Nov. 24, 2020. YouTube video. https://www.youtube.com/watch?v=Z-krkZaTzcE.

"Welcome, Garrard." Produced by Mattachine Society of Washington, DC. October 8, 2018. YouTube video. https://www.youtube.com/watch?v=o5CbjaDy3N8.

White Papers

McDermott Will & Emery. "America's Promise of Reconciliation and Redemption: The Need for an Official Acknowledgment and Apology for the Historic Government Assault on LGBT Federal Employees and Military Personnel." June 17, 2021. White paper. www.mwe.com/media/mcdermott-mattachine-society.

McDermott Will & Emery. "The Pernicious Myth of Conversion Therapy: How Love in Action Perpetrated a Fraud on America." October 12, 2018. White paper. https://stopconversiontherapy.org/wp-content/uploads/2019/07/Mattachine-Society-Conversion-Therapy-White-Paper-Redacted.pdf?6bfec1&6bfec1.

Index